EDEN™

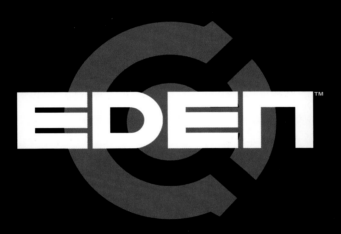

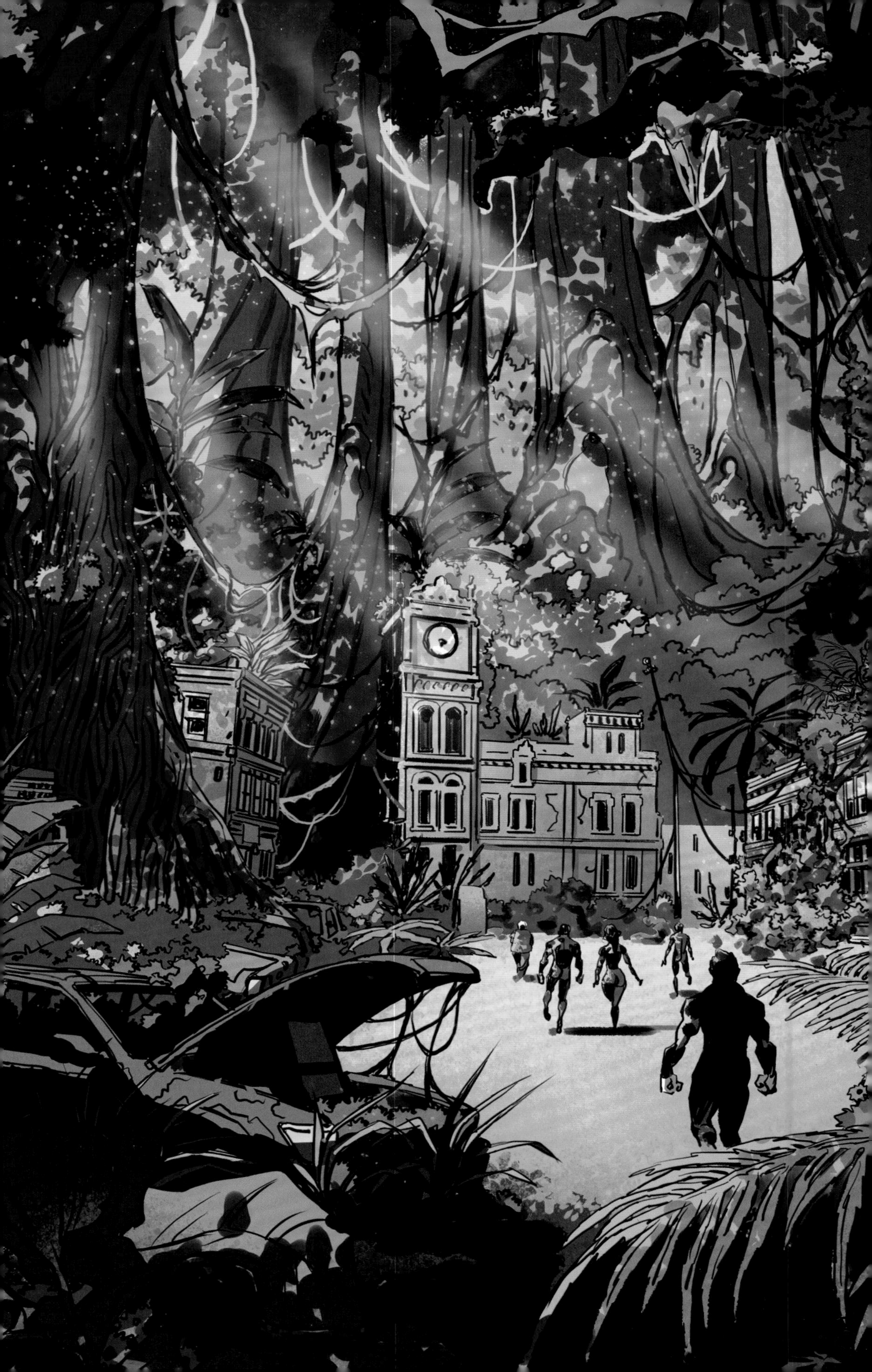

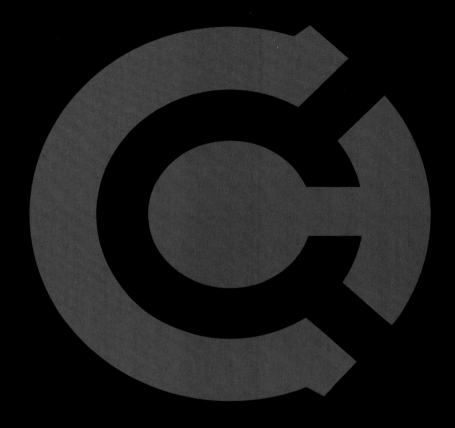

WRITTEN BY **MATTHEW ARNOLD** // ART BY **RICCARDO BURCHIELLI**
COLORED BY **LUCA SALCE** // LETTERED BY **ED DUKESHIRE**
EDITED BY **WILL DENNIS**
SPECIAL THANKS TO **GIANMARCO VERONESI**

DARK HORSE BOOKS

DARK HORSE TEAM

PRESIDENT AND PUBLISHER
MIKE RICHARDSON

EDITOR
DANIEL CHABON

ASSISTANT EDITORS
CHUCK HOWITT
MISHA GEHR

DESIGNER
KATHLEEN BARNETT

DIGITAL ART TECHNICIAN
JASON RICKERD

SPECIAL THANKS TO **DAVID STEINBERGER**,
CHIP MOSHER, AND **BRYCE GOLD**.

NEIL HANKERSON EXECUTIVE VICE PRESIDENT / **TOM WEDDLE** CHIEF FINANCIAL OFFICER / **DALE LaFOUNTAIN** CHIEF INFORMATION OFFICER / **TIM WIESCH** VICE PRESIDENT OF LICENSING / **MATT PARKINSON** VICE PRESIDENT OF MARKETING / **VANESSA TODD-HOLMES** VICE PRESIDENT OF PRODUCTION AND SCHEDULING / **MARK BERNARDI** VICE PRESIDENT OF BOOK TRADE AND DIGITAL SALES / **RANDY LAHRMAN** VICE PRESIDENT OF PRODUCT DEVELOPMENT / **KEN LIZZI** GENERAL COUNSEL / **DAVE MARSHALL** EDITOR IN CHIEF / **DAVEY ESTRADA** EDITORIAL DIRECTOR / **CHRIS WARNER** SENIOR BOOKS EDITOR / **CARY GRAZZINI** DIRECTOR OF SPECIALTY PROJECTS / **LIA RIBACCHI** ART DIRECTOR / **MATT DRYER** DIRECTOR OF DIGITAL ART AND PREPRESS / **MICHAEL GOMBOS** SENIOR DIRECTOR OF LICENSED PUBLICATIONS / **KARI YADRO** DIRECTOR OF CUSTOM PROGRAMS / **KARI TORSON** DIRECTOR OF INTERNATIONAL LICENSING

Published by Dark Horse Books
A division of Dark Horse Comics LLC
10956 SE Main Street
Milwaukie, OR 97222

First edition: July 2022
Trade paperback ISBN 978-1-50673-090-5

1 3 5 7 9 10 8 6 4 2
Printed in China

Comic Shop Locator Service: comicshoplocator.com

Eden

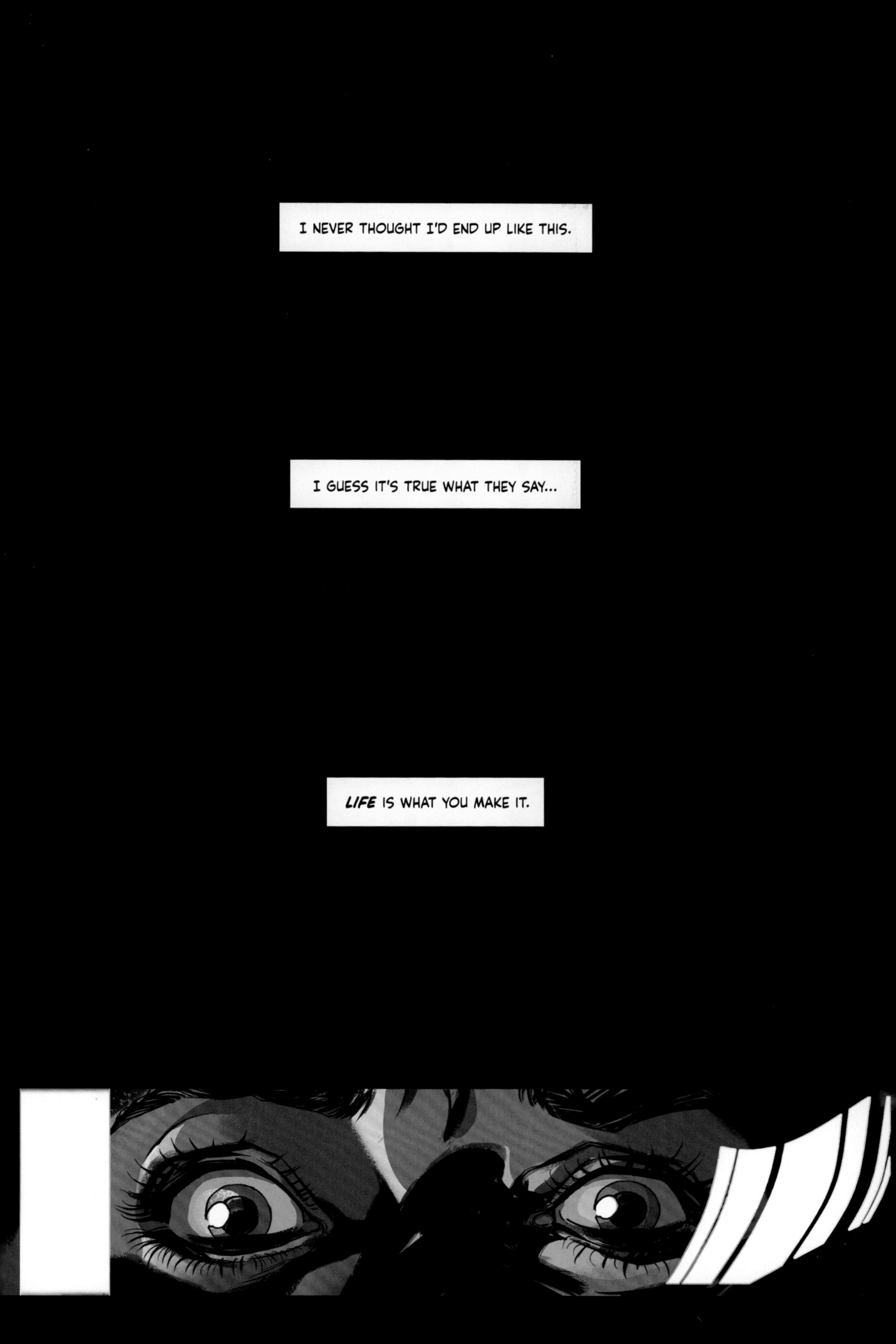
I NEVER THOUGHT I'D END UP LIKE THIS.
I GUESS IT'S TRUE WHAT THEY SAY...
LIFE IS WHAT YOU MAKE IT.

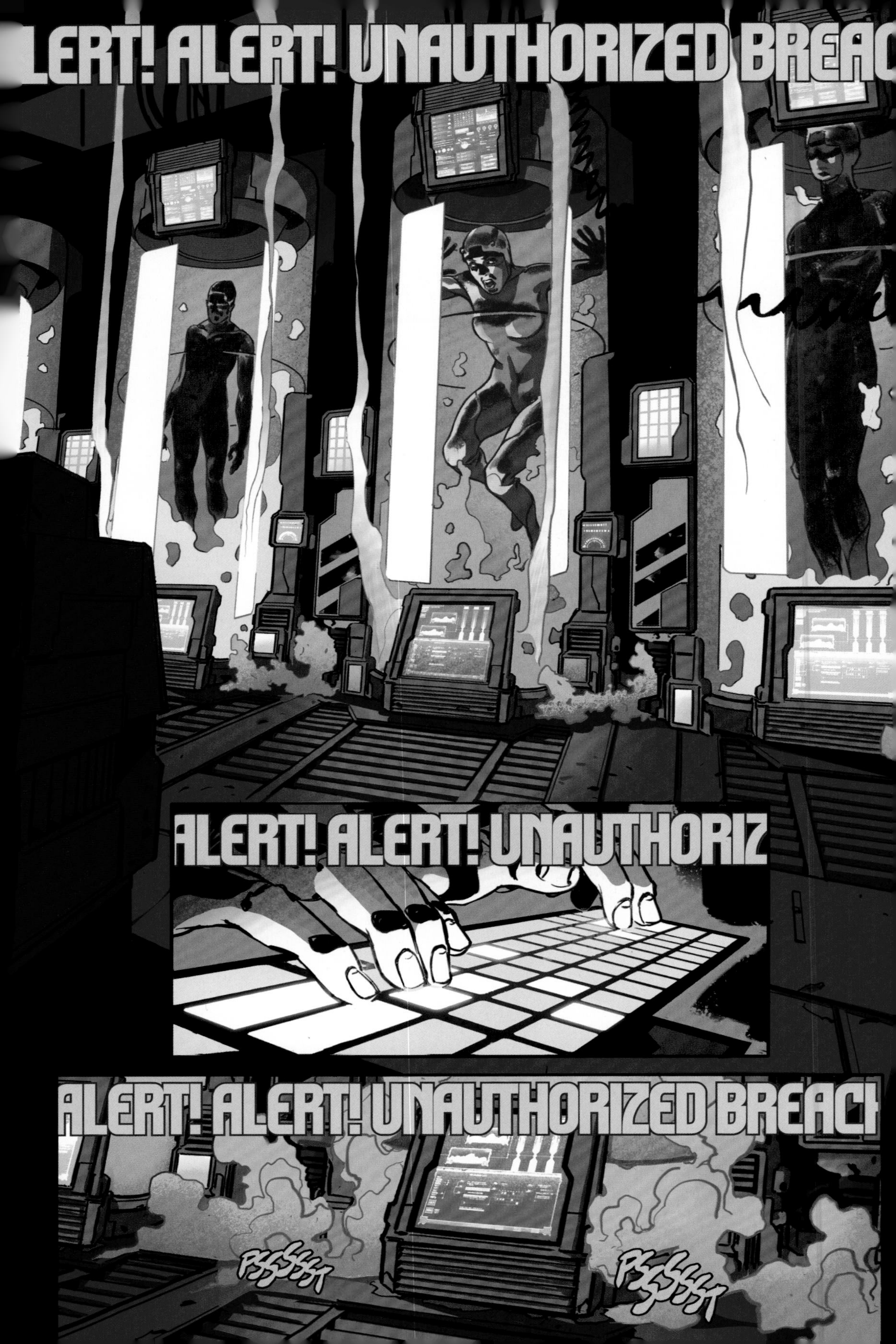
LERT! ALERT! UNAUTHORIZED BREAC
ALERT! ALERT! UNAUTHORIZ
ALERT! ALERT! UNAUTHORIZED BREAC
PSSSSST
PSSSSST

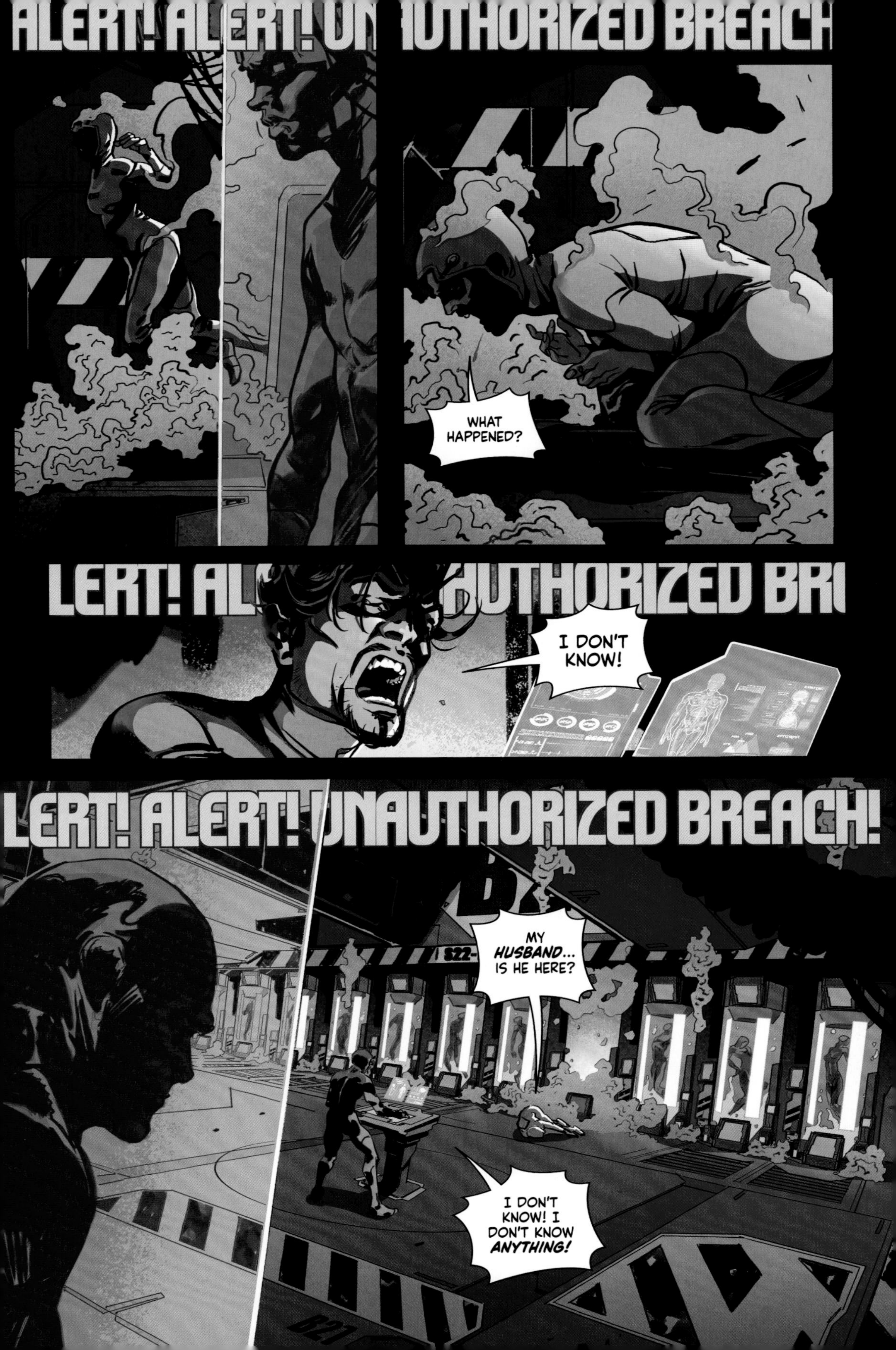
ALERT! ALERT! UNAUTHORIZED BREACH
WHAT HAPPENED?
LERT! AL UTHORIZED BRI
I DON'T KNOW!
LERT! ALERT! UNAUTHORIZED BREACH!
MY *HUSBAND*... IS HE HERE?
I DON'T KNOW! I DON'T KNOW *ANYTHING!*

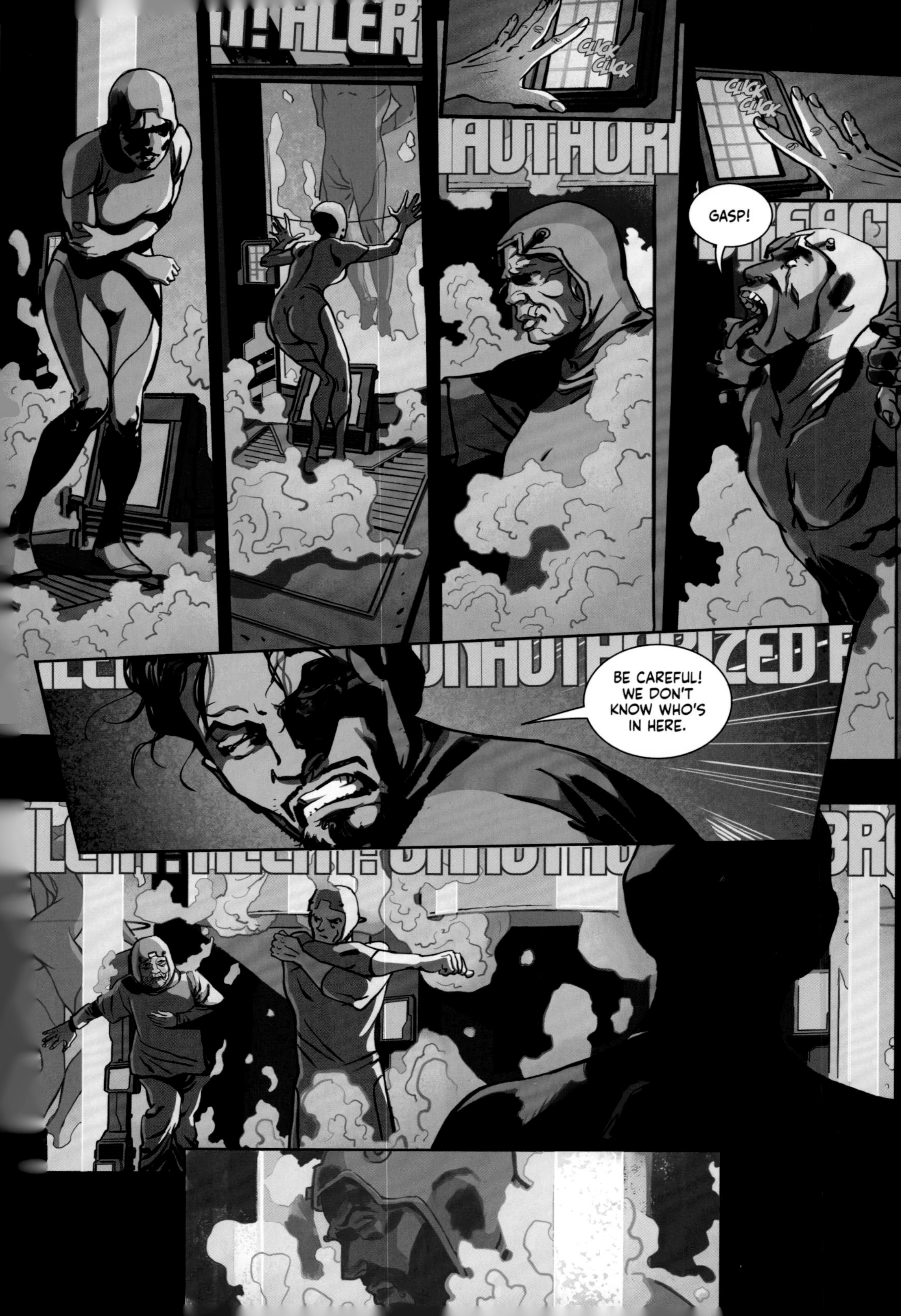
CLICK CLICK
CLICK CLICK
GASP!
BE CAREFUL! WE DON'T KNOW WHO'S IN HERE.

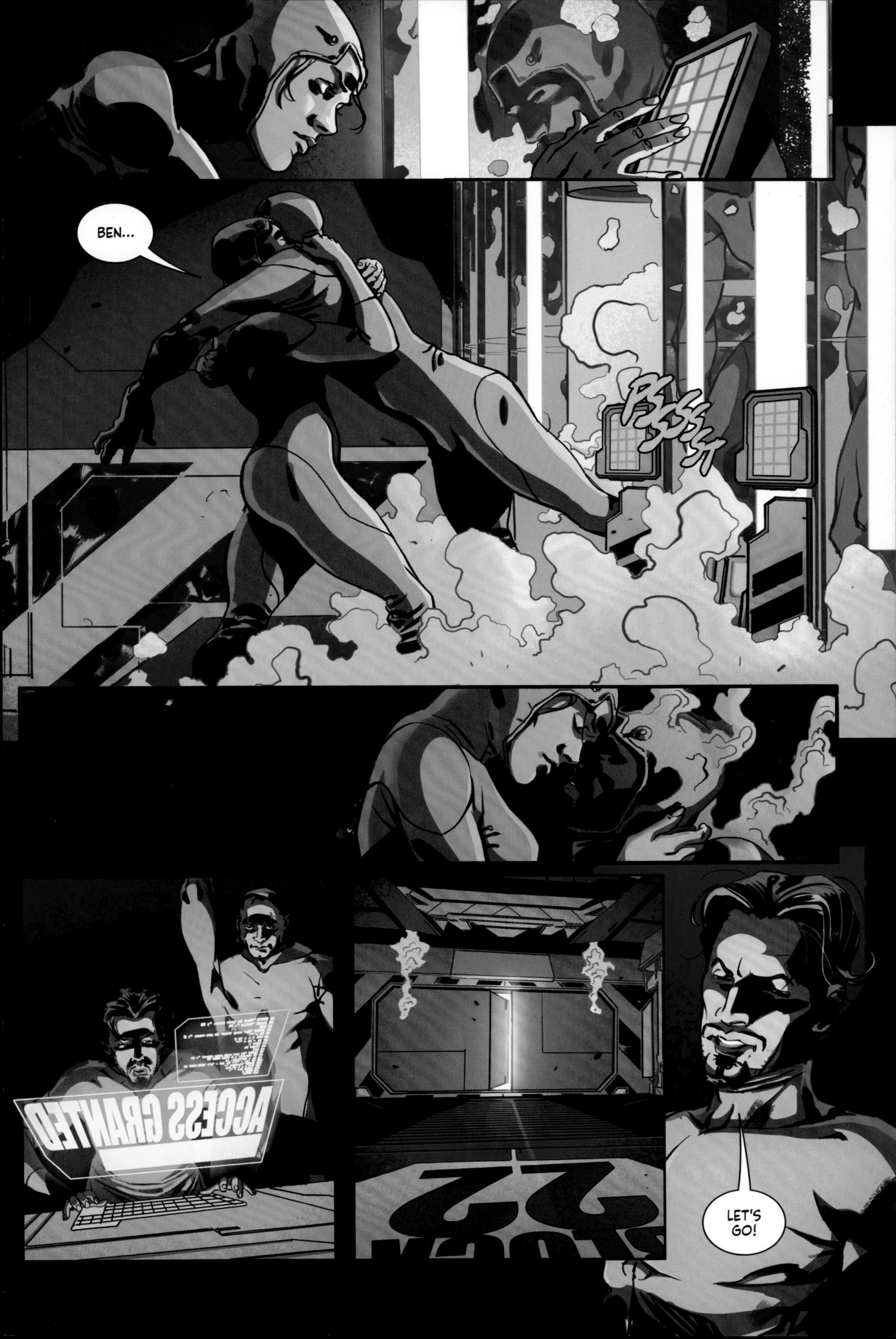
BEN...
PSSSST
ACCESS GRANTED
LET'S GO!

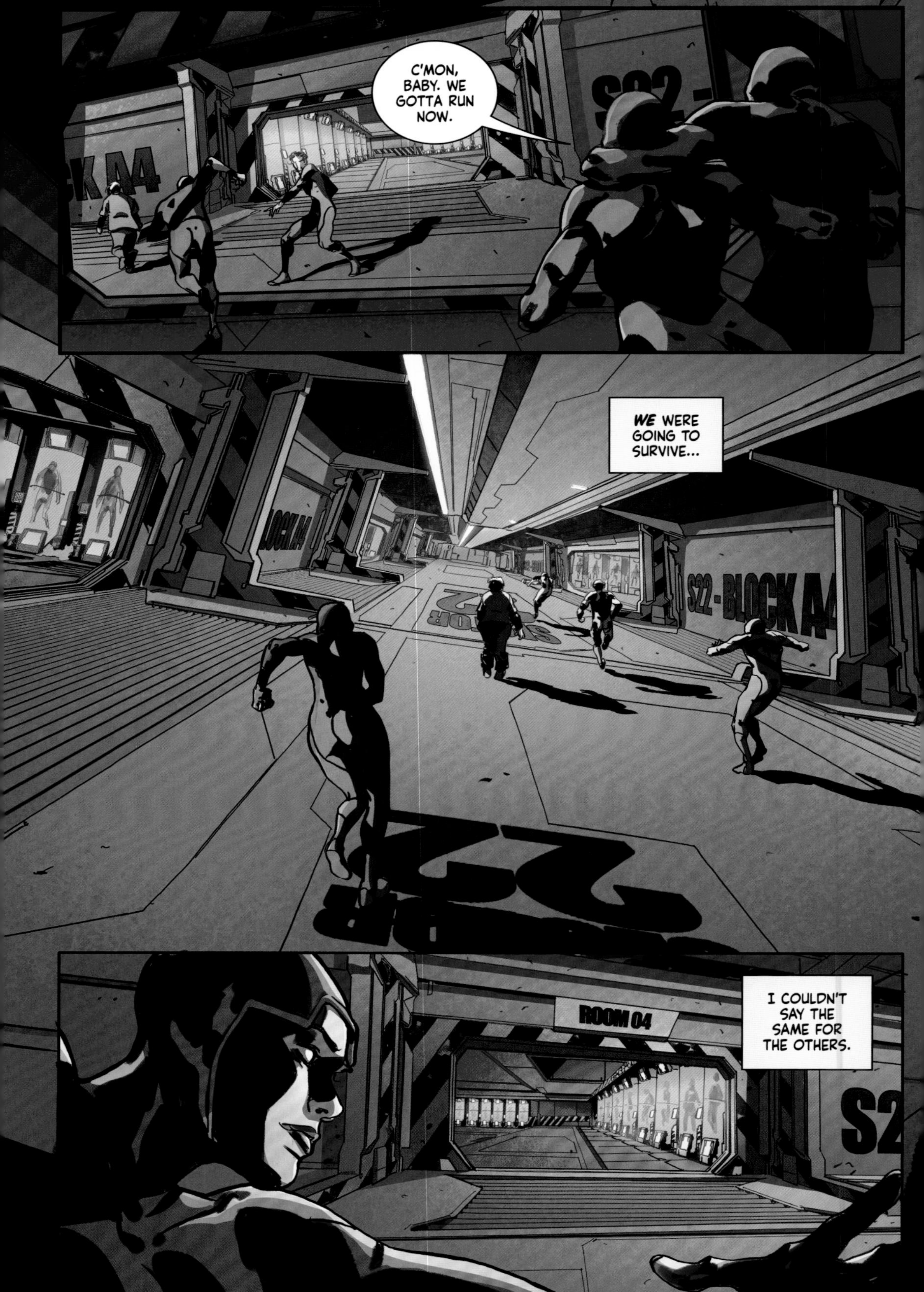

S22-
CK A4
C'MON, BABY. WE GOTTA RUN NOW.
WE WERE GOING TO SURVIVE...
LOCK A4
S22-BLOCK A4
ROOM 04
I COULDN'T SAY THE SAME FOR THE OTHERS.
S2

EDEN™

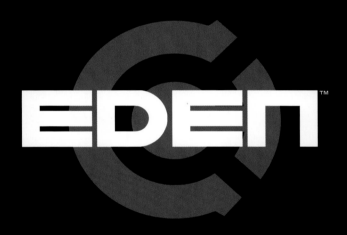

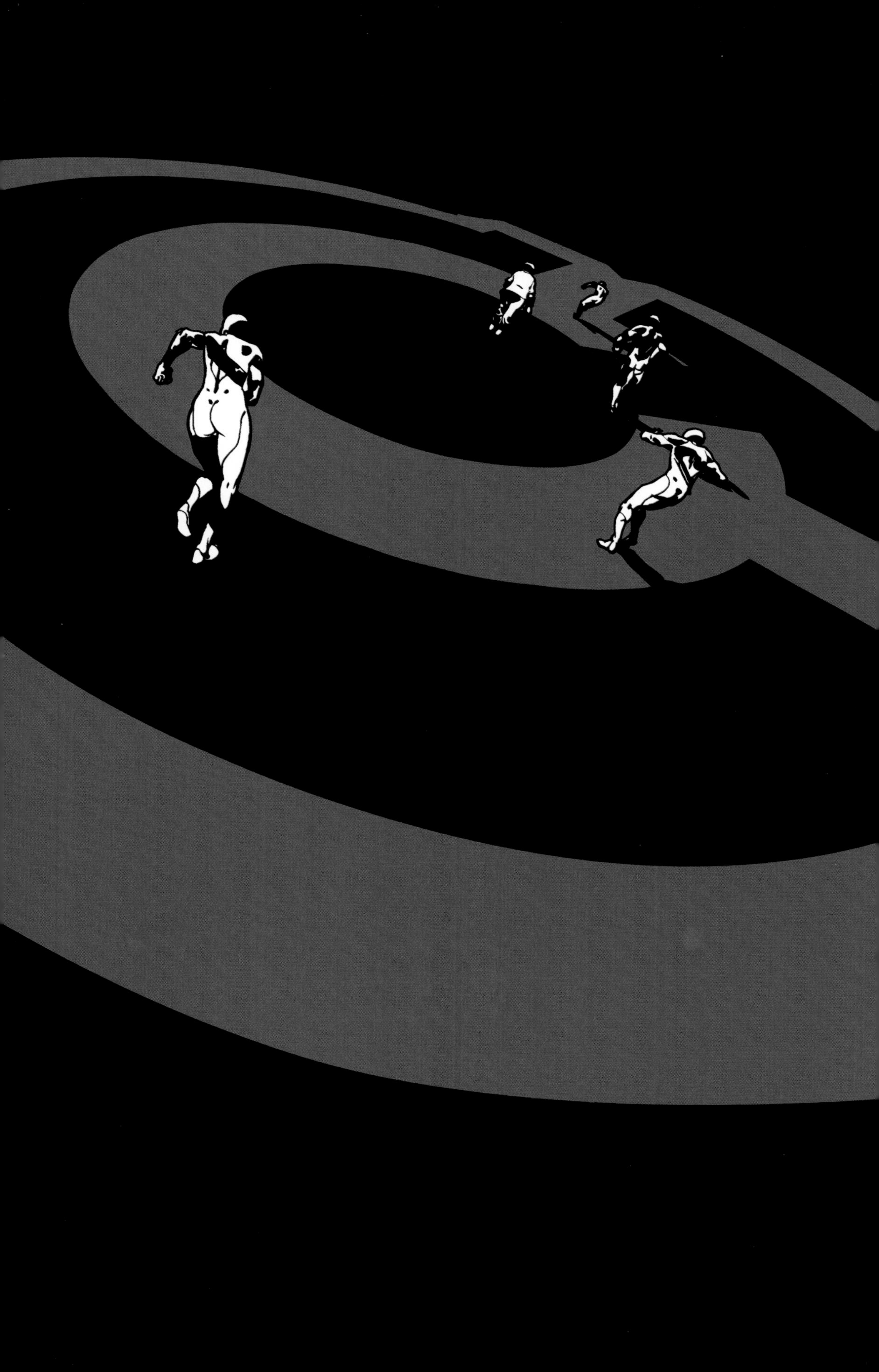

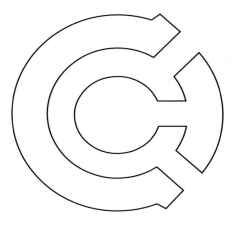

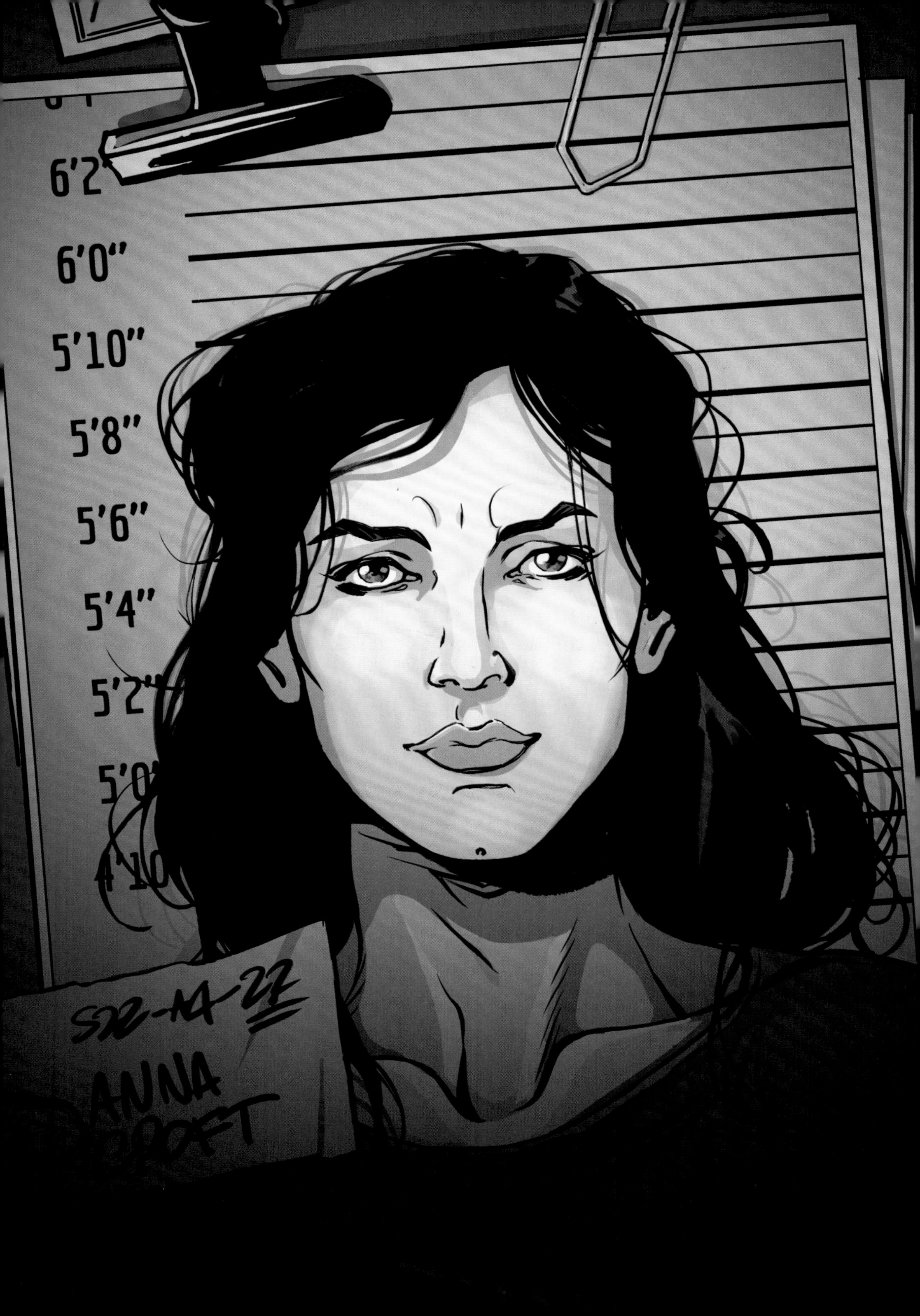
6'2"
6'0"
5'10"
5'8"
5'6"
5'4"
S22-14-22
ANNA

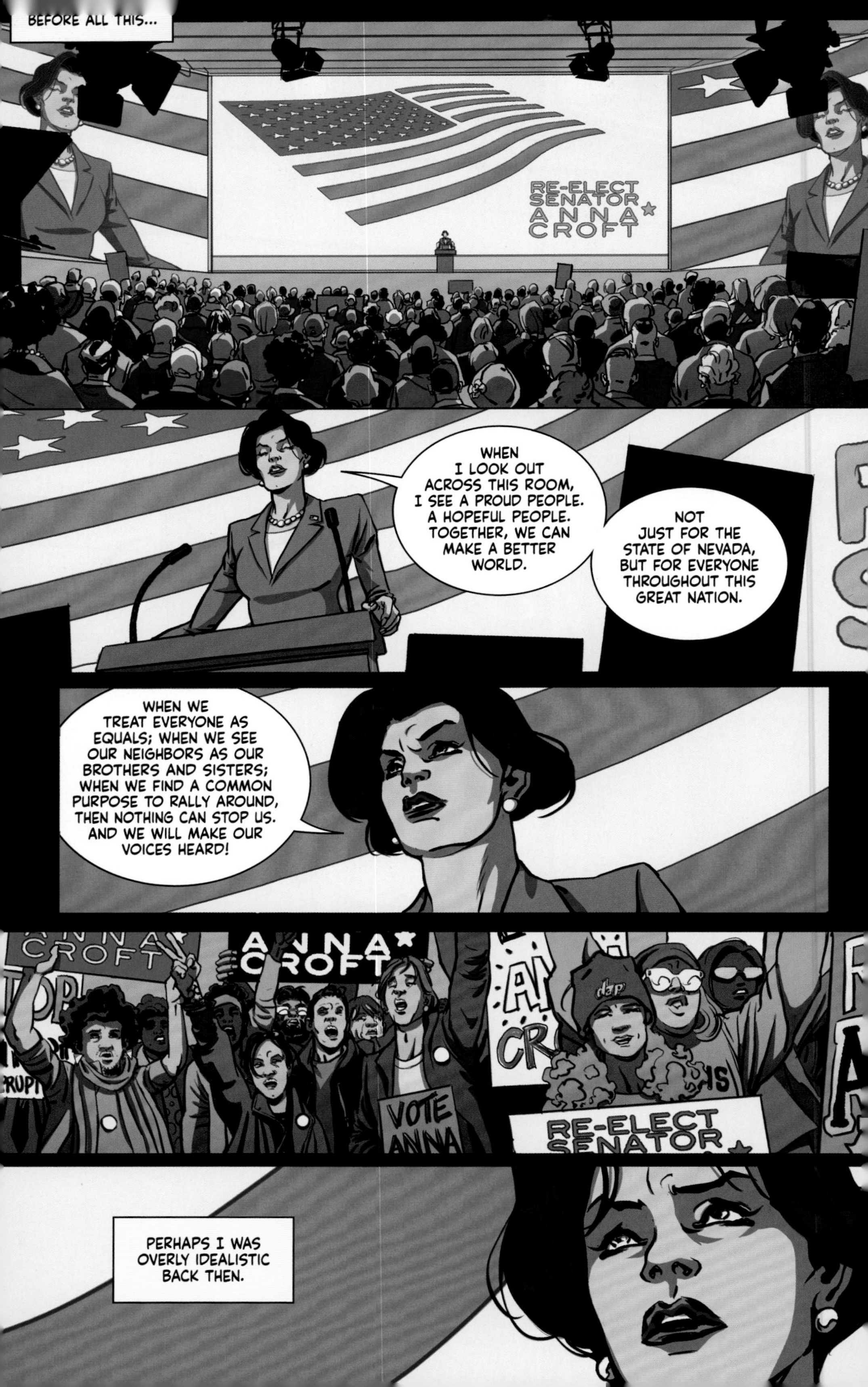
BEFORE ALL THIS...
RE-ELECT SENATOR ANNA CROFT
WHEN I LOOK OUT ACROSS THIS ROOM, I SEE A PROUD PEOPLE. A HOPEFUL PEOPLE. TOGETHER, WE CAN MAKE A BETTER WORLD.
NOT JUST FOR THE STATE OF NEVADA, BUT FOR EVERYONE THROUGHOUT THIS GREAT NATION.
WHEN WE TREAT EVERYONE AS EQUALS; WHEN WE SEE OUR NEIGHBORS AS OUR BROTHERS AND SISTERS; WHEN WE FIND A COMMON PURPOSE TO RALLY AROUND, THEN NOTHING CAN STOP US. AND WE WILL MAKE OUR VOICES HEARD!
ANNA CROFT
ANNA CROFT
VOTE ANNA
RE-ELECT SENATOR
PERHAPS I WAS OVERLY IDEALISTIC BACK THEN.

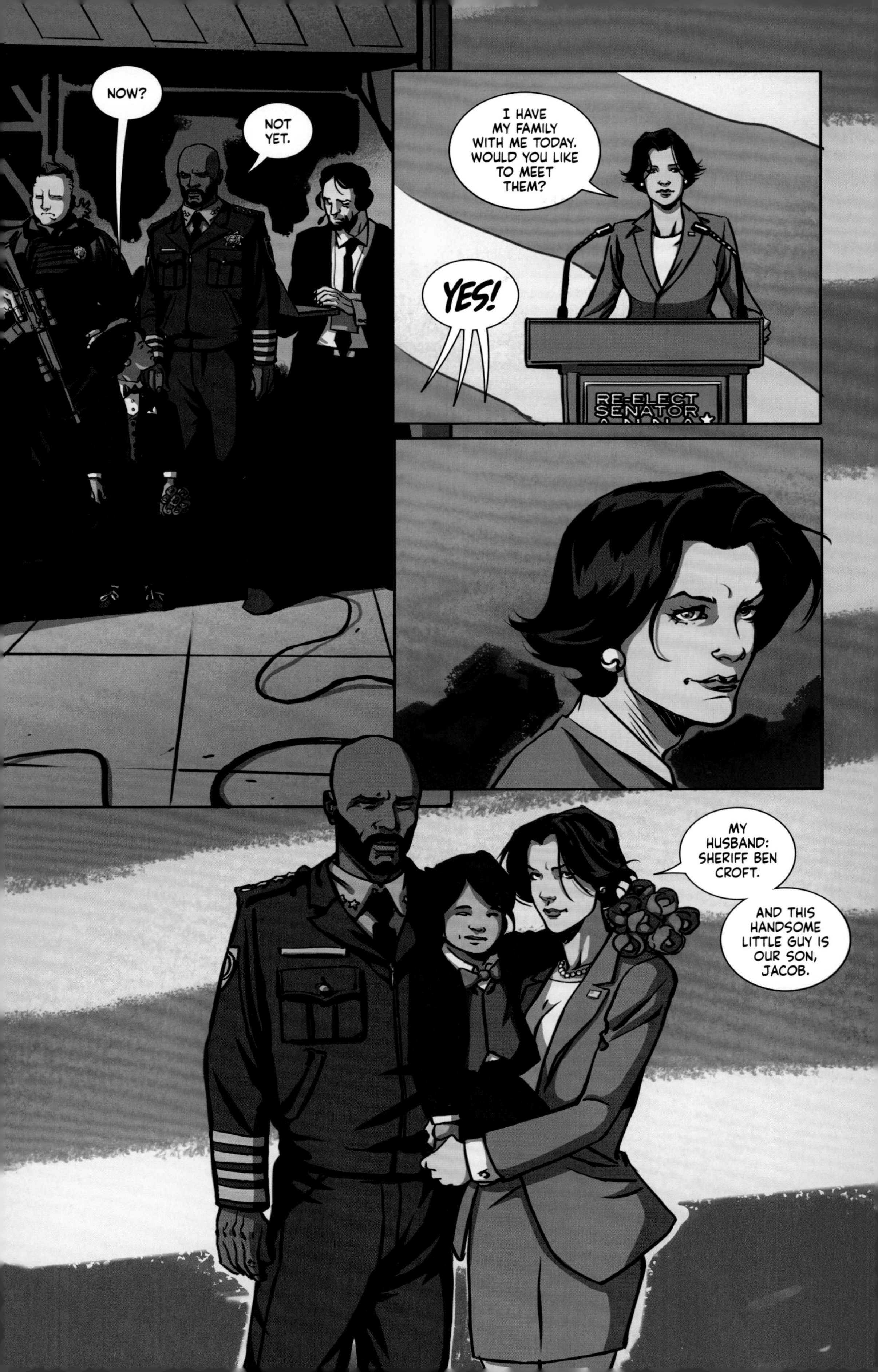
NOW?
NOT YET.
I HAVE MY FAMILY WITH ME TODAY. WOULD YOU LIKE TO MEET THEM?
YES!
RE-ELECT SENATOR
MY HUSBAND: SHERIFF BEN CROFT.
AND THIS HANDSOME LITTLE GUY IS OUR SON, JACOB.

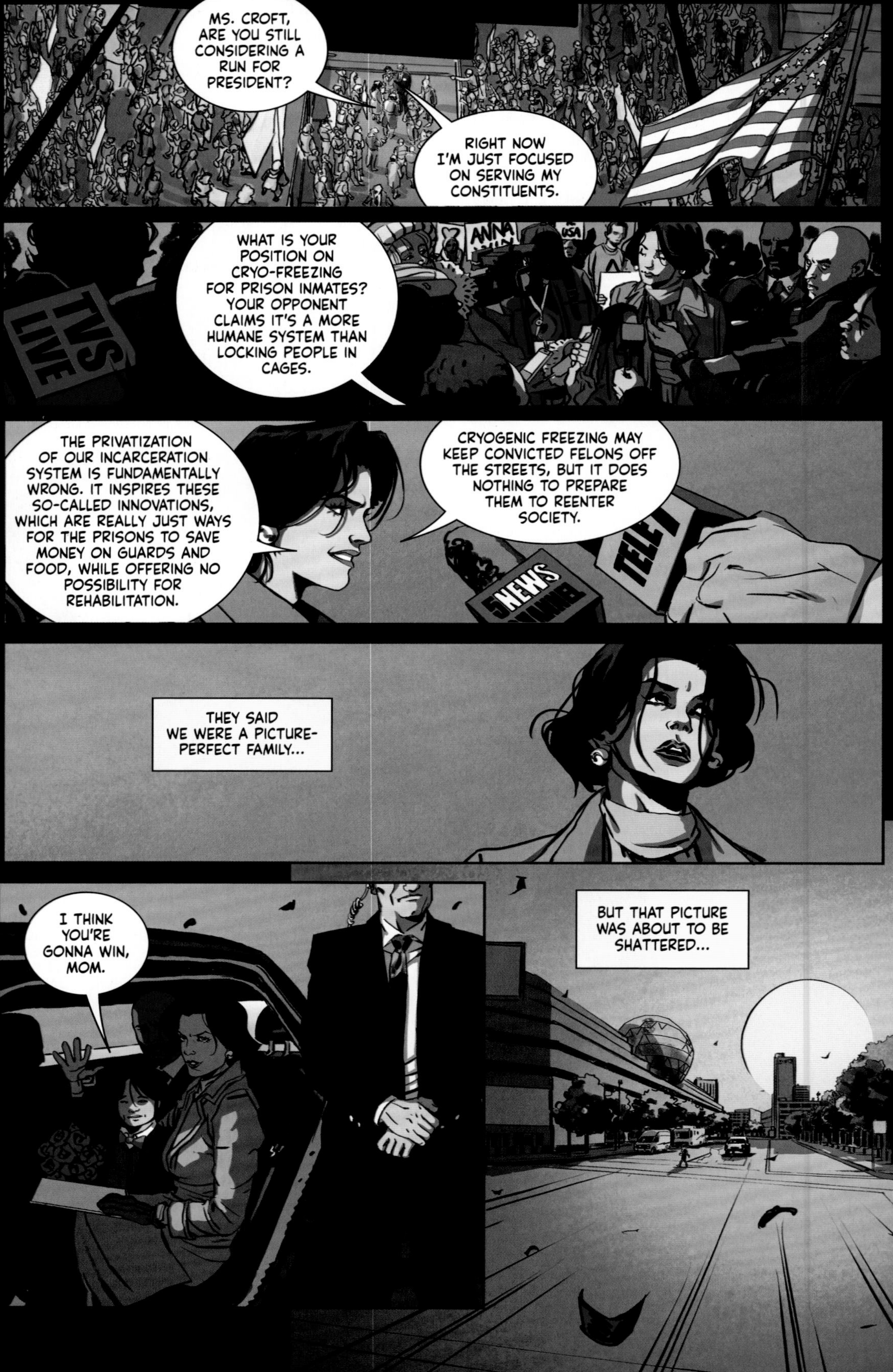
MS. CROFT, ARE YOU STILL CONSIDERING A RUN FOR PRESIDENT?
RIGHT NOW I'M JUST FOCUSED ON SERVING MY CONSTITUENTS.
TVS LIVE
WHAT IS YOUR POSITION ON CRYO-FREEZING FOR PRISON INMATES? YOUR OPPONENT CLAIMS IT'S A MORE HUMANE SYSTEM THAN LOCKING PEOPLE IN CAGES.
THE PRIVATIZATION OF OUR INCARCERATION SYSTEM IS FUNDAMENTALLY WRONG. IT INSPIRES THESE SO-CALLED INNOVATIONS, WHICH ARE REALLY JUST WAYS FOR THE PRISONS TO SAVE MONEY ON GUARDS AND FOOD, WHILE OFFERING NO POSSIBILITY FOR REHABILITATION.
CRYOGENIC FREEZING MAY KEEP CONVICTED FELONS OFF THE STREETS, BUT IT DOES NOTHING TO PREPARE THEM TO REENTER SOCIETY.
THEY SAID WE WERE A PICTURE-PERFECT FAMILY...
I THINK YOU'RE GONNA WIN, MOM.
BUT THAT PICTURE WAS ABOUT TO BE SHATTERED...

TRAGEDY STRIKES THE FAMILY OF SENATOR ANNA CROFT TODAY...

THE RENO POLICE DEPARTMENT IS REPORTING THAT THE FIVE-YEAR-OLD SON OF THE SENATOR WAS APPARENTLY KIDNAPPED SOMETIME LATE YESTERDAY AFTERNOON. WE GO NOW TO A PRESS CONFERENCE ALREADY IN PROGRESS...

HEADLINE NEWS LIVE AMERICA

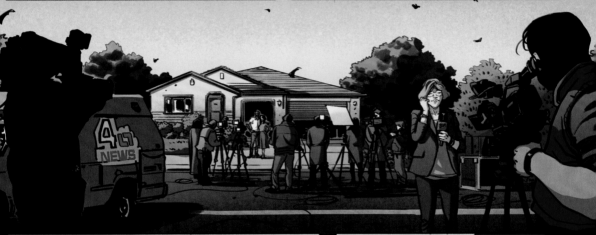

IF ANYONE HAS ANY INFORMATION, PLEASE COME FORWARD. WE *LOVE* OUR BOY AND WE DESPERATELY WANT HIM BACK.

SENATOR CROFT...IS THERE SOMETHING YOU WANT TO SAY TO THE PERSON WHO DID THIS?

I...JUST DON'T KNOW WHAT TO SAY. NO COMMENT NOW.

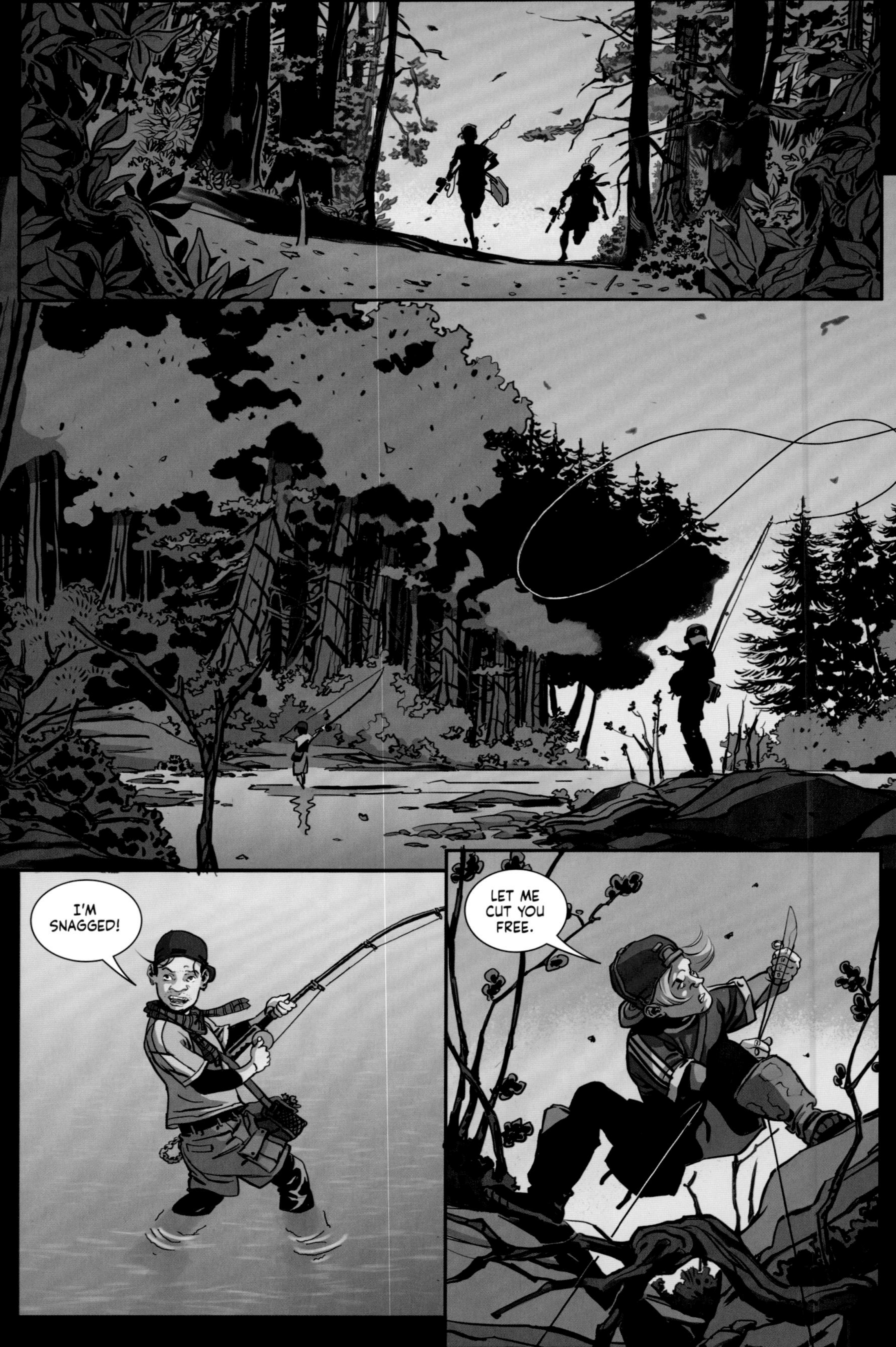
I'M SNAGGED!
LET ME CUT YOU FREE.

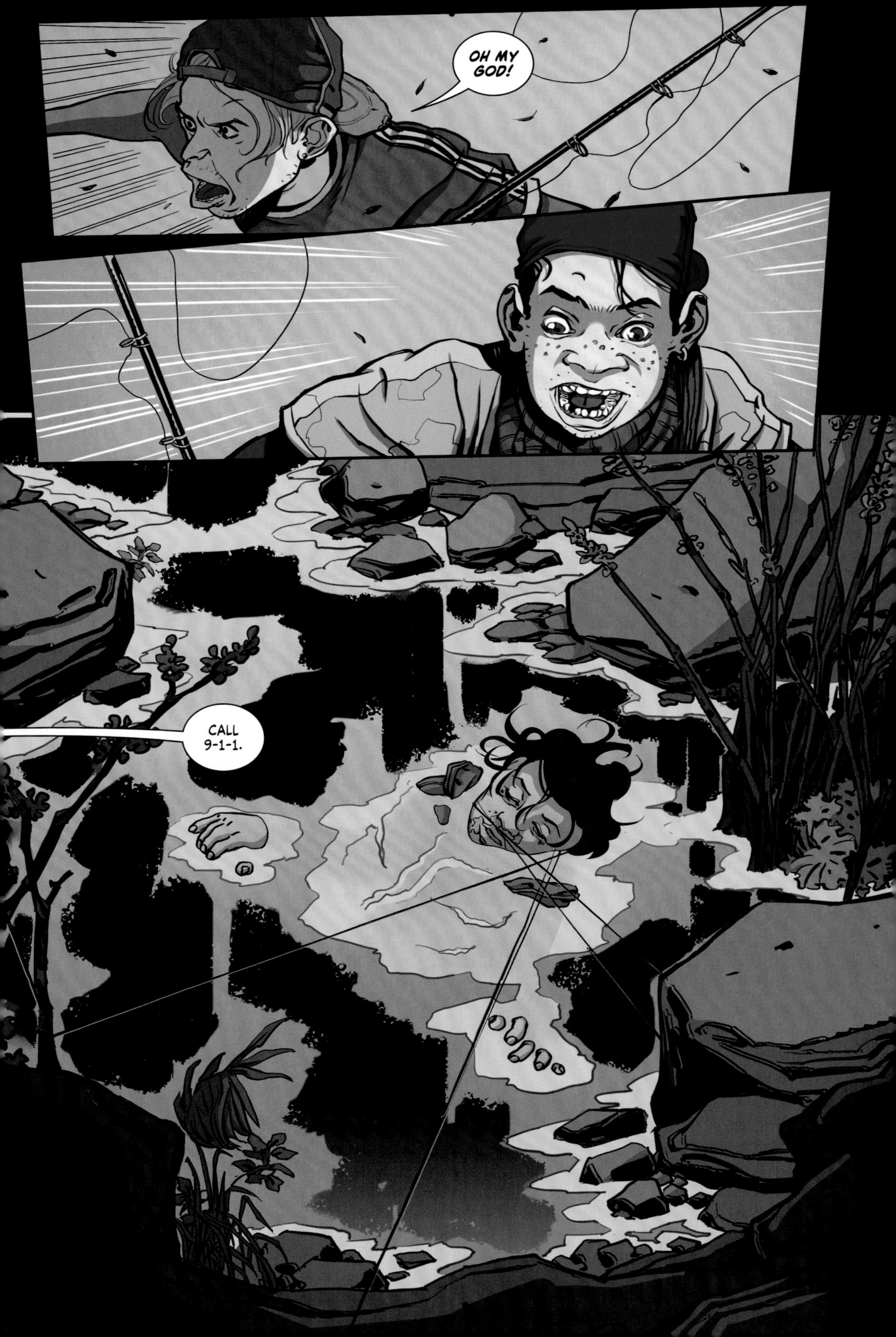
OH MY GOD!
CALL 9-1-1.

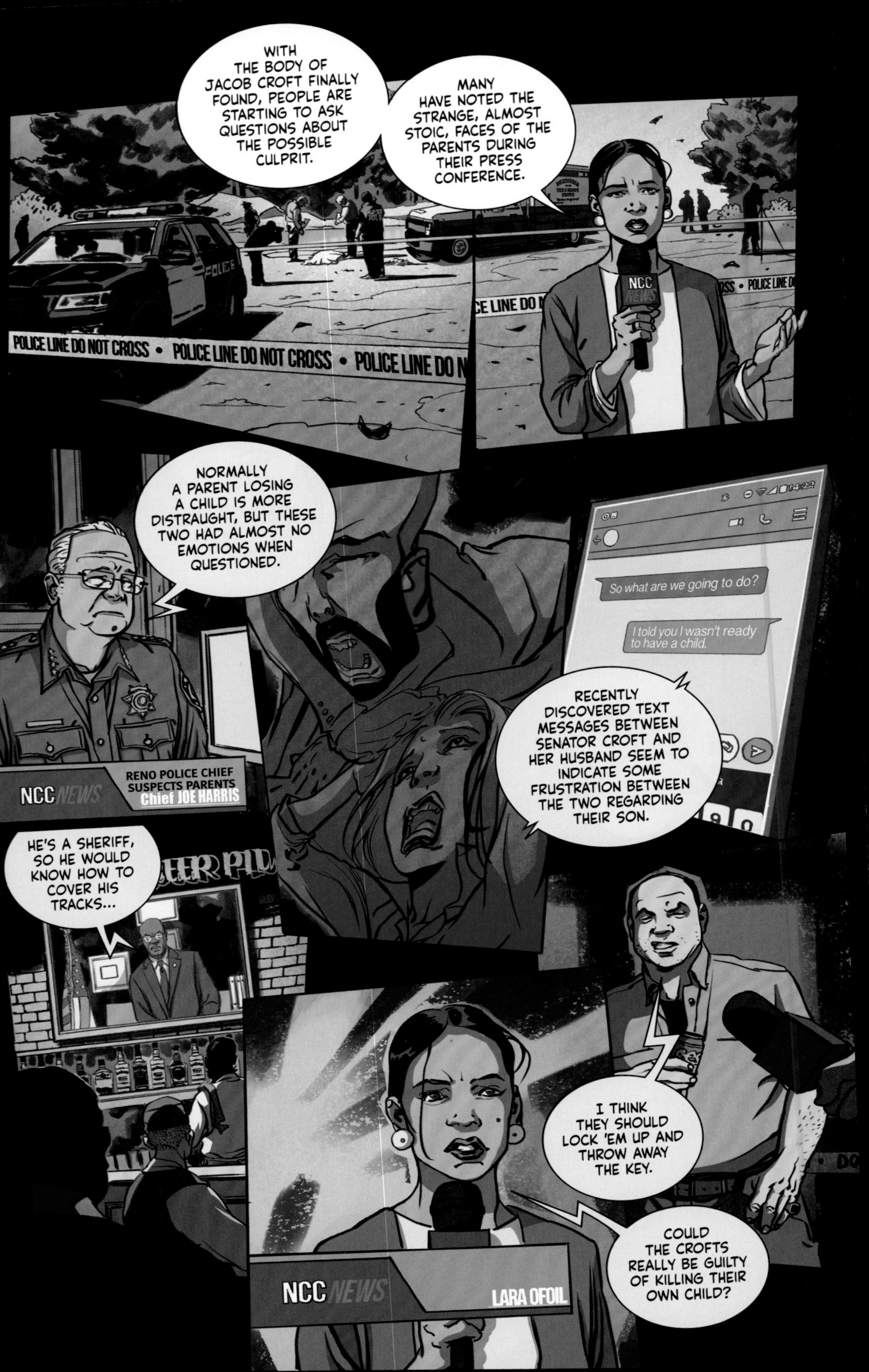
WITH THE BODY OF JACOB CROFT FINALLY FOUND, PEOPLE ARE STARTING TO ASK QUESTIONS ABOUT THE POSSIBLE CULPRIT.
MANY HAVE NOTED THE STRANGE, ALMOST STOIC, FACES OF THE PARENTS DURING THEIR PRESS CONFERENCE.
POLICE LINE DO NOT CROSS • POLICE LINE DO NOT CROSS • POLICE LINE DO N
POLICE
NCC NEWS
NORMALLY A PARENT LOSING A CHILD IS MORE DISTRAUGHT, BUT THESE TWO HAD ALMOST NO EMOTIONS WHEN QUESTIONED.
NCC NEWS
RENO POLICE CHIEF SUSPECTS PARENTS
Chief JOE HARRIS
So what are we going to do?
I told you I wasn't ready to have a child.
RECENTLY DISCOVERED TEXT MESSAGES BETWEEN SENATOR CROFT AND HER HUSBAND SEEM TO INDICATE SOME FRUSTRATION BETWEEN THE TWO REGARDING THEIR SON.
HE'S A SHERIFF, SO HE WOULD KNOW HOW TO COVER HIS TRACKS...
I THINK THEY SHOULD LOCK 'EM UP AND THROW AWAY THE KEY.
NCC NEWS
LARA OFOIL
COULD THE CROFTS REALLY BE GUILTY OF KILLING THEIR OWN CHILD?

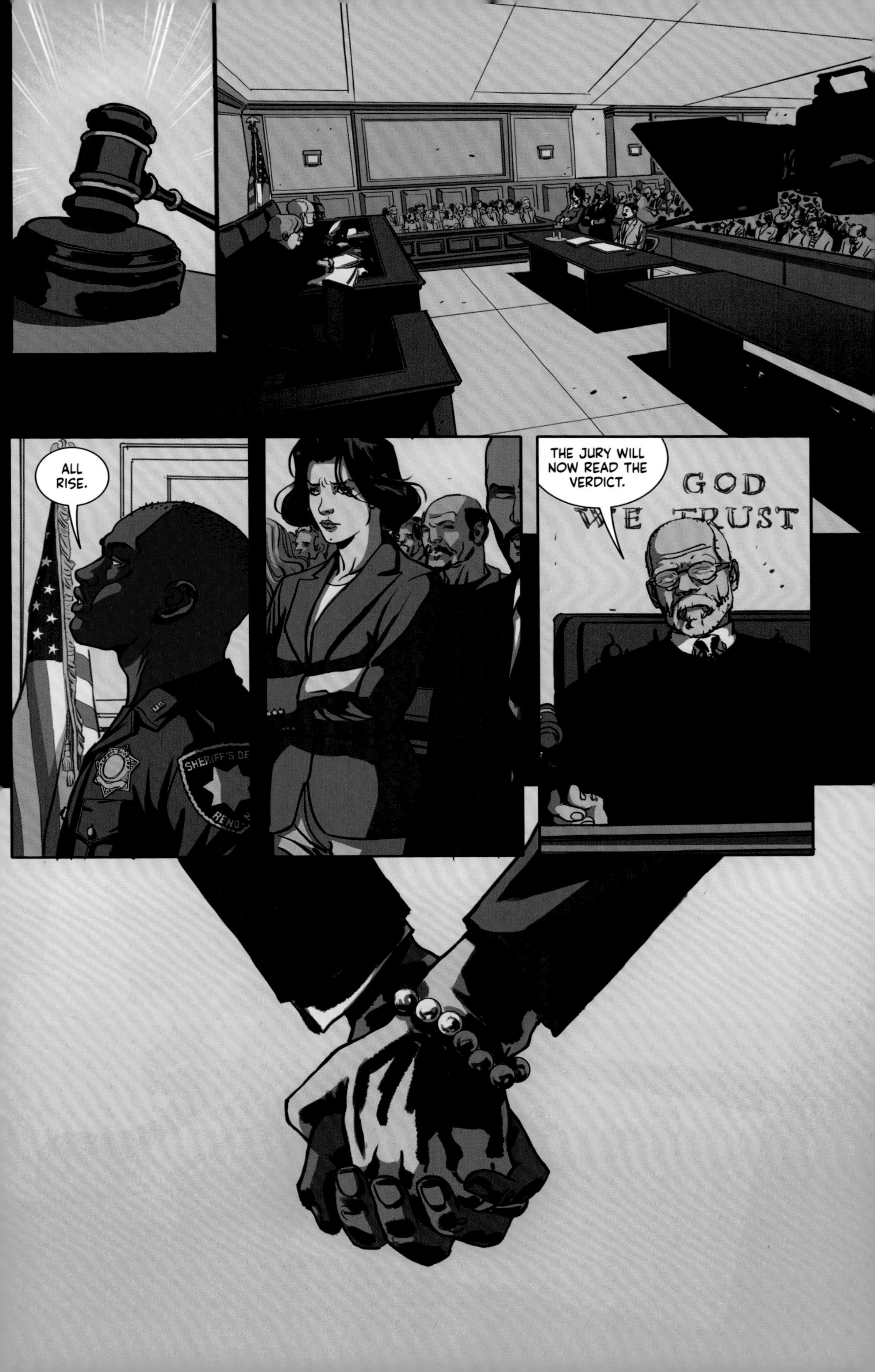
ALL RISE.
SHERIFF'S DE
RENO
THE JURY WILL NOW READ THE VERDICT.
GOD
WE TRUST

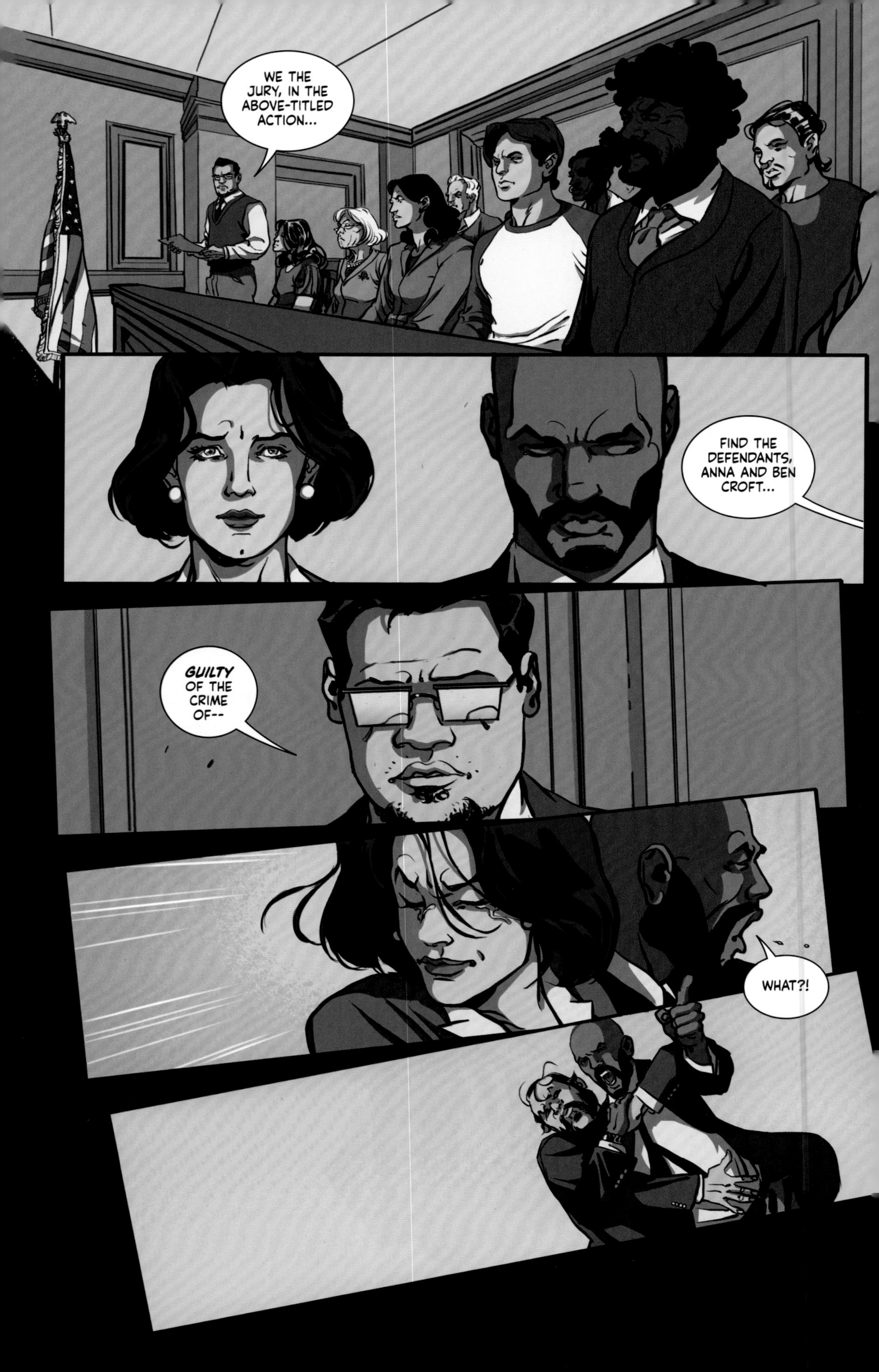
WE THE JURY, IN THE ABOVE-TITLED ACTION...
FIND THE DEFENDANTS, ANNA AND BEN CROFT...
GUILTY OF THE CRIME OF--
WHAT?!

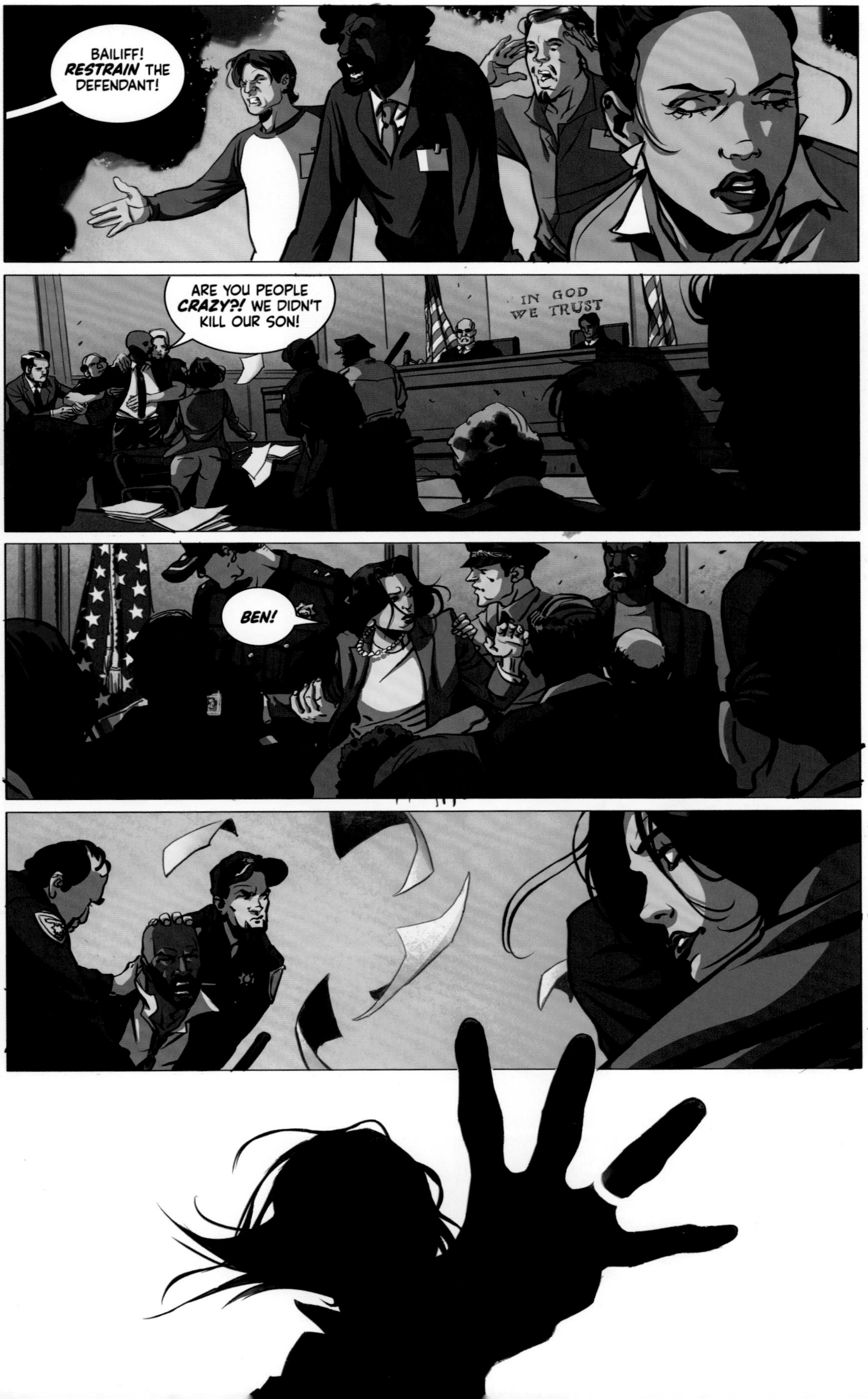
BAILIFF! RESTRAIN THE DEFENDANT!
ARE YOU PEOPLE CRAZY?! WE DIDN'T KILL OUR SON!
IN GOD WE TRUST
BEN!

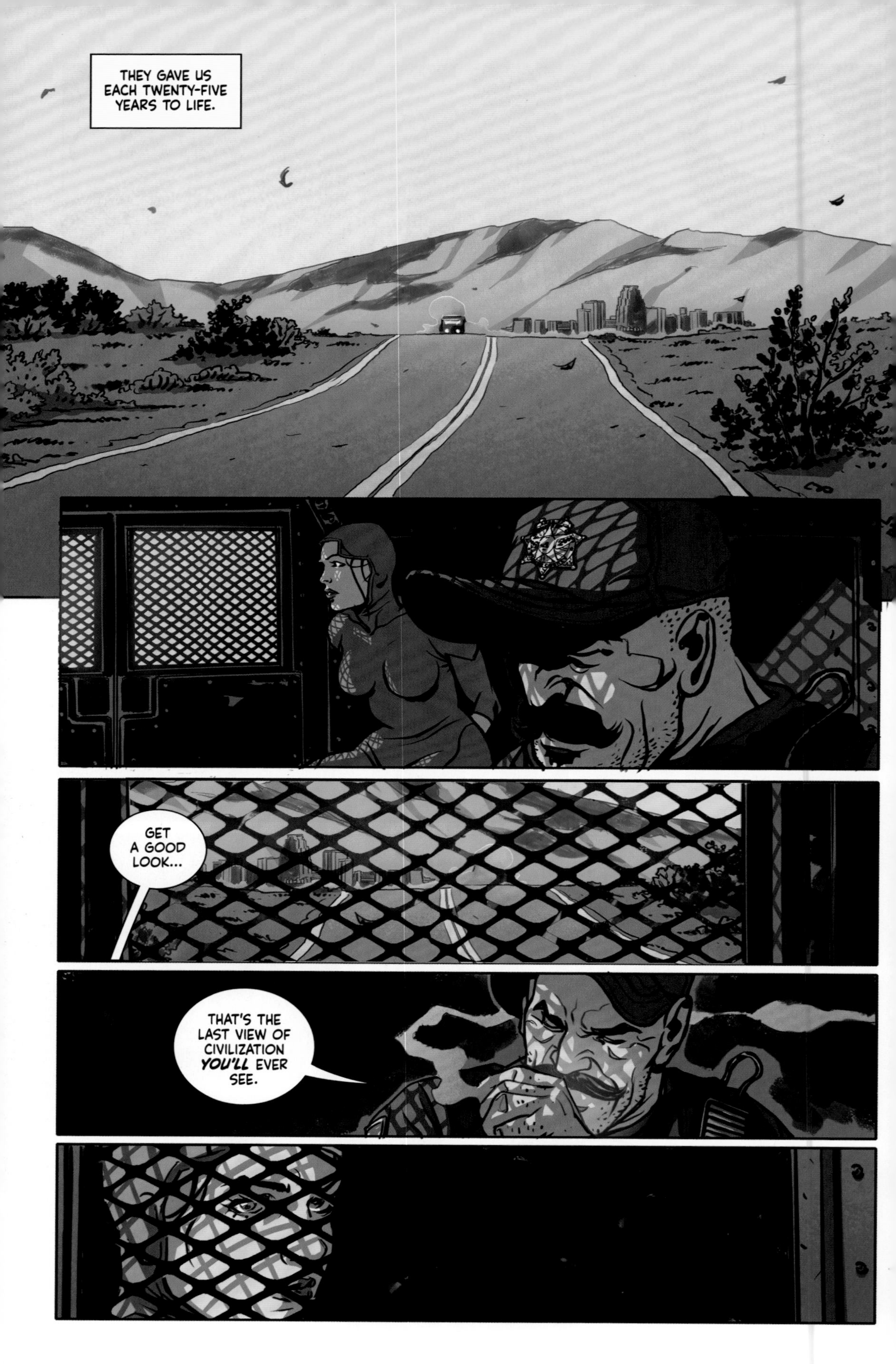
THEY GAVE US EACH TWENTY-FIVE YEARS TO LIFE.
GET A GOOD LOOK...
THAT'S THE LAST VIEW OF CIVILIZATION *YOU'LL* EVER SEE.

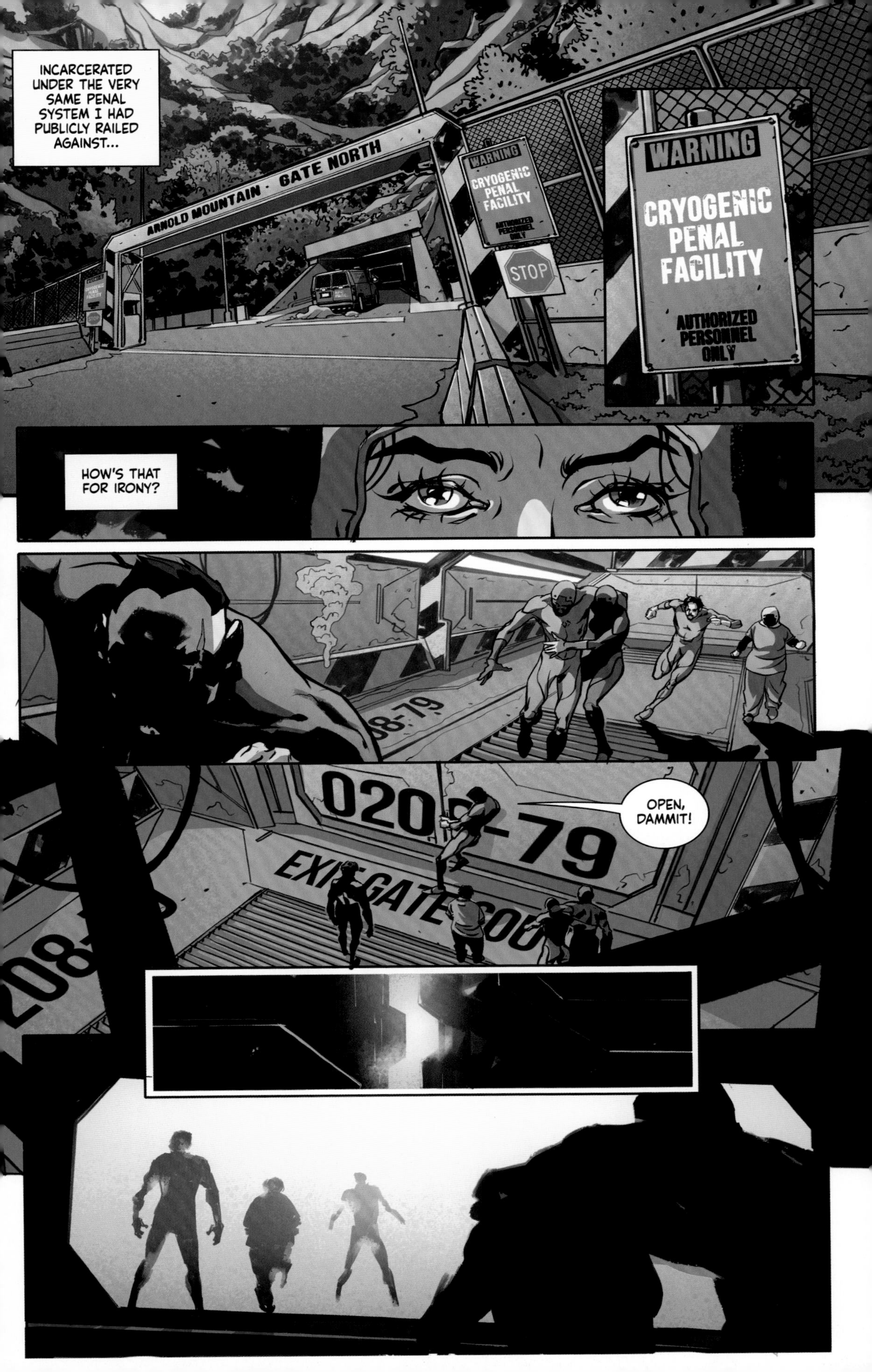
INCARCERATED UNDER THE VERY SAME PENAL SYSTEM I HAD PUBLICLY RAILED AGAINST...
ARNOLD MOUNTAIN · GATE NORTH
WARNING
CRYOGENIC PENAL FACILITY
AUTHORIZED PERSONNEL ONLY
STOP
WARNING
CRYOGENIC PENAL FACILITY
AUTHORIZED PERSONNEL ONLY
HOW'S THAT FOR IRONY?
OPEN, DAMMIT!

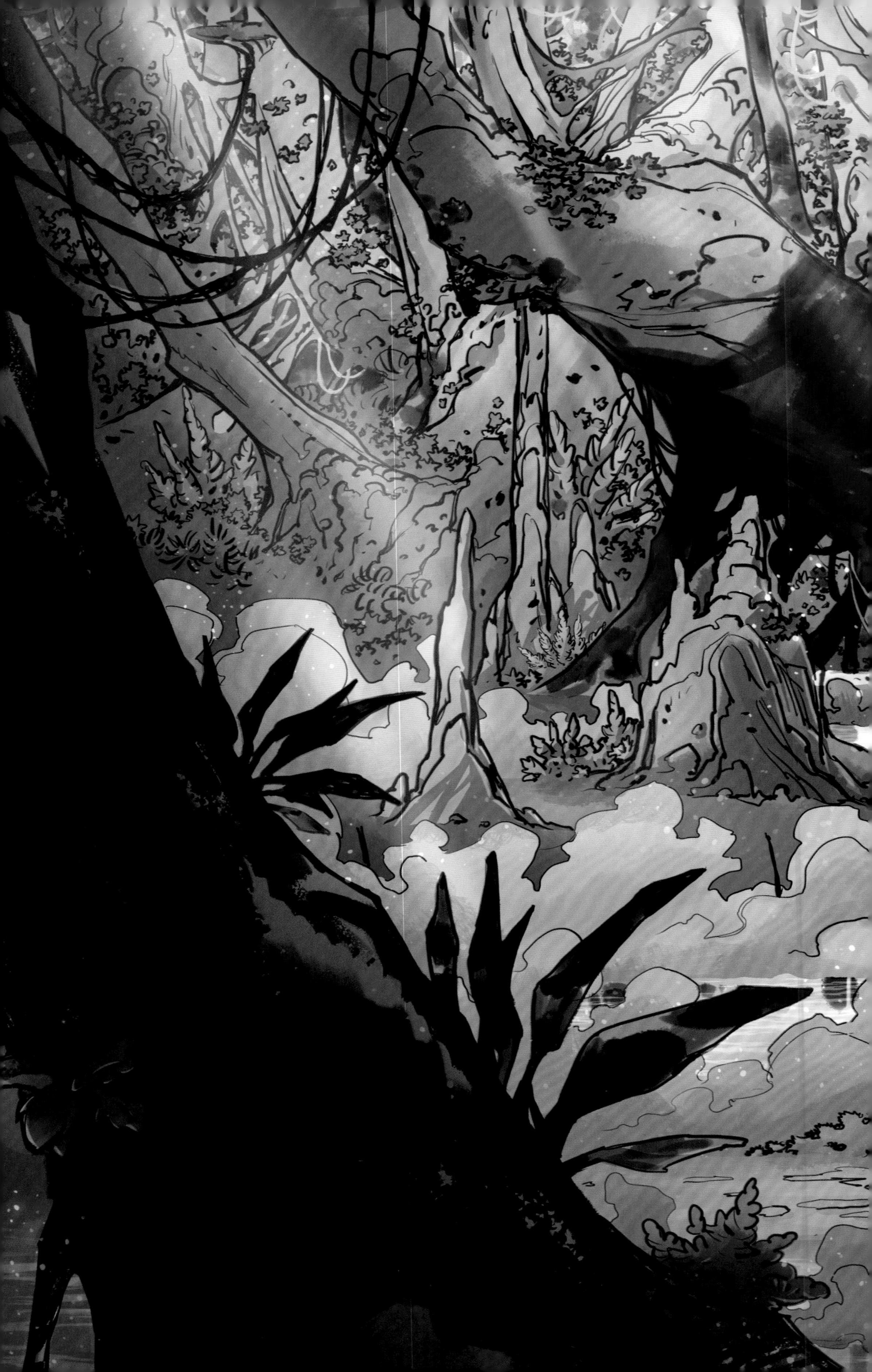

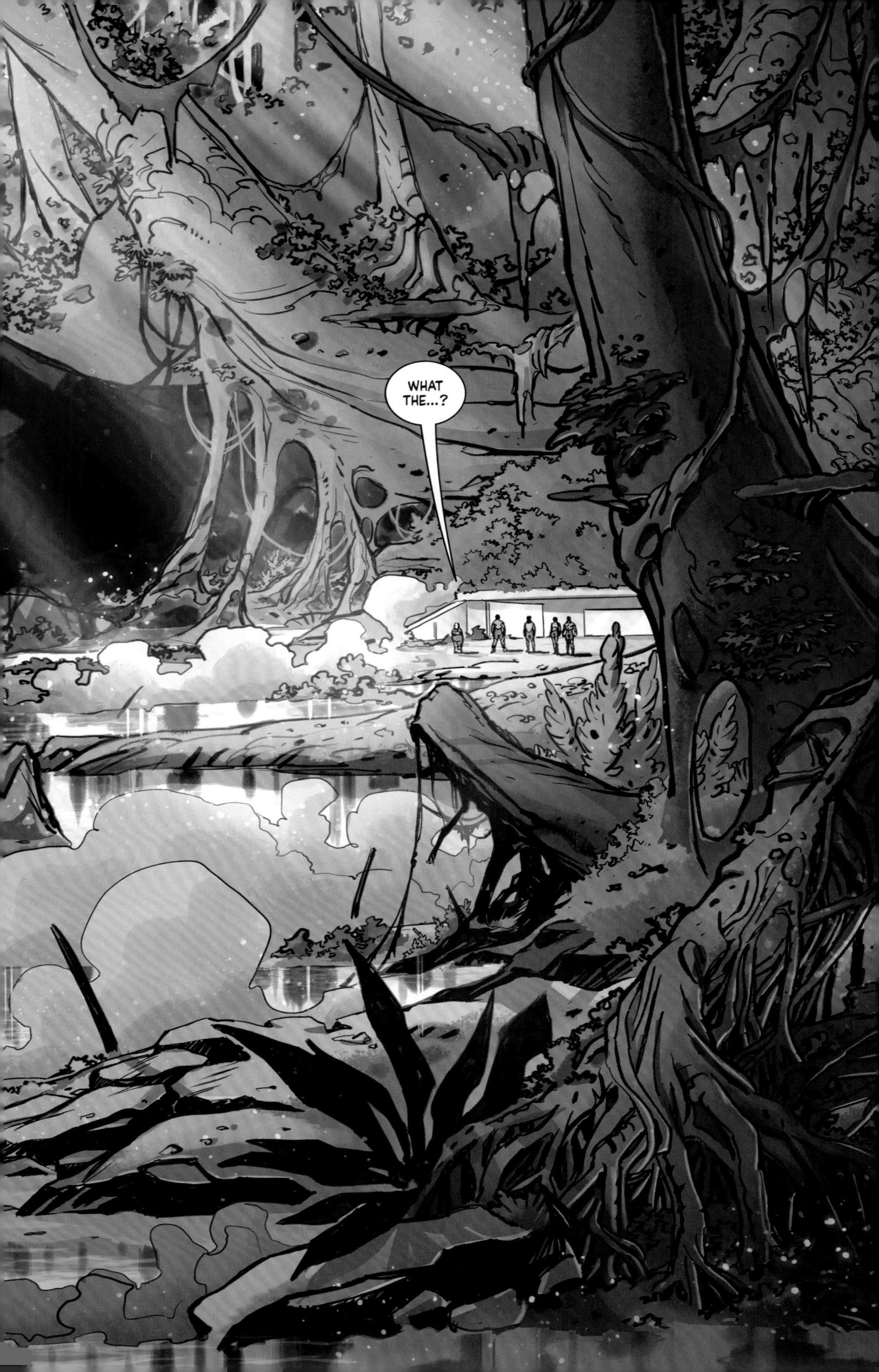
WHAT THE...?

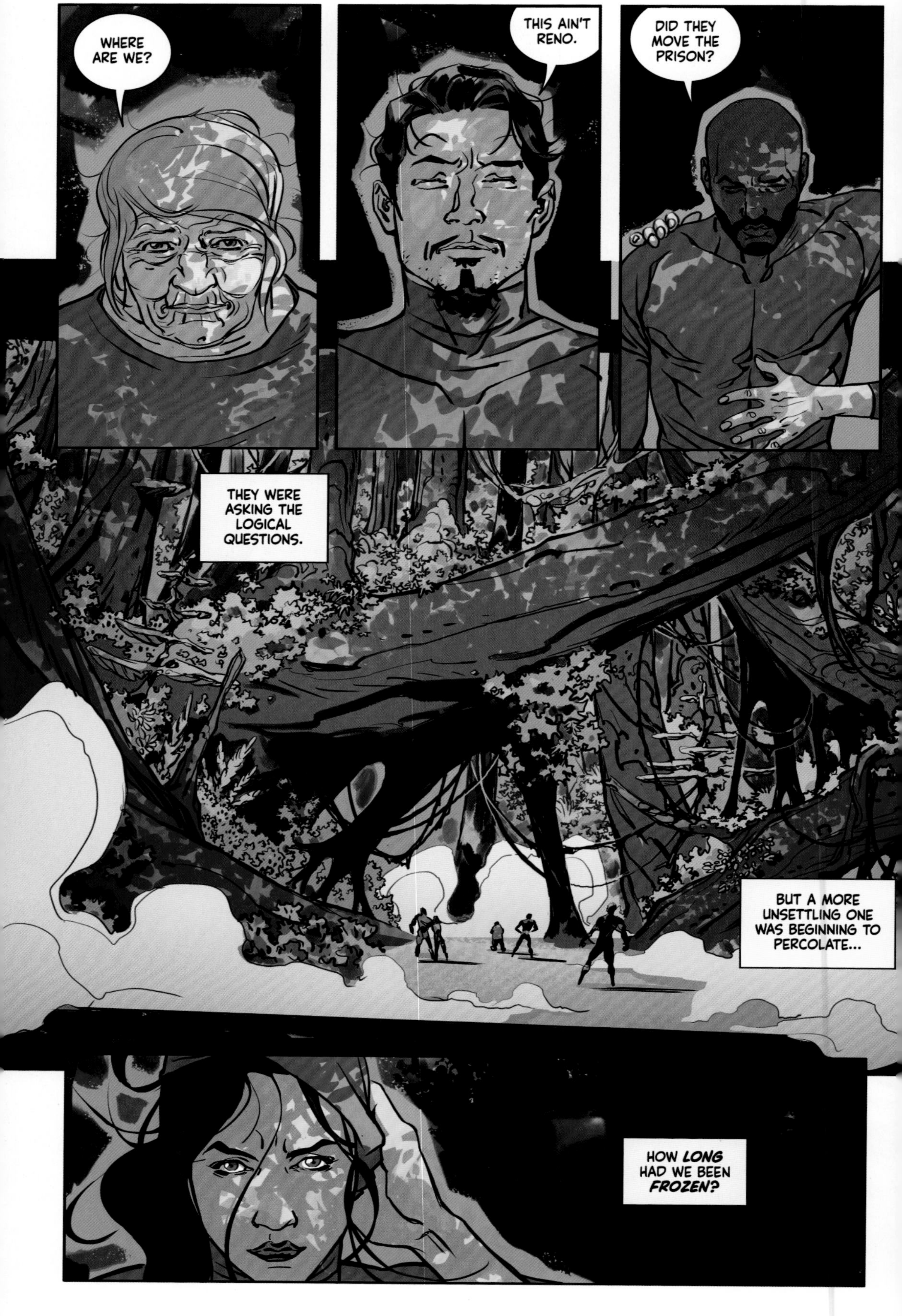
WHERE ARE WE?
THIS AIN'T RENO.
DID THEY MOVE THE PRISON?
THEY WERE ASKING THE LOGICAL QUESTIONS.
BUT A MORE UNSETTLING ONE WAS BEGINNING TO PERCOLATE...
HOW LONG HAD WE BEEN FROZEN?

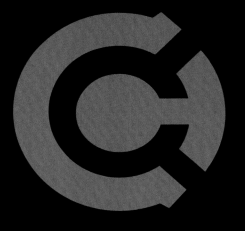

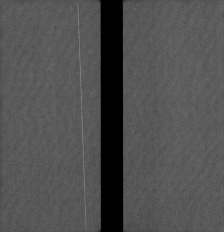

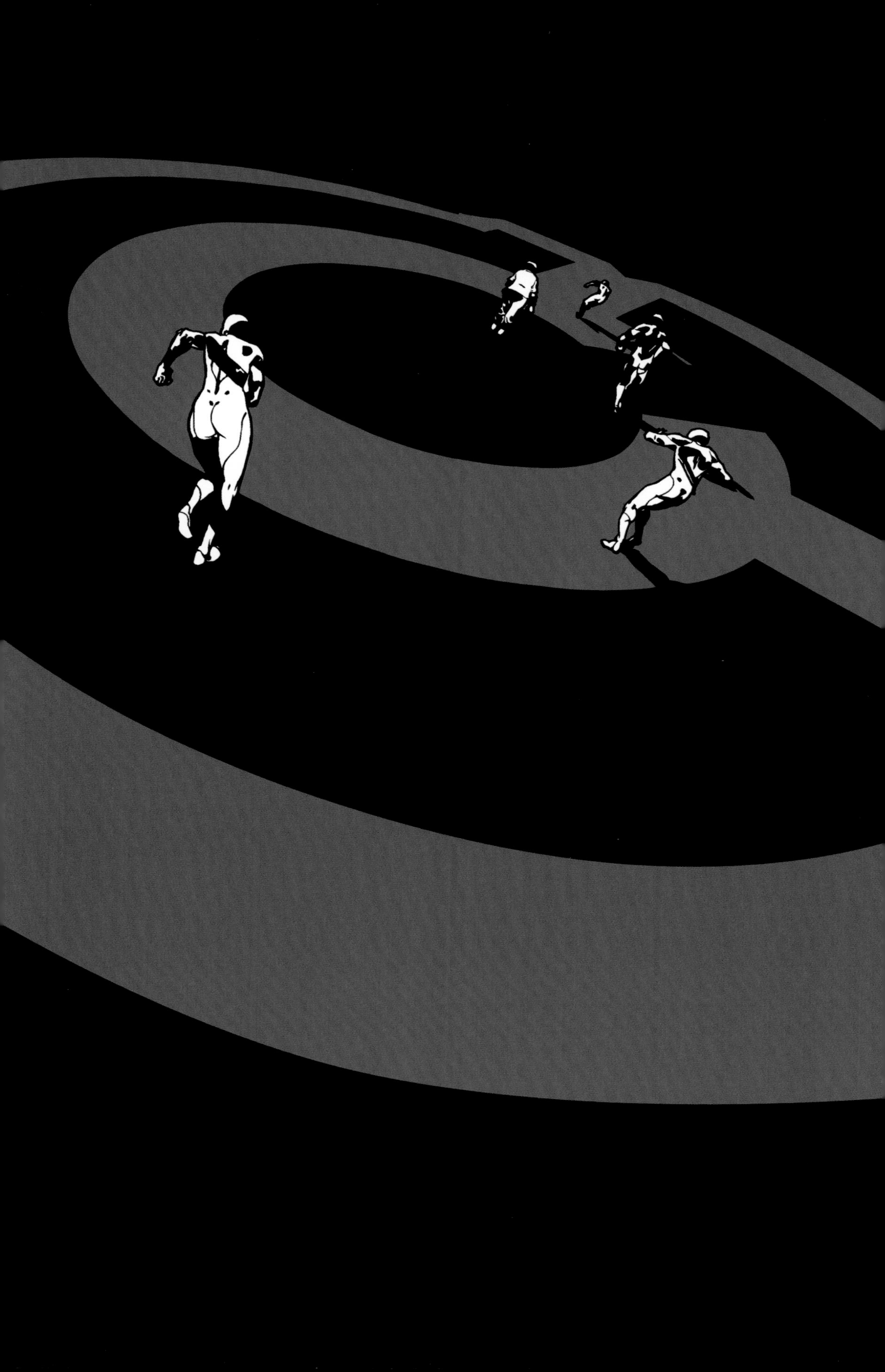

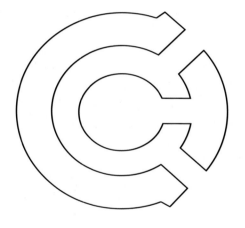

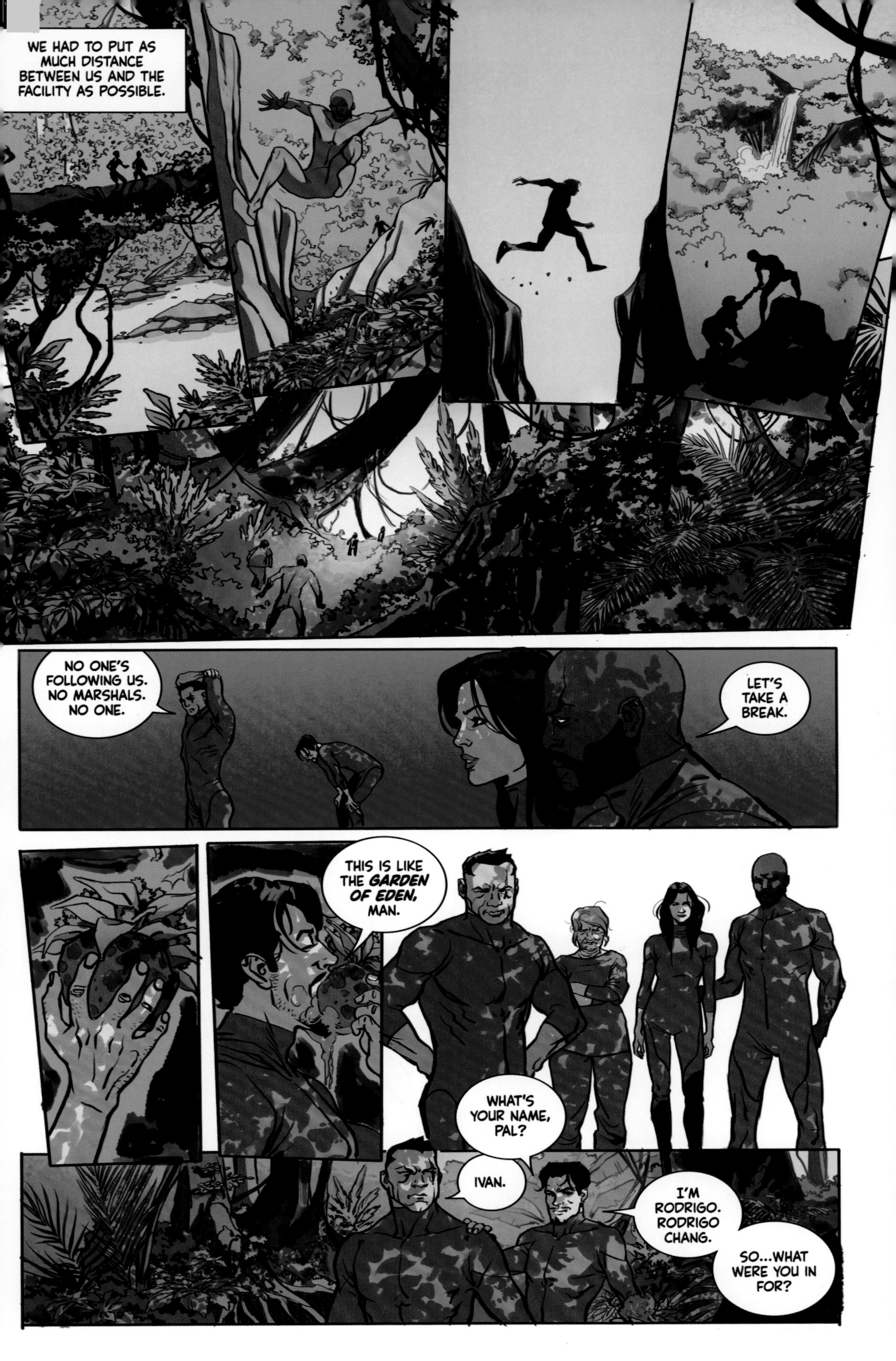
WE HAD TO PUT AS MUCH DISTANCE BETWEEN US AND THE FACILITY AS POSSIBLE.
NO ONE'S FOLLOWING US. NO MARSHALS. NO ONE.
LET'S TAKE A BREAK.
THIS IS LIKE THE *GARDEN OF EDEN,* MAN.
WHAT'S YOUR NAME, PAL?
IVAN.
I'M RODRIGO. RODRIGO CHANG.
SO...WHAT WERE YOU IN FOR?

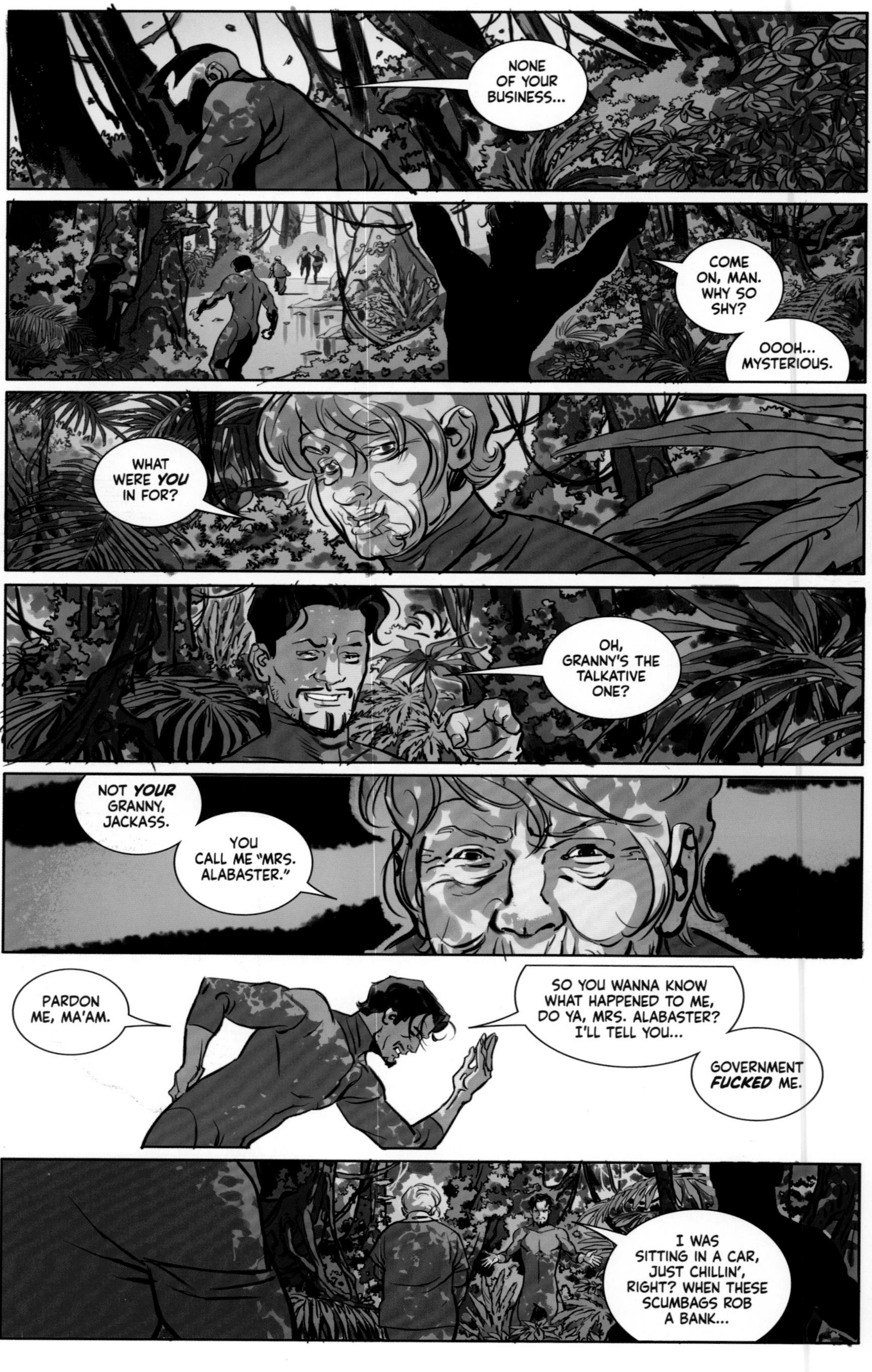
NONE OF YOUR BUSINESS...
COME ON, MAN. WHY SO SHY?
OOOH... MYSTERIOUS.
WHAT WERE *YOU* IN FOR?
OH, GRANNY'S THE TALKATIVE ONE?
NOT *YOUR* GRANNY, JACKASS.
YOU CALL ME "MRS. ALABASTER."
PARDON ME, MA'AM.
SO YOU WANNA KNOW WHAT HAPPENED TO ME, DO YA, MRS. ALABASTER? I'LL TELL YOU...
GOVERNMENT *FUCKED* ME.
I WAS SITTING IN A CAR, JUST CHILLIN', RIGHT? WHEN THESE SCUMBAGS ROB A BANK...

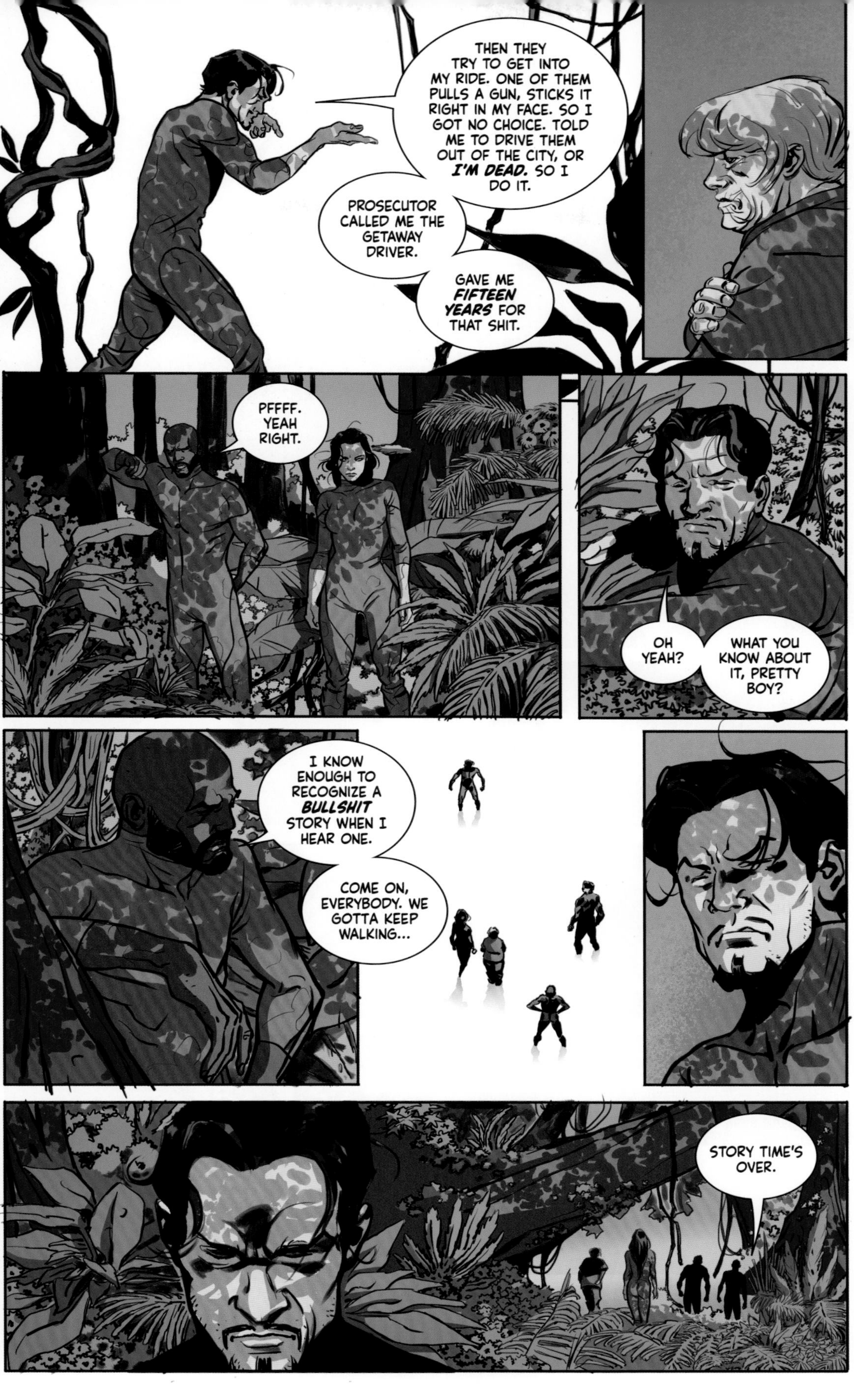
THEN THEY TRY TO GET INTO MY RIDE. ONE OF THEM PULLS A GUN, STICKS IT RIGHT IN MY FACE. SO I GOT NO CHOICE. TOLD ME TO DRIVE THEM OUT OF THE CITY, OR I'M DEAD. SO I DO IT.
PROSECUTOR CALLED ME THE GETAWAY DRIVER.
GAVE ME FIFTEEN YEARS FOR THAT SHIT.
PFFFF. YEAH RIGHT.
OH YEAH?
WHAT YOU KNOW ABOUT IT, PRETTY BOY?
I KNOW ENOUGH TO RECOGNIZE A BULLSHIT STORY WHEN I HEAR ONE.
COME ON, EVERYBODY. WE GOTTA KEEP WALKING...
STORY TIME'S OVER.

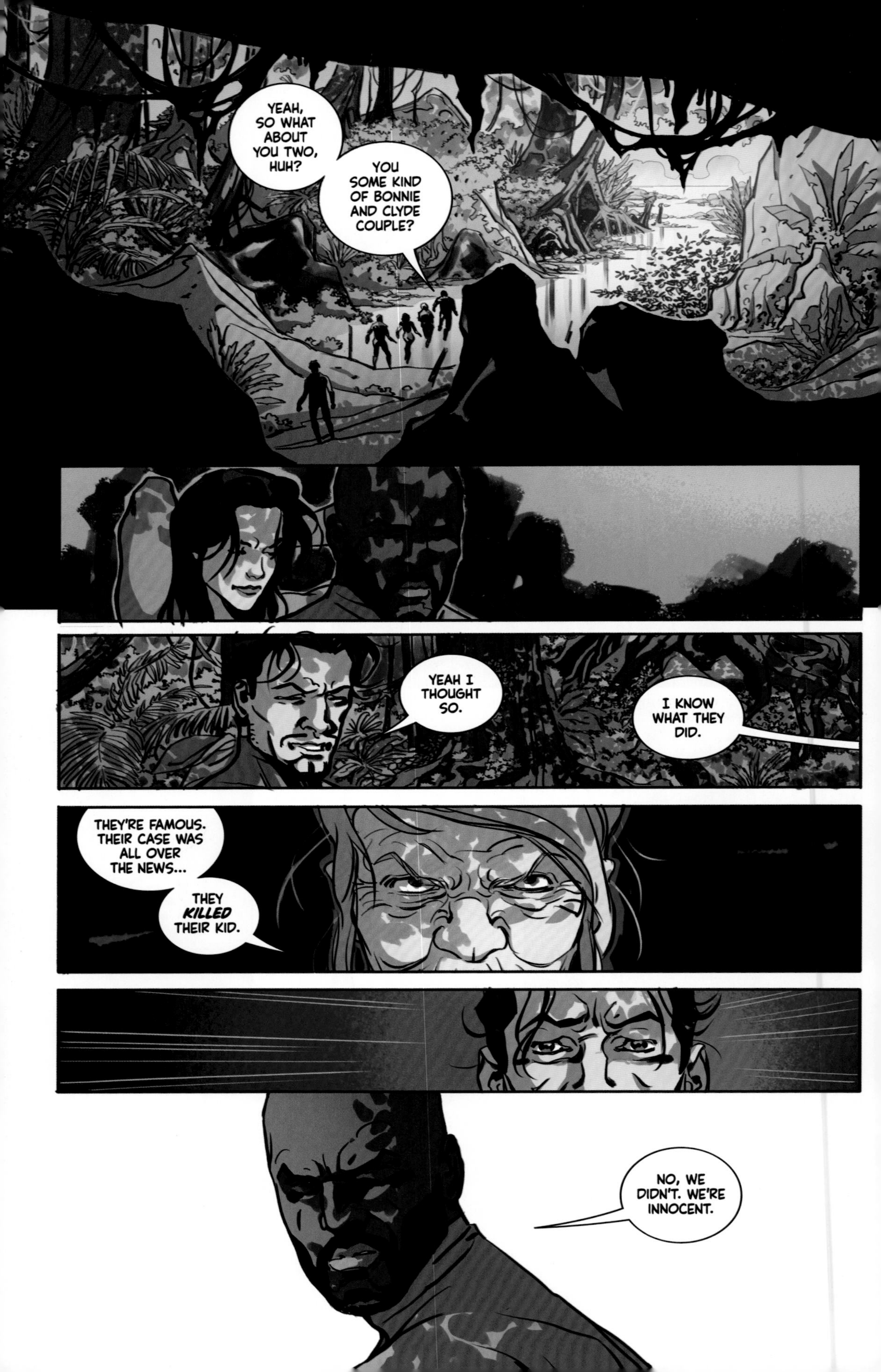
YEAH, SO WHAT ABOUT YOU TWO, HUH?
YOU SOME KIND OF BONNIE AND CLYDE COUPLE?
YEAH I THOUGHT SO.
I KNOW WHAT THEY DID.
THEY'RE FAMOUS. THEIR CASE WAS ALL OVER THE NEWS...
THEY *KILLED* THEIR KID.
NO, WE DIDN'T. WE'RE INNOCENT.

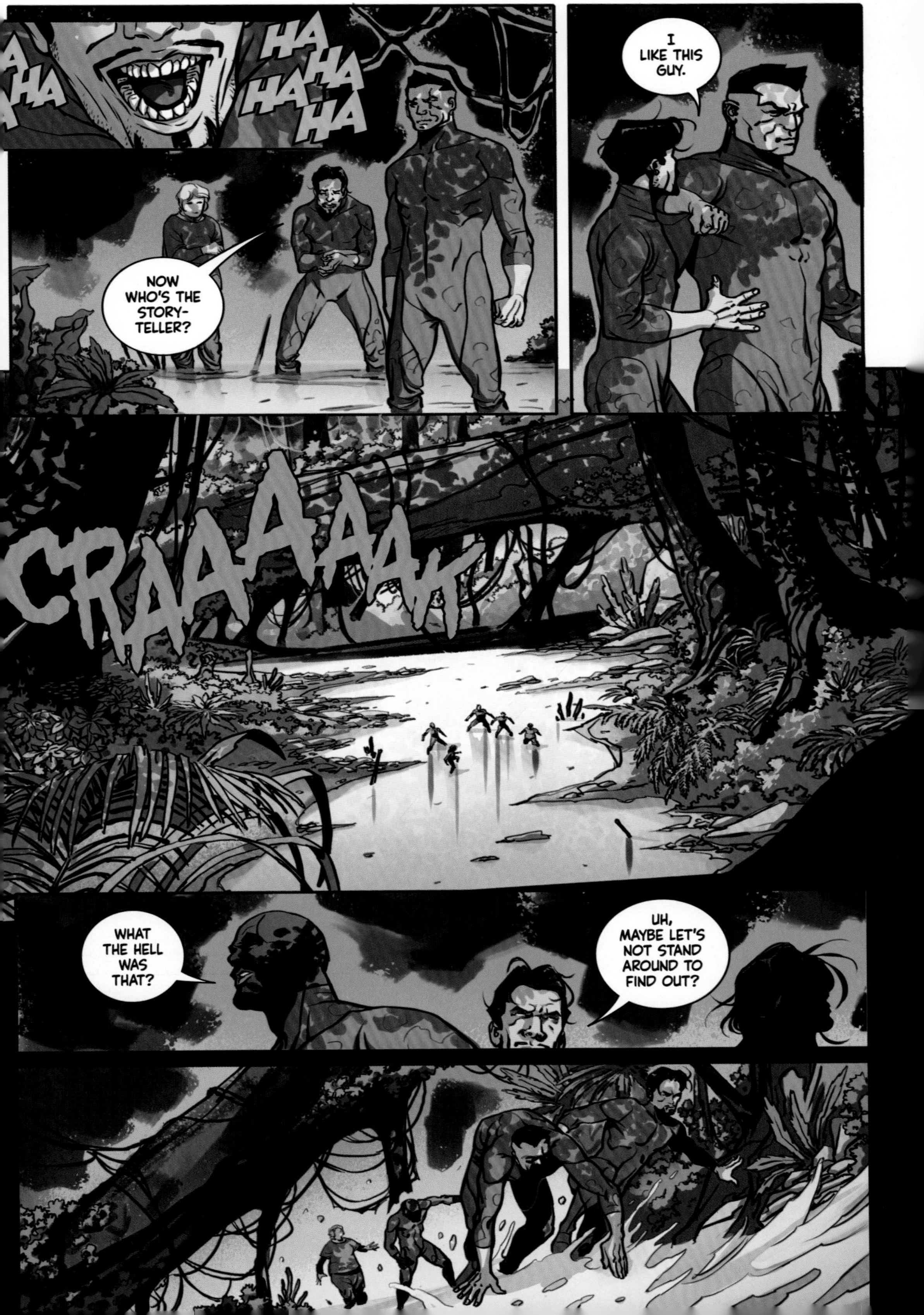
HA HA HA HA
HA HA HA HA
I LIKE THIS GUY.
NOW WHO'S THE STORY-TELLER?
CRAAAAAK
WHAT THE HELL WAS THAT?
UH, MAYBE LET'S NOT STAND AROUND TO FIND OUT?

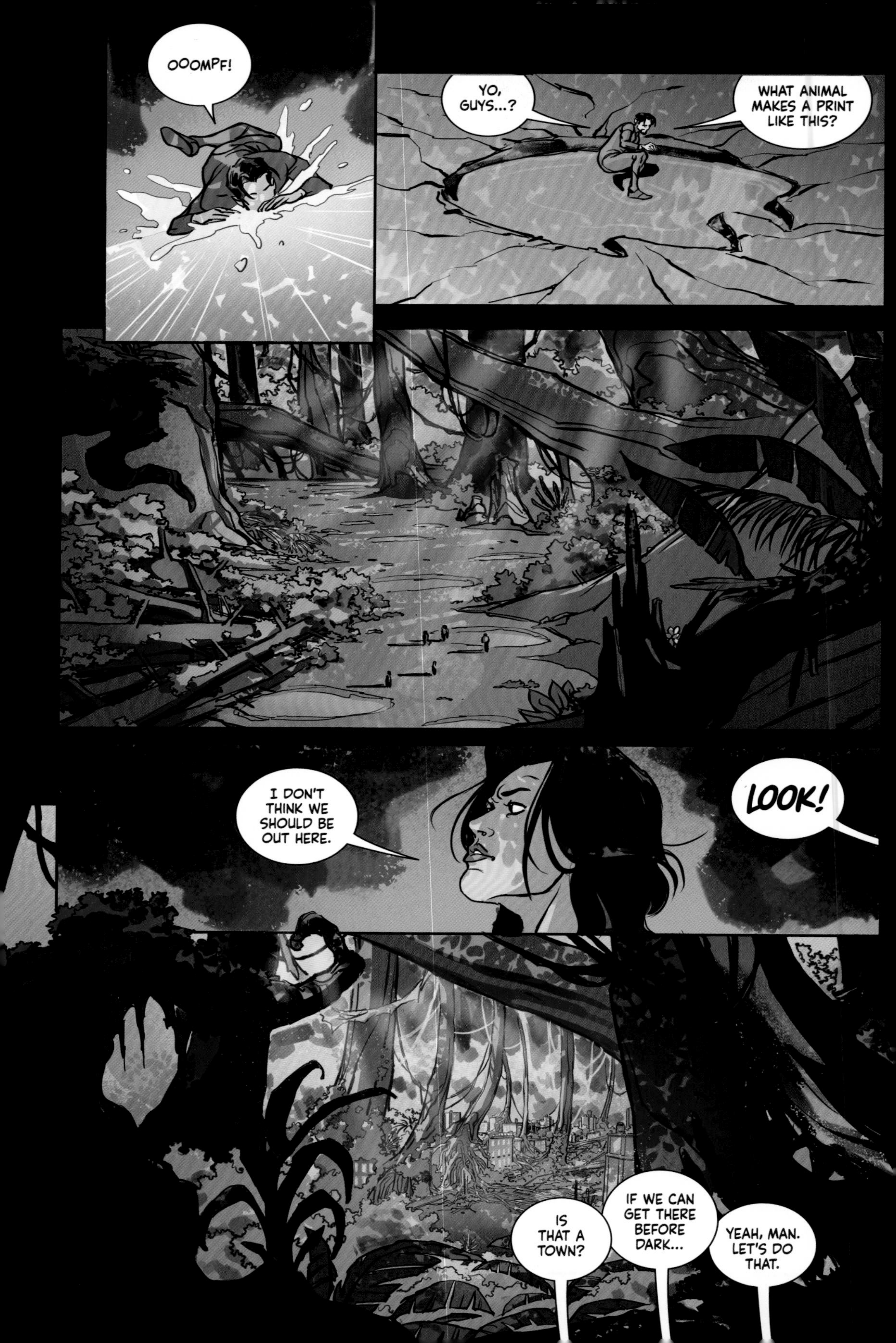
OOOMPF!
YO, GUYS...?
WHAT ANIMAL MAKES A PRINT LIKE THIS?
I DON'T THINK WE SHOULD BE OUT HERE.
LOOK!
IS THAT A TOWN?
IF WE CAN GET THERE BEFORE DARK...
YEAH, MAN. LET'S DO THAT.

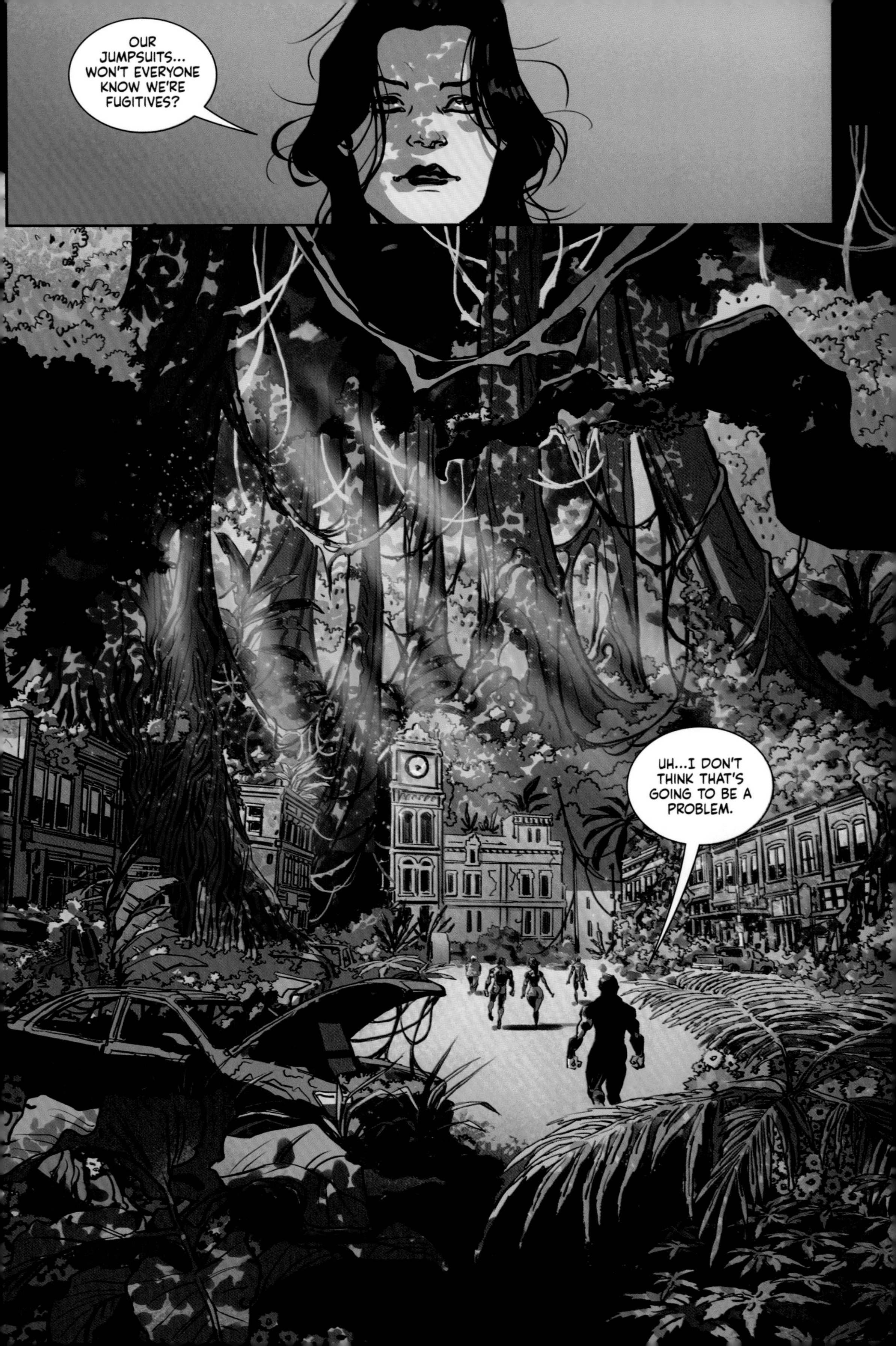
OUR JUMPSUITS... WON'T EVERYONE KNOW WE'RE FUGITIVES?
UH...I DON'T THINK THAT'S GOING TO BE A PROBLEM.

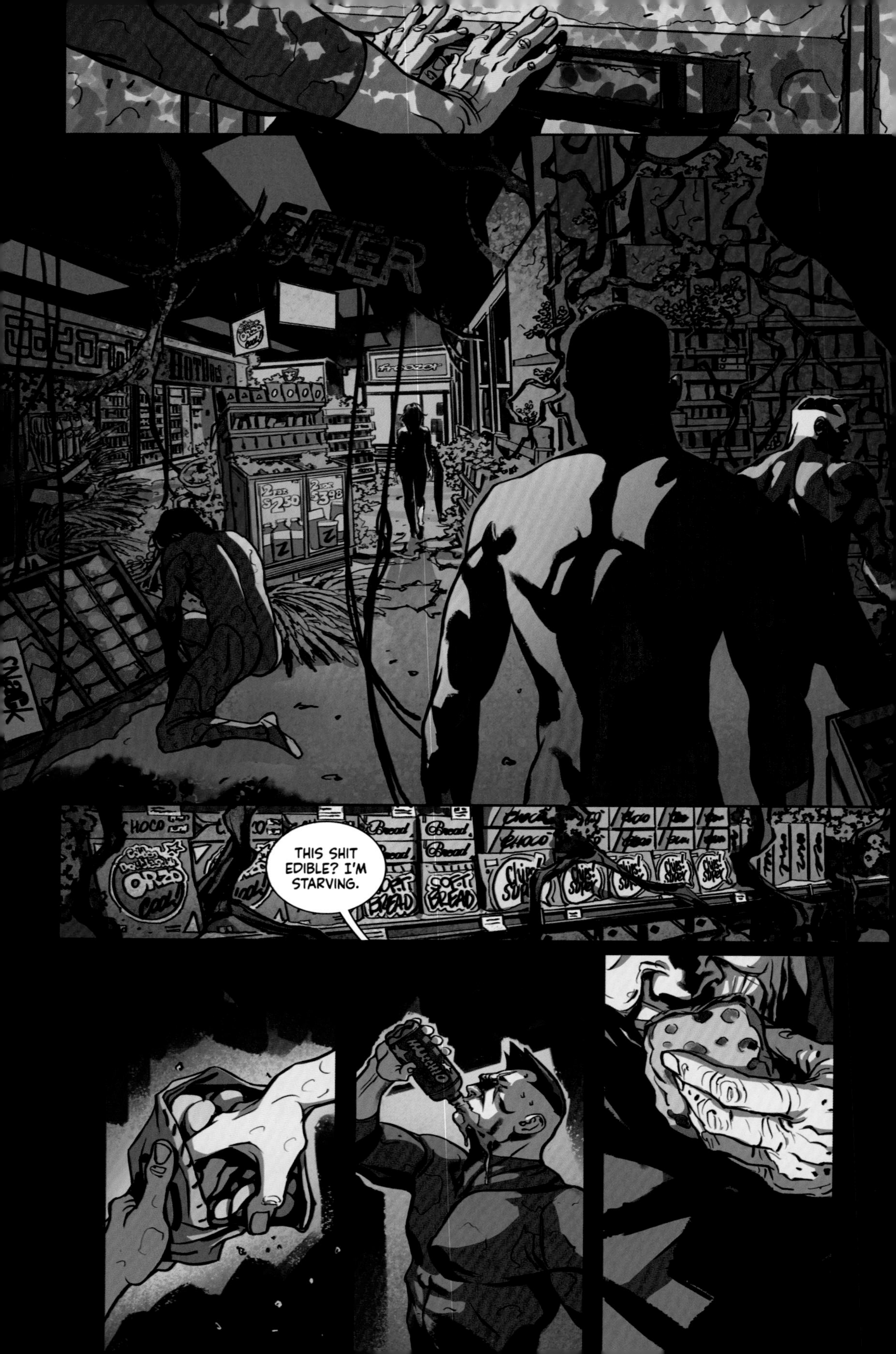
THIS SHIT EDIBLE? I'M STARVING.
SOFT BREAD

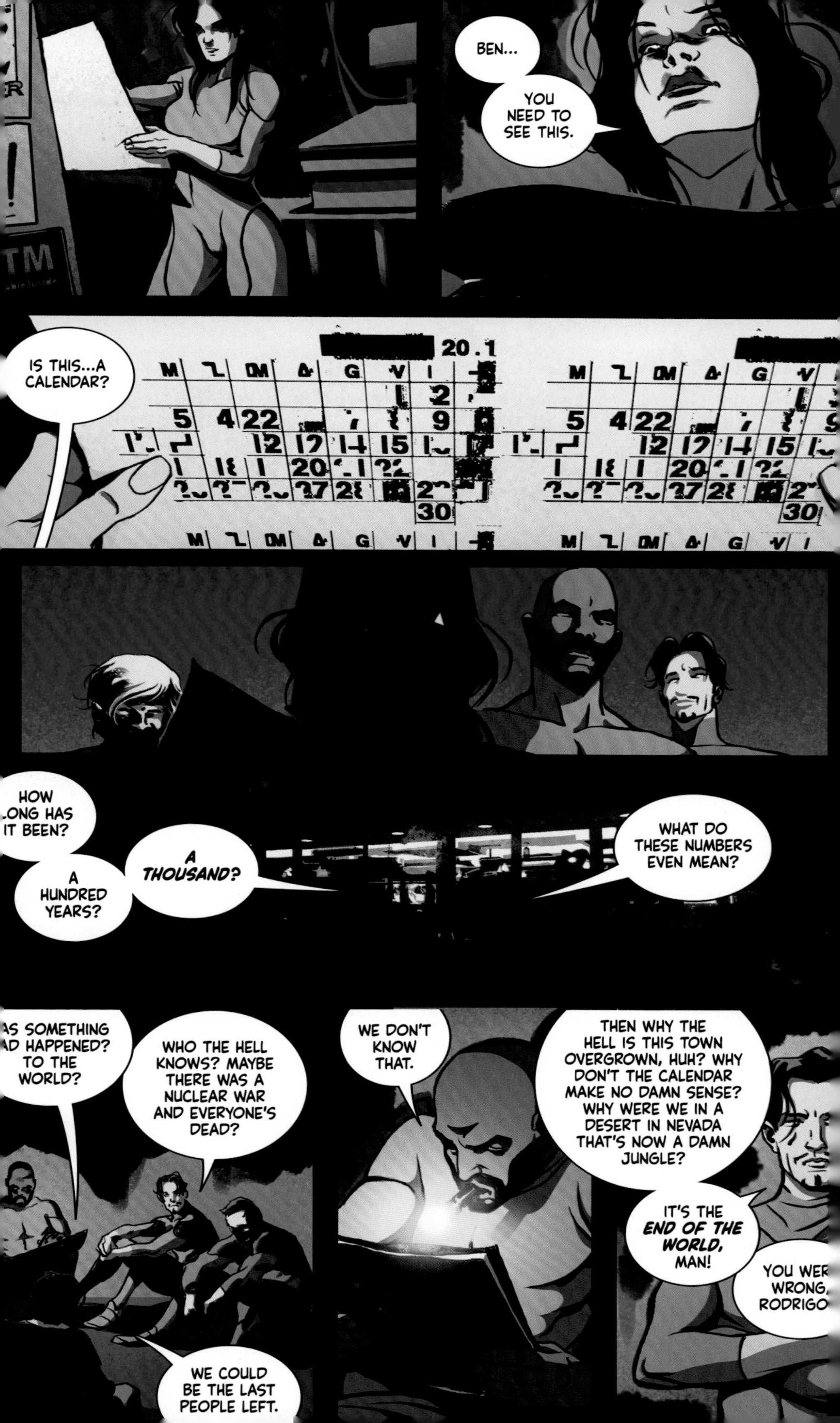

BEN...
YOU NEED TO SEE THIS.
IS THIS...A CALENDAR?
HOW
ONG HAS
IT BEEN?
A HUNDRED YEARS?
A THOUSAND?
WHAT DO THESE NUMBERS EVEN MEAN?
AS SOMETHING
AD HAPPENED?
TO THE WORLD?
WHO THE HELL KNOWS? MAYBE THERE WAS A NUCLEAR WAR AND EVERYONE'S DEAD?
WE COULD BE THE LAST PEOPLE LEFT.
WE DON'T KNOW THAT.
THEN WHY THE HELL IS THIS TOWN OVERGROWN, HUH? WHY DON'T THE CALENDAR MAKE NO DAMN SENSE? WHY WERE WE IN A DESERT IN NEVADA THAT'S NOW A DAMN JUNGLE?
IT'S THE END OF THE WORLD, MAN!
YOU WER
WRONG,
RODRIGO

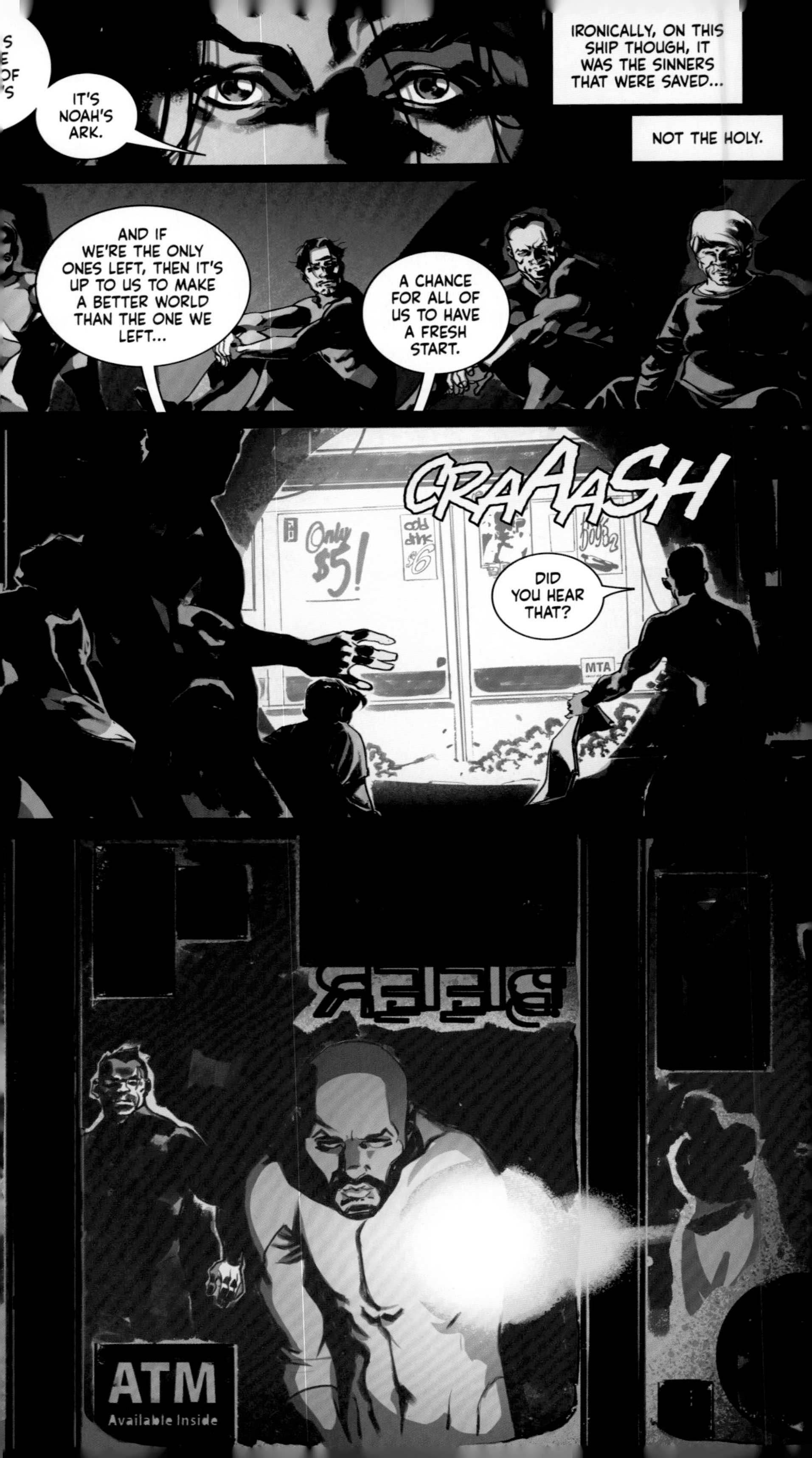

IT'S NOAH'S ARK.
IRONICALLY, ON THIS SHIP THOUGH, IT WAS THE SINNERS THAT WERE SAVED...
NOT THE HOLY.
AND IF WE'RE THE ONLY ONES LEFT, THEN IT'S UP TO US TO MAKE A BETTER WORLD THAN THE ONE WE LEFT...
A CHANCE FOR ALL OF US TO HAVE A FRESH START.
CRAAASH
Only $5!
cold drink $6
DID YOU HEAR THAT?
MTA
ATM
Available Inside

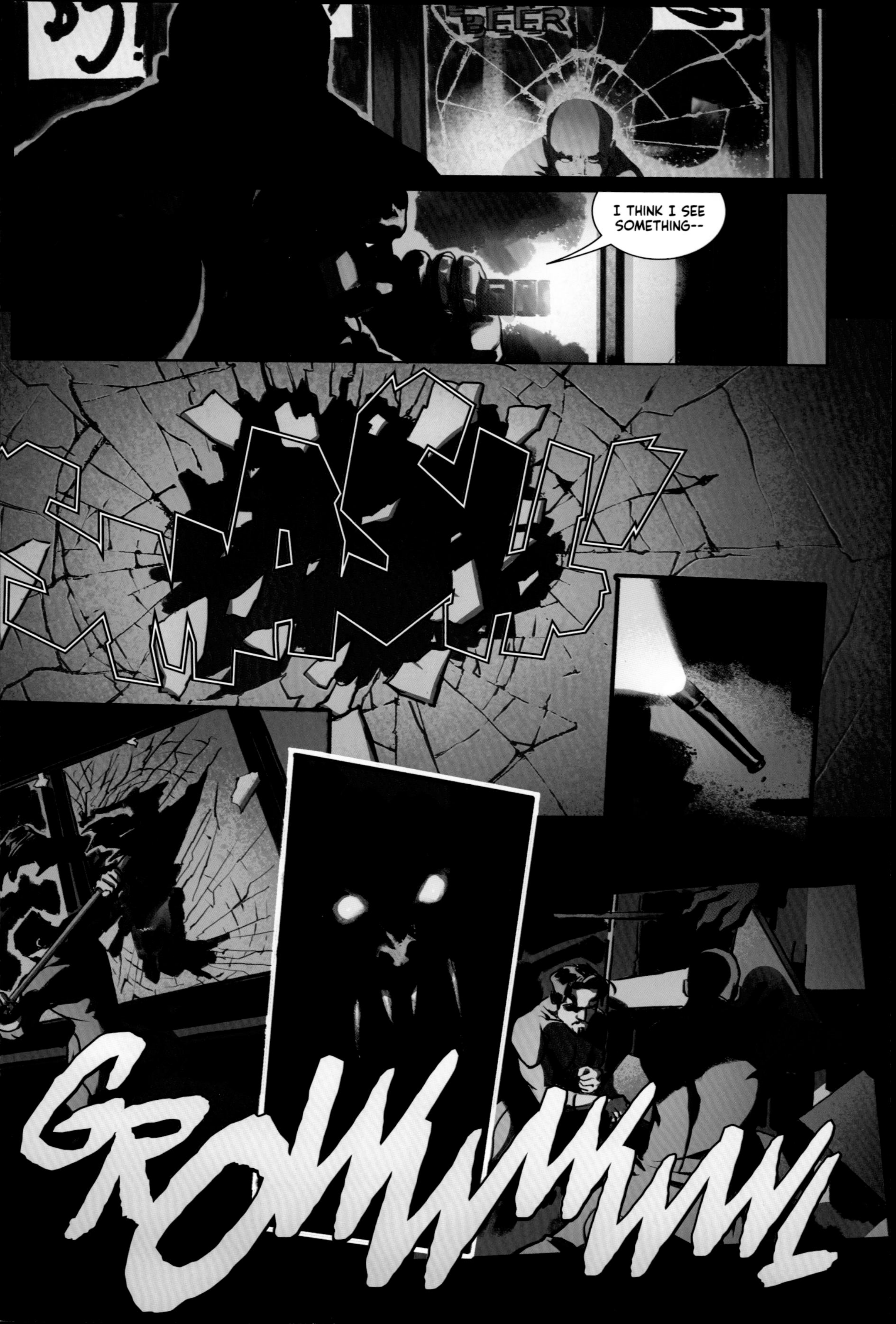
BEER
I THINK I SEE SOMETHING--

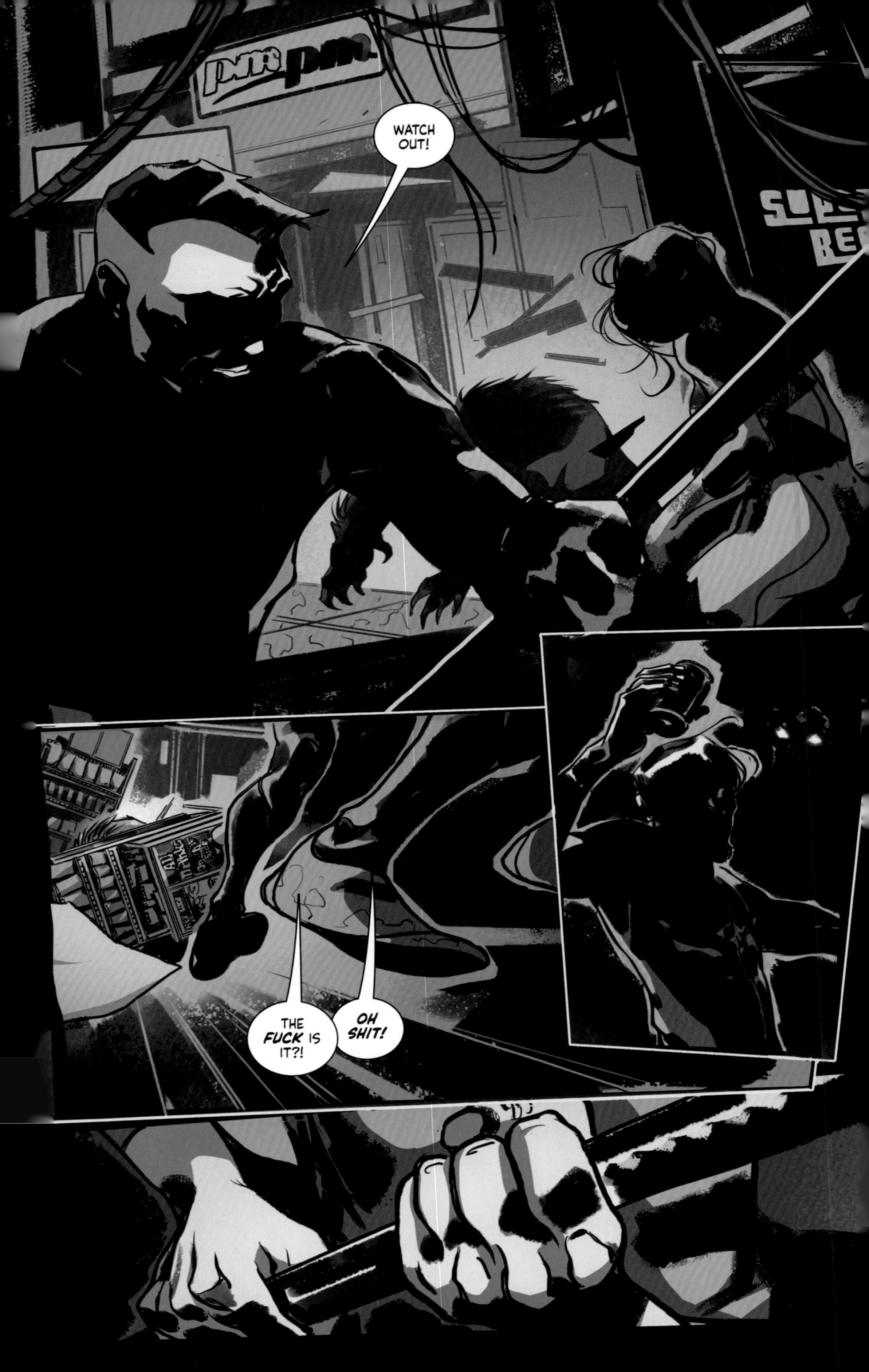

WATCH OUT!
THE *FUCK* IS IT?!
OH SHIT!

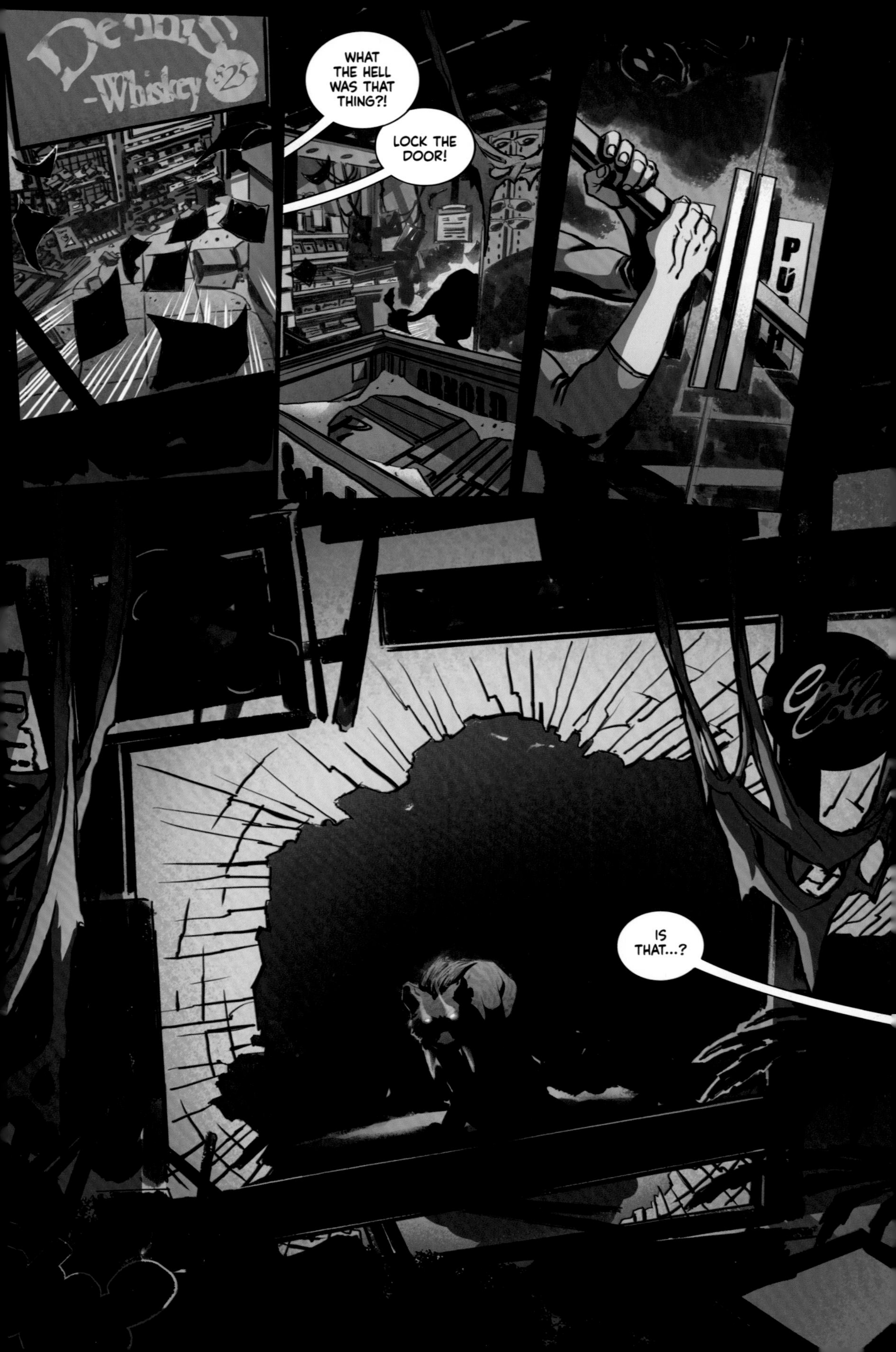

Whiskey $25
WHAT THE HELL WAS THAT THING?!
LOCK THE DOOR!
ARNOLD
IS THAT...?

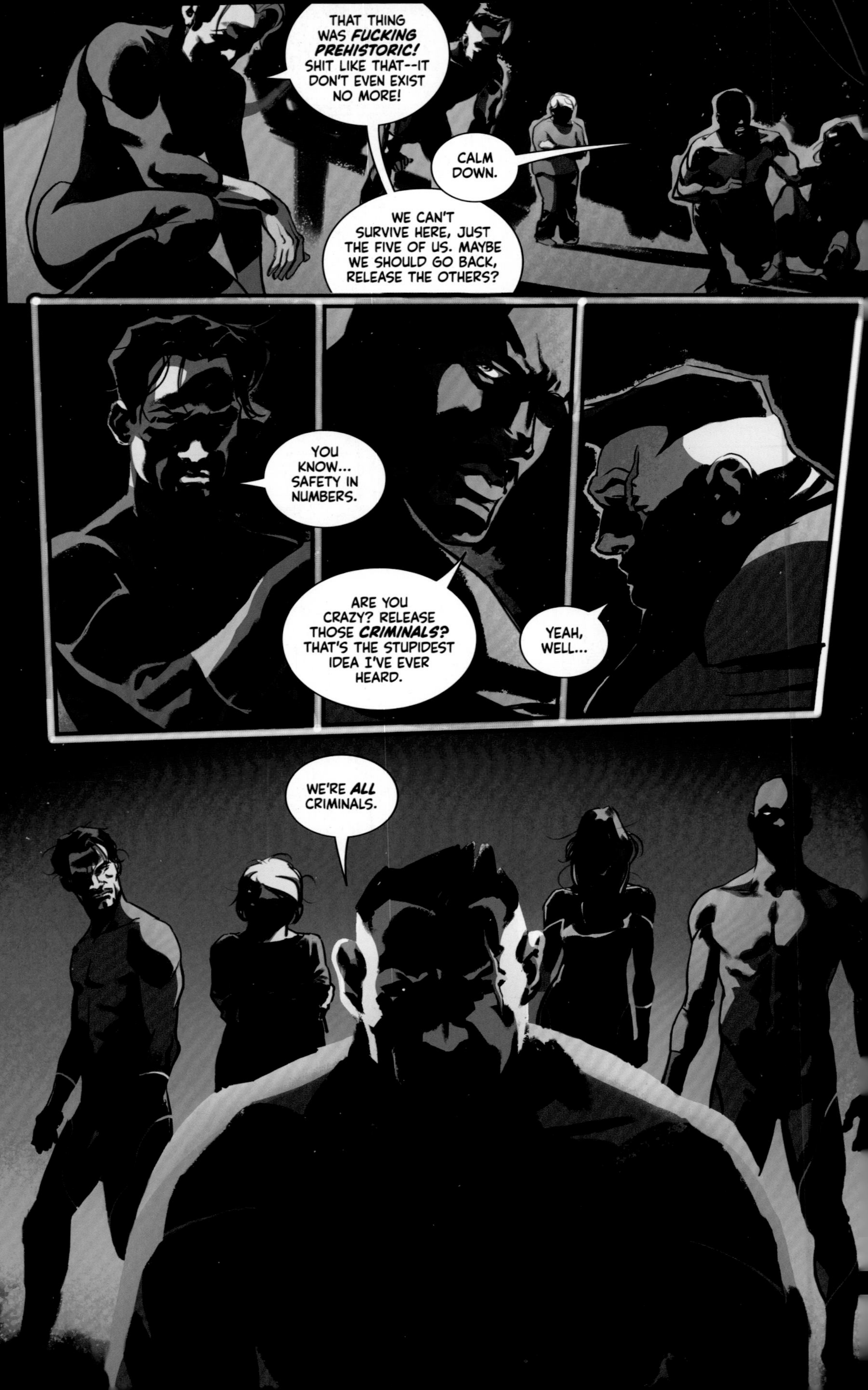
THAT THING WAS FUCKING PREHISTORIC! SHIT LIKE THAT--IT DON'T EVEN EXIST NO MORE!
CALM DOWN.
WE CAN'T SURVIVE HERE, JUST THE FIVE OF US. MAYBE WE SHOULD GO BACK, RELEASE THE OTHERS?
YOU KNOW... SAFETY IN NUMBERS.
ARE YOU CRAZY? RELEASE THOSE CRIMINALS? THAT'S THE STUPIDEST IDEA I'VE EVER HEARD.
YEAH, WELL...
WE'RE ALL CRIMINALS.

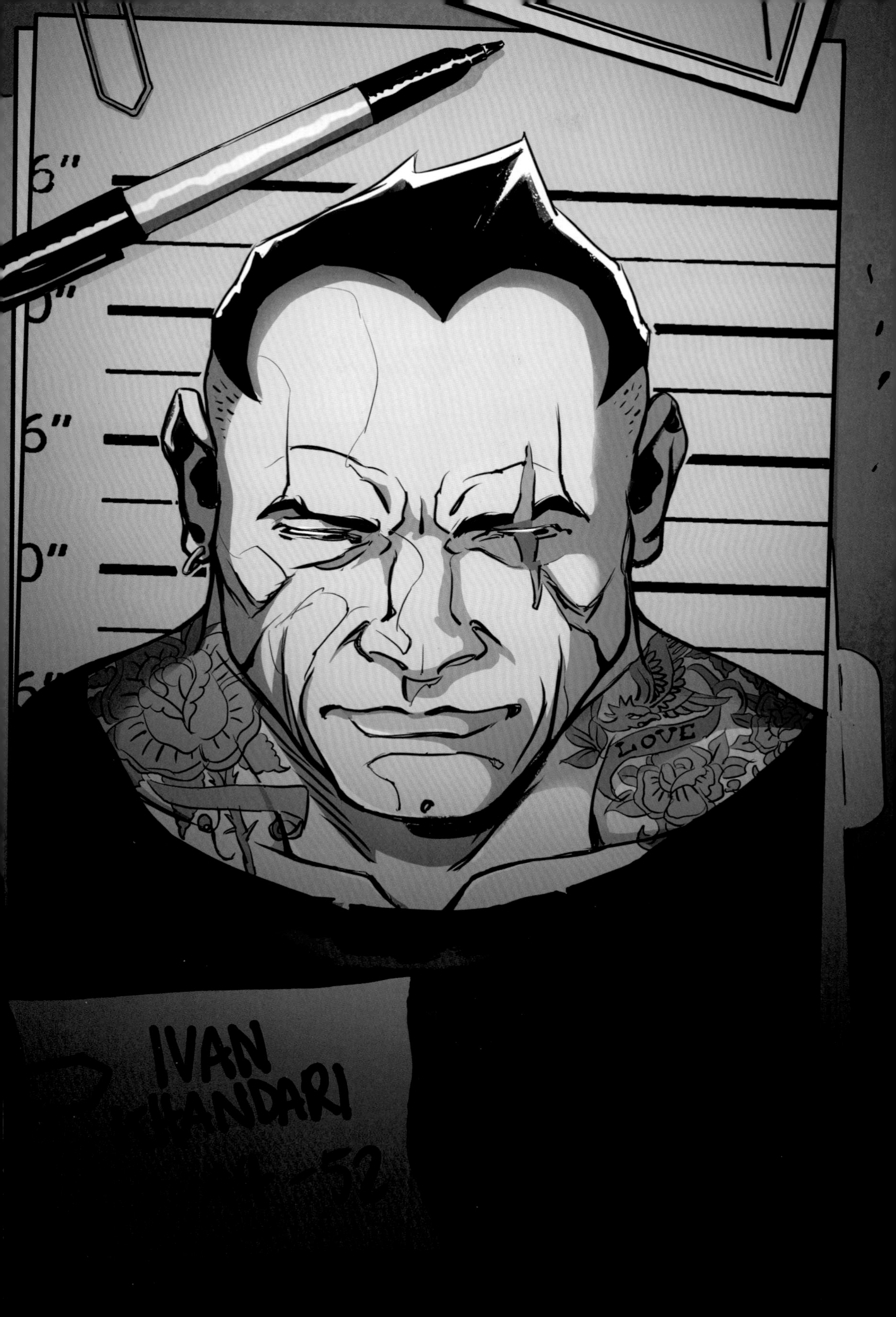
LOVE
IVAN
HANDARI

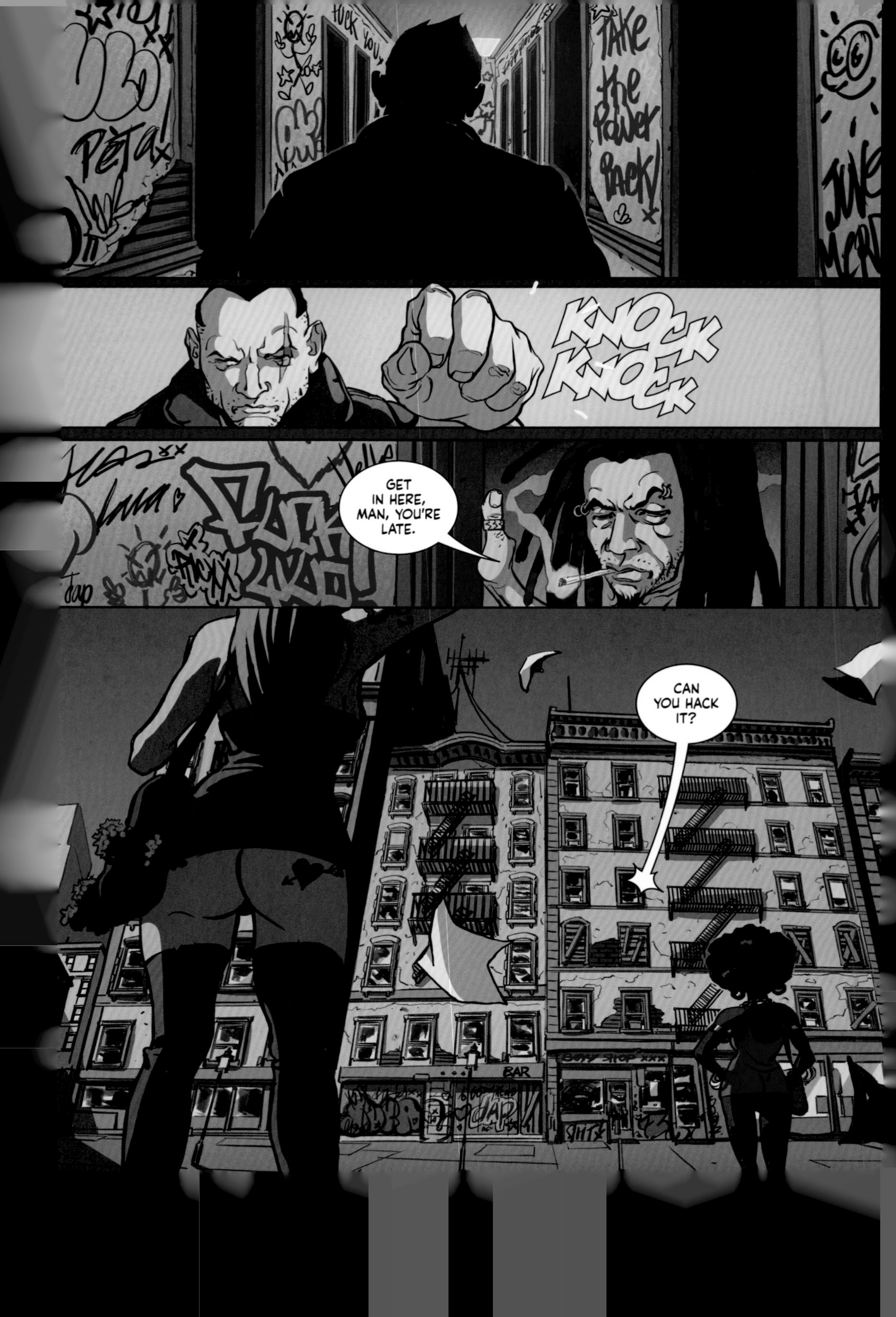

KNOCK KNOCK
GET IN HERE, MAN, YOU'RE LATE.
CAN YOU HACK IT?

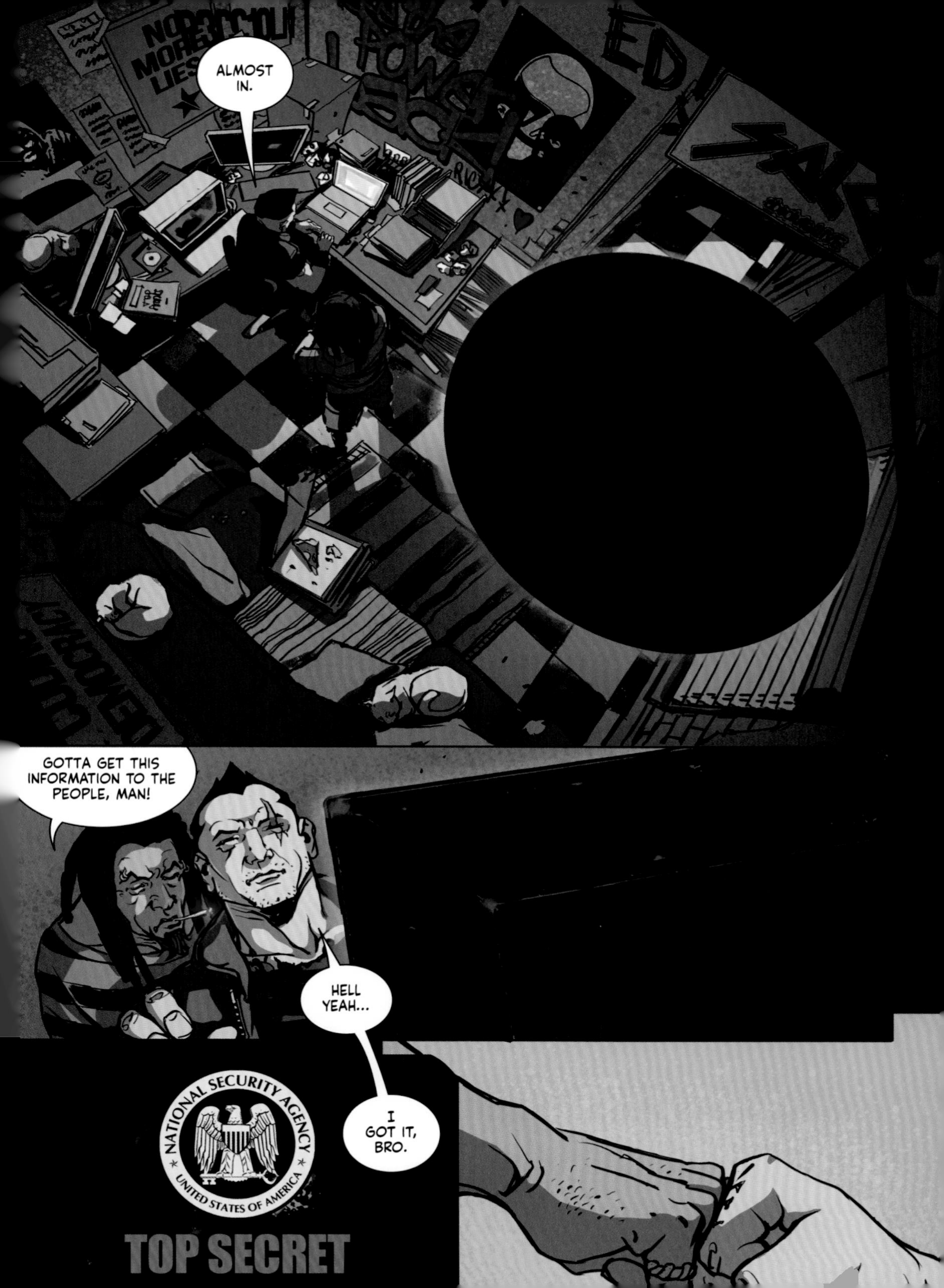
ALMOST IN.
GOTTA GET THIS INFORMATION TO THE PEOPLE, MAN!
HELL YEAH...
I GOT IT, BRO.
NATIONAL SECURITY AGENCY
UNITED STATES OF AMERICA
TOP SECRET

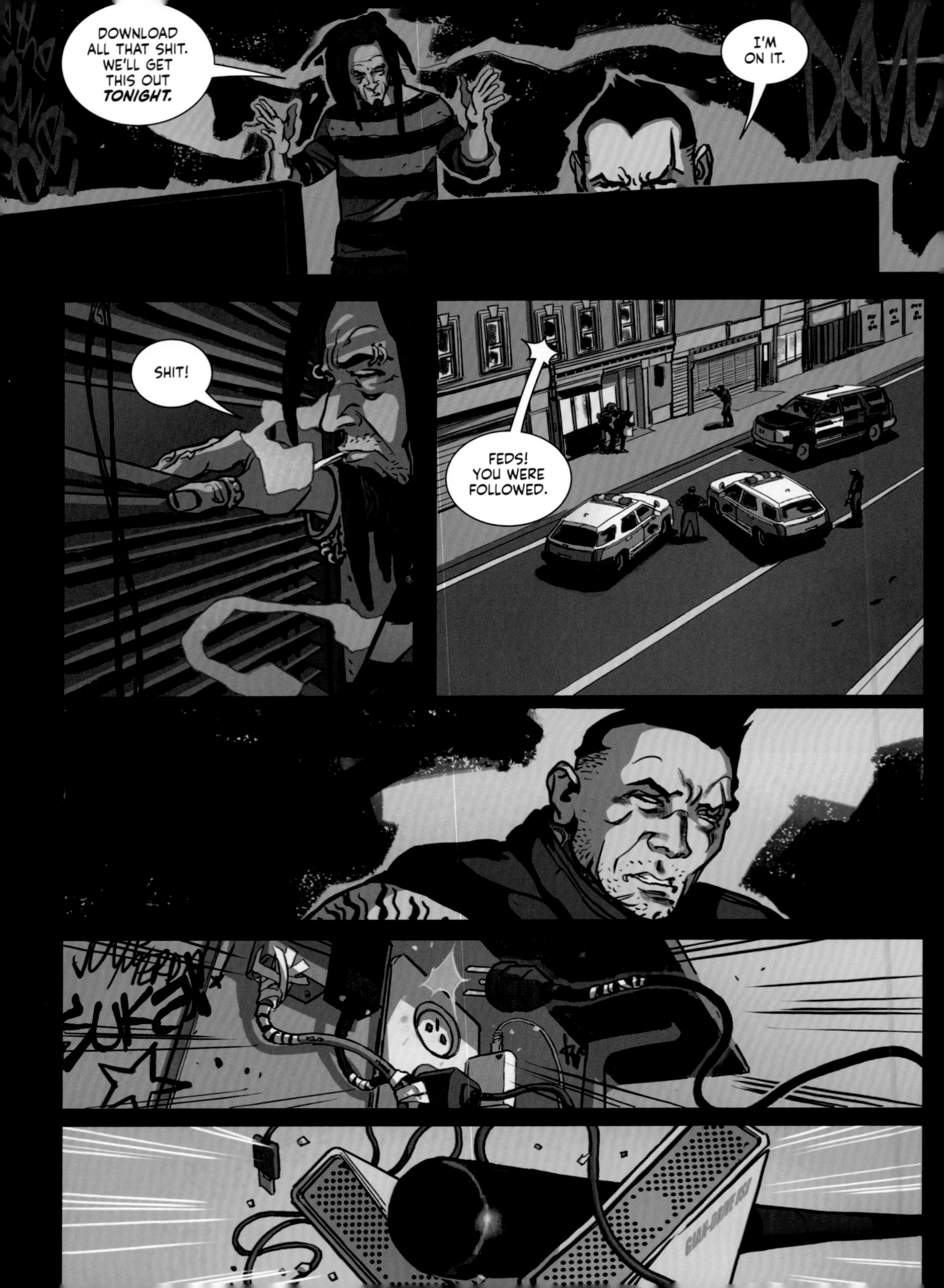
DOWNLOAD ALL THAT SHIT. WE'LL GET THIS OUT *TONIGHT.*
I'M ON IT.
SHIT!
FEDS! YOU WERE FOLLOWED.

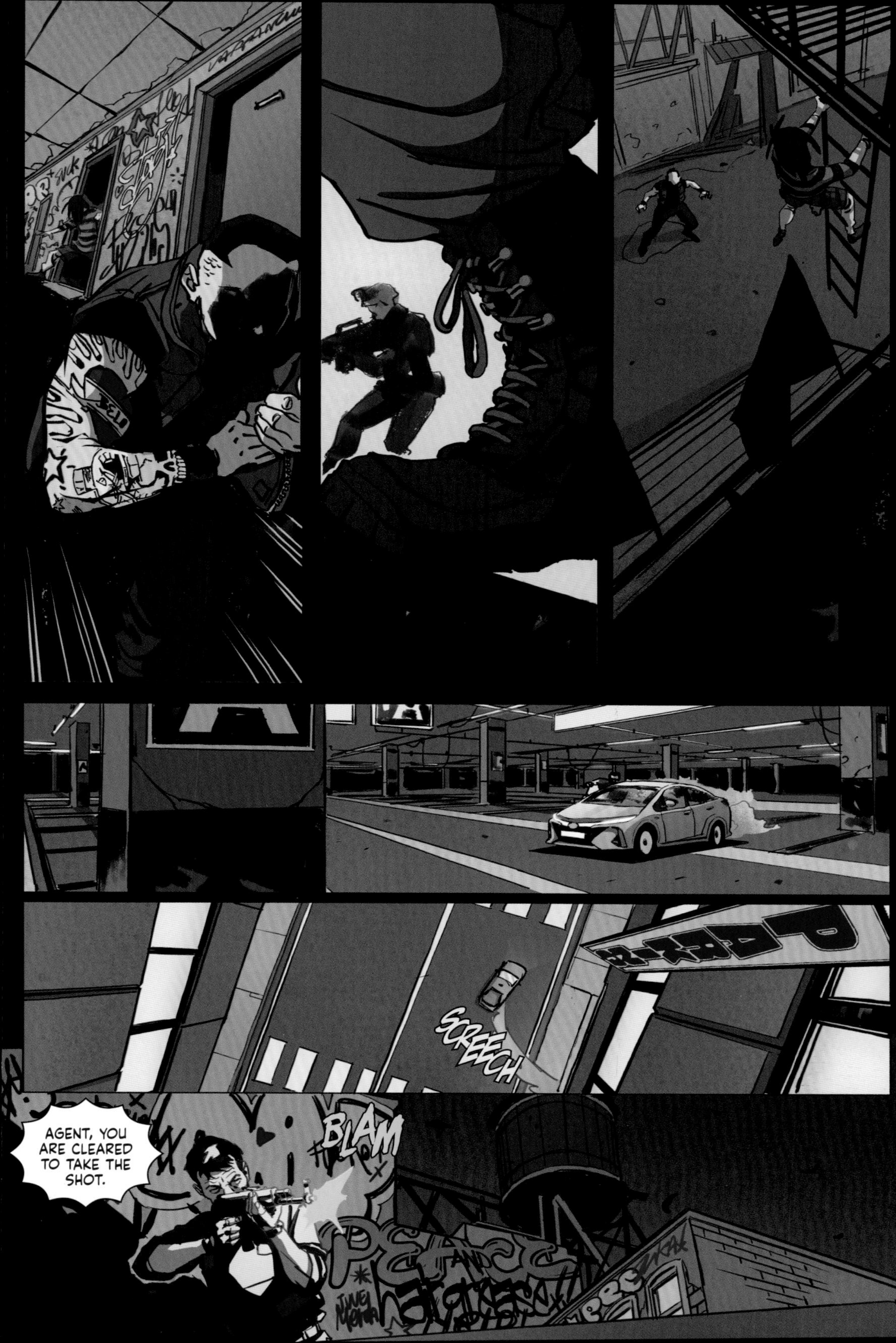
SCREEECH
AGENT, YOU ARE CLEARED TO TAKE THE SHOT.
BLAM

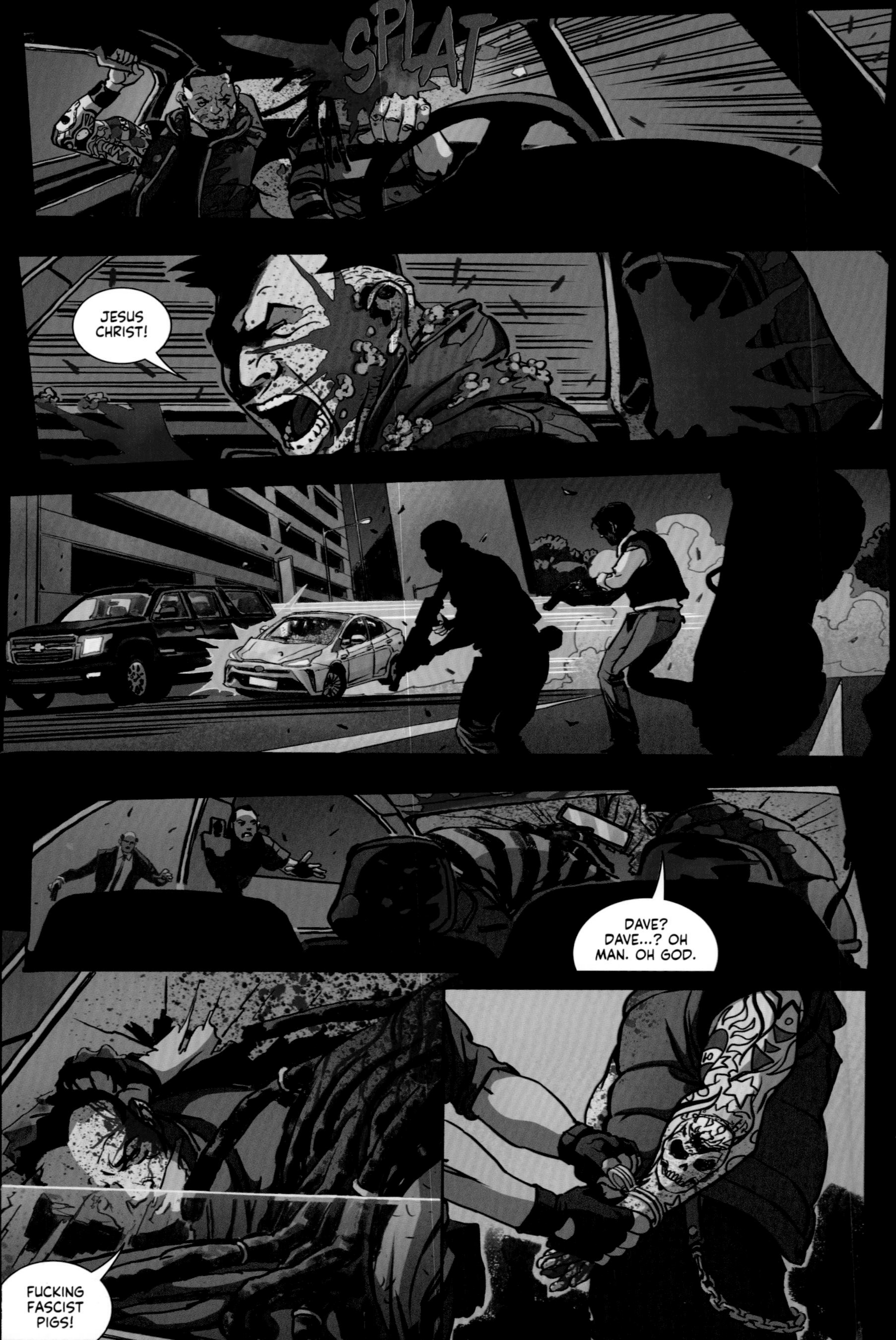
SPLAT
JESUS CHRIST!
DAVE? DAVE...? OH MAN. OH GOD.
FUCKING FASCIST PIGS!

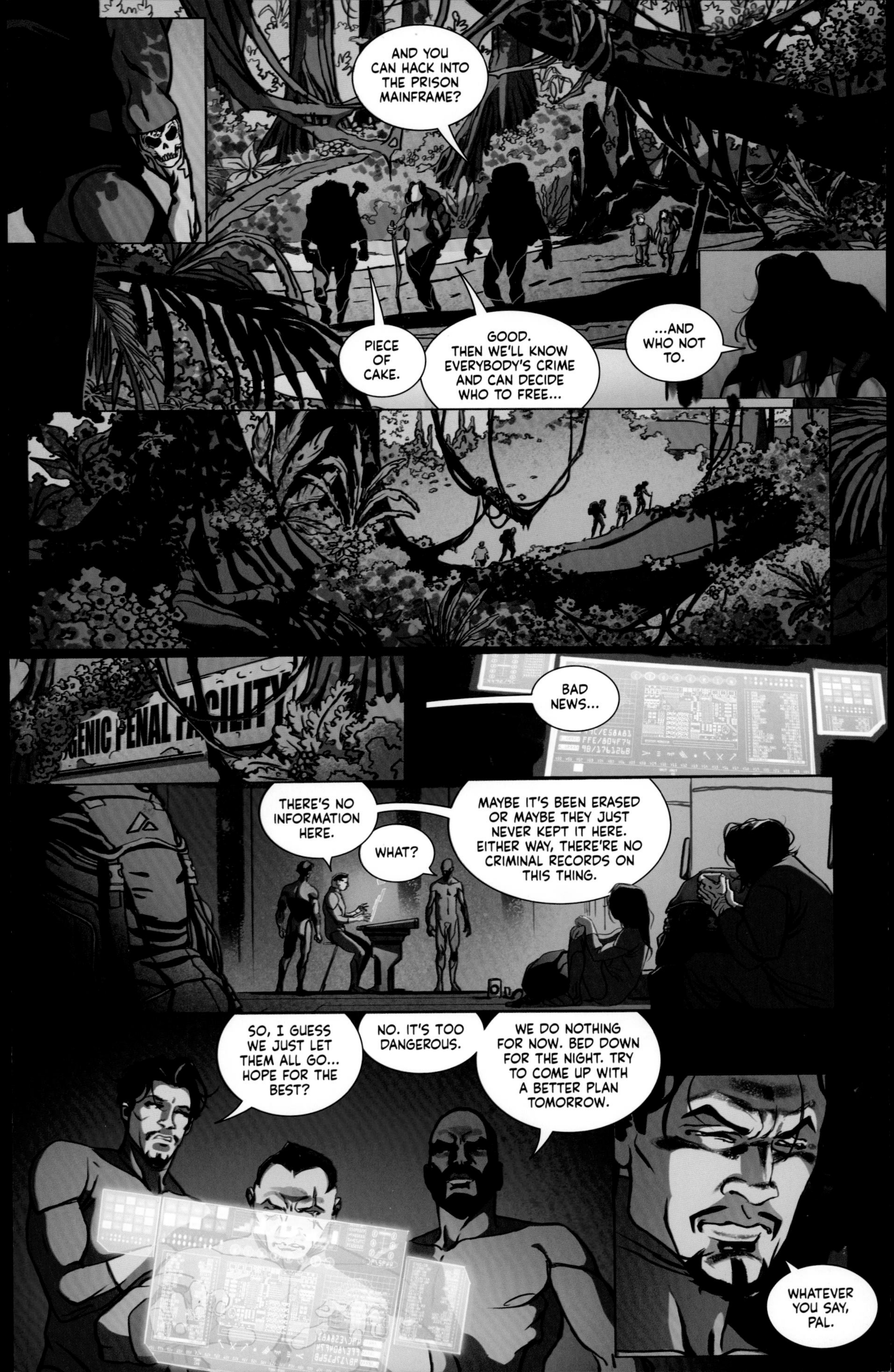
AND YOU CAN HACK INTO THE PRISON MAINFRAME?
PIECE OF CAKE.
GOOD. THEN WE'LL KNOW EVERYBODY'S CRIME AND CAN DECIDE WHO TO FREE...
...AND WHO NOT TO.
GENIC PENAL FACILITY
BAD NEWS...
THERE'S NO INFORMATION HERE.
WHAT?
MAYBE IT'S BEEN ERASED OR MAYBE THEY JUST NEVER KEPT IT HERE. EITHER WAY, THERE'RE NO CRIMINAL RECORDS ON THIS THING.
SO, I GUESS WE JUST LET THEM ALL GO... HOPE FOR THE BEST?
NO. IT'S TOO DANGEROUS.
WE DO NOTHING FOR NOW. BED DOWN FOR THE NIGHT. TRY TO COME UP WITH A BETTER PLAN TOMORROW.
WHATEVER YOU SAY, PAL.

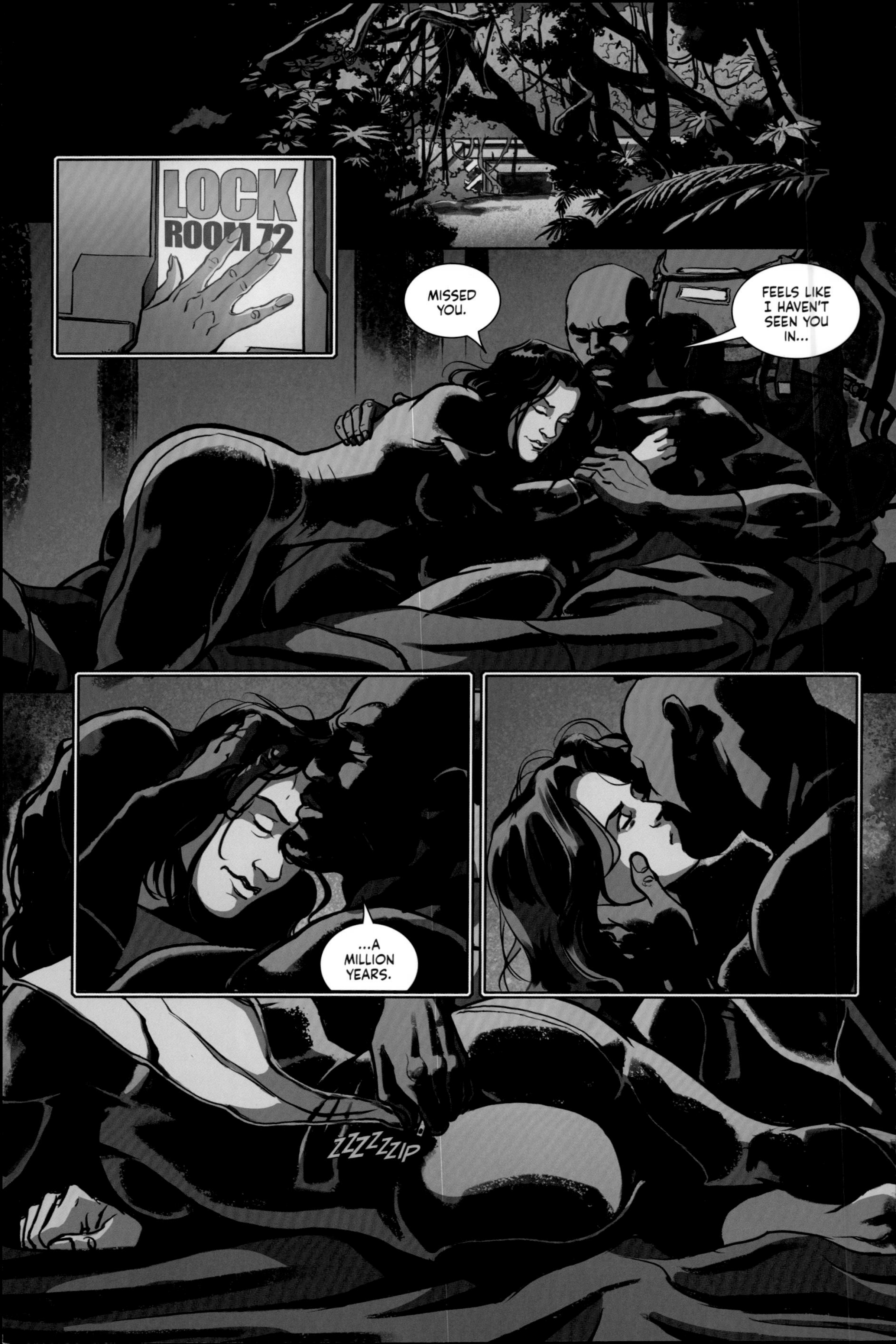
LOCK
ROOM 72
MISSED YOU.
FEELS LIKE I HAVEN'T SEEN YOU IN...
...A MILLION YEARS.
ZZZZZZIP

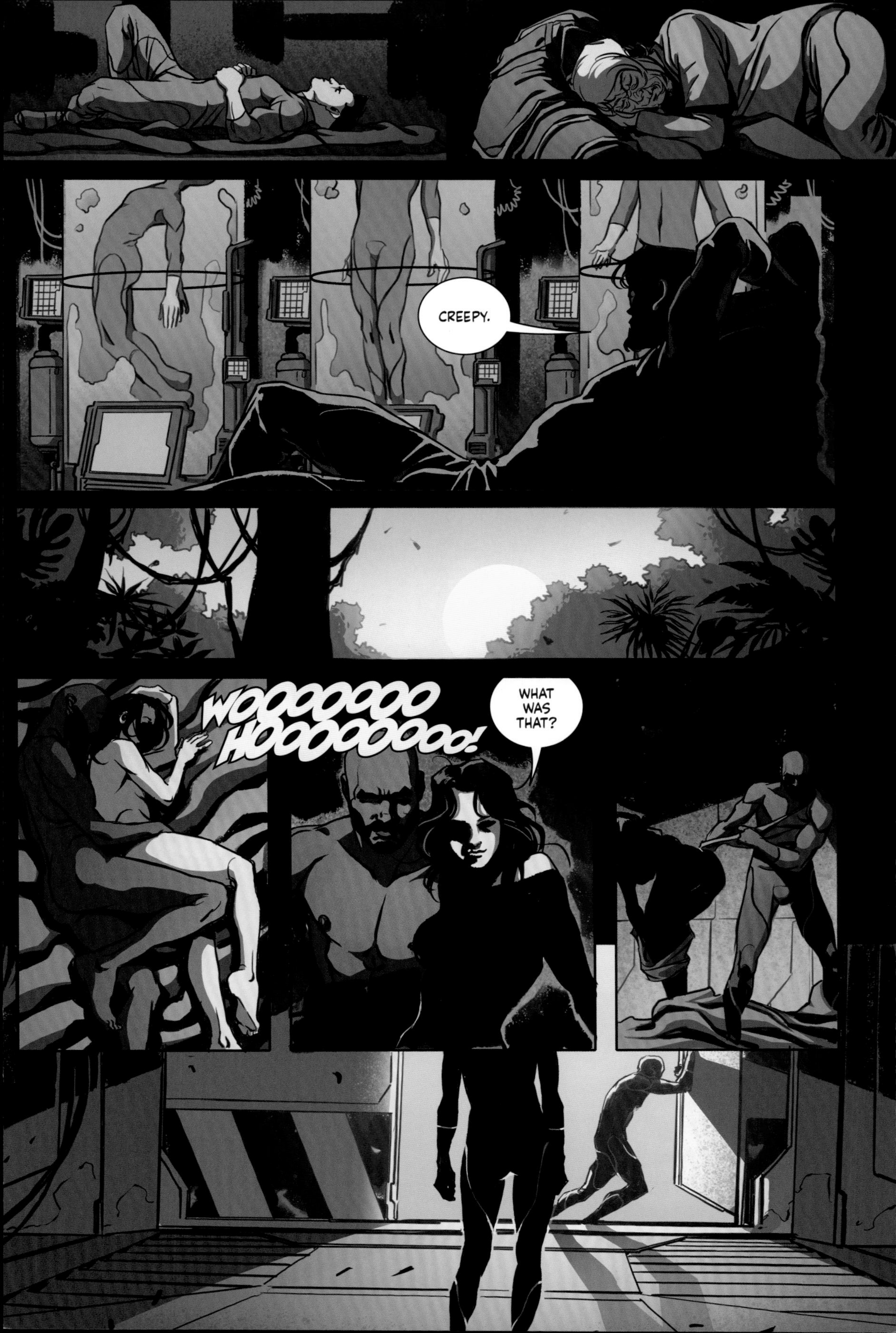
CREEPY.
WOOOOOOO HOOOOOOOOO!
WHAT WAS THAT?

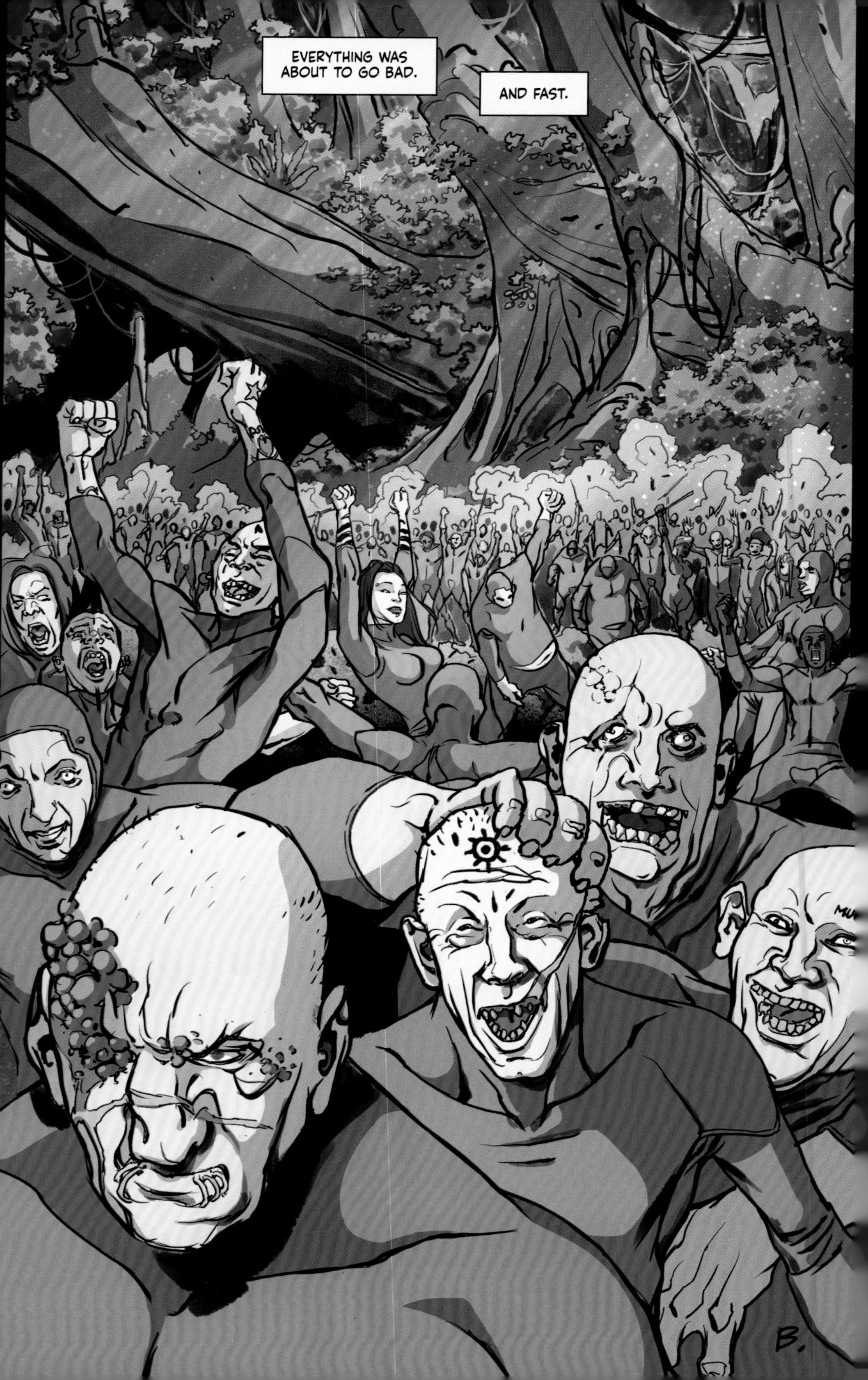
EVERYTHING WAS
ABOUT TO GO BAD.
AND FAST.

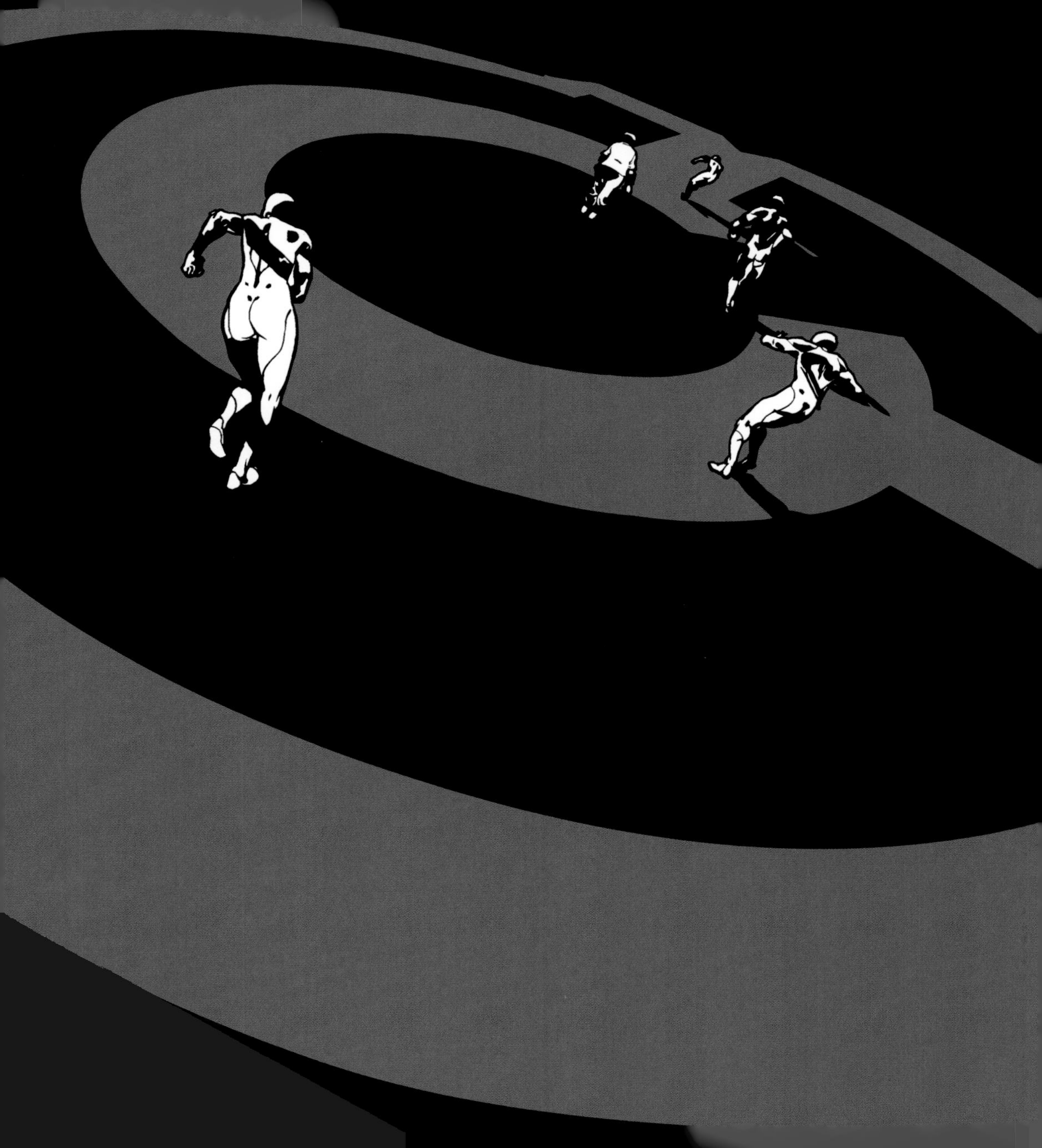

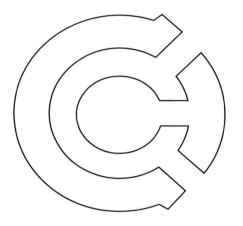

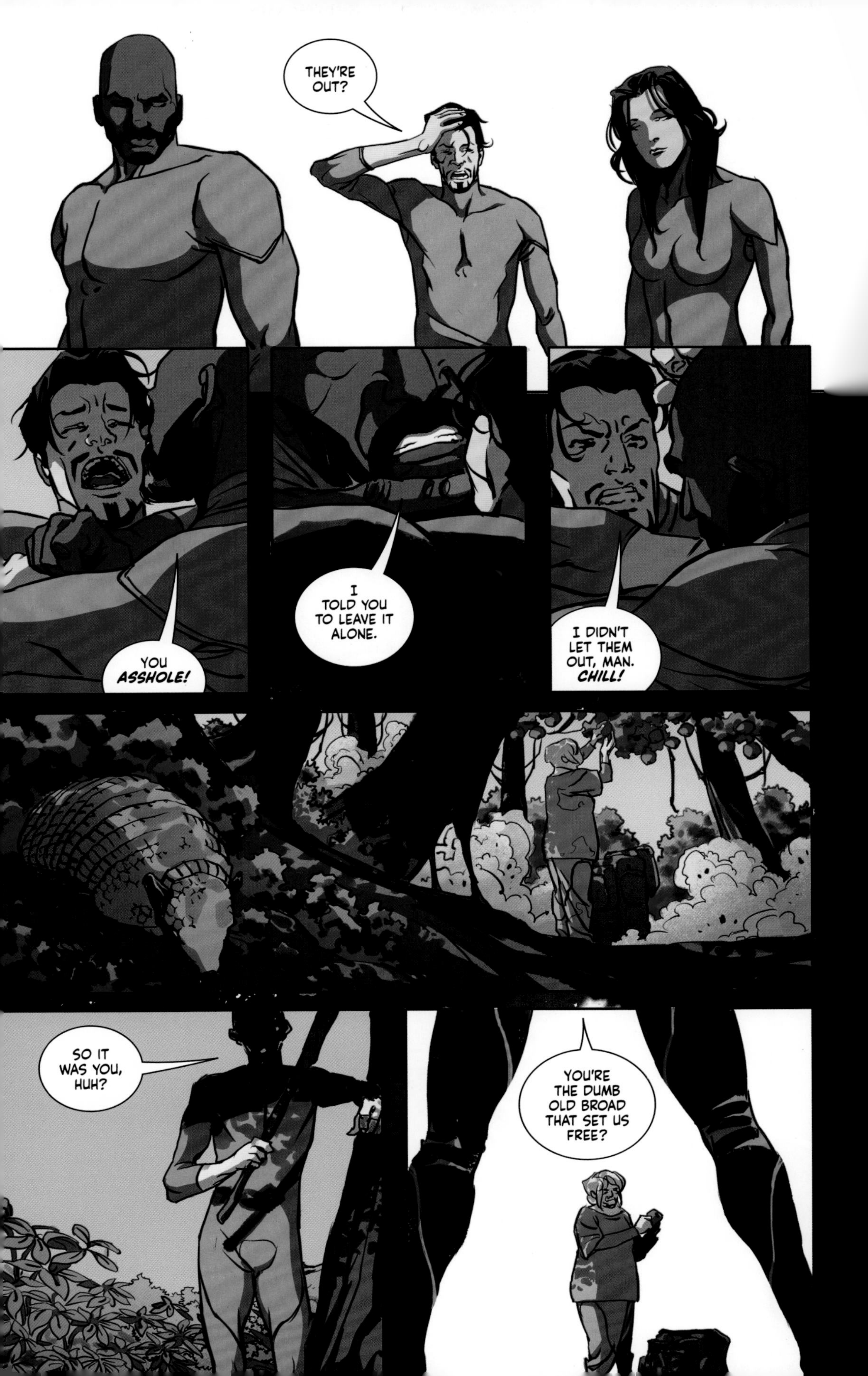
THEY'RE OUT?
YOU **ASSHOLE!**
I TOLD YOU TO LEAVE IT ALONE.
I DIDN'T LET THEM OUT, MAN. **CHILL!**
SO IT WAS YOU, HUH?
YOU'RE THE DUMB OLD BROAD THAT SET US FREE?

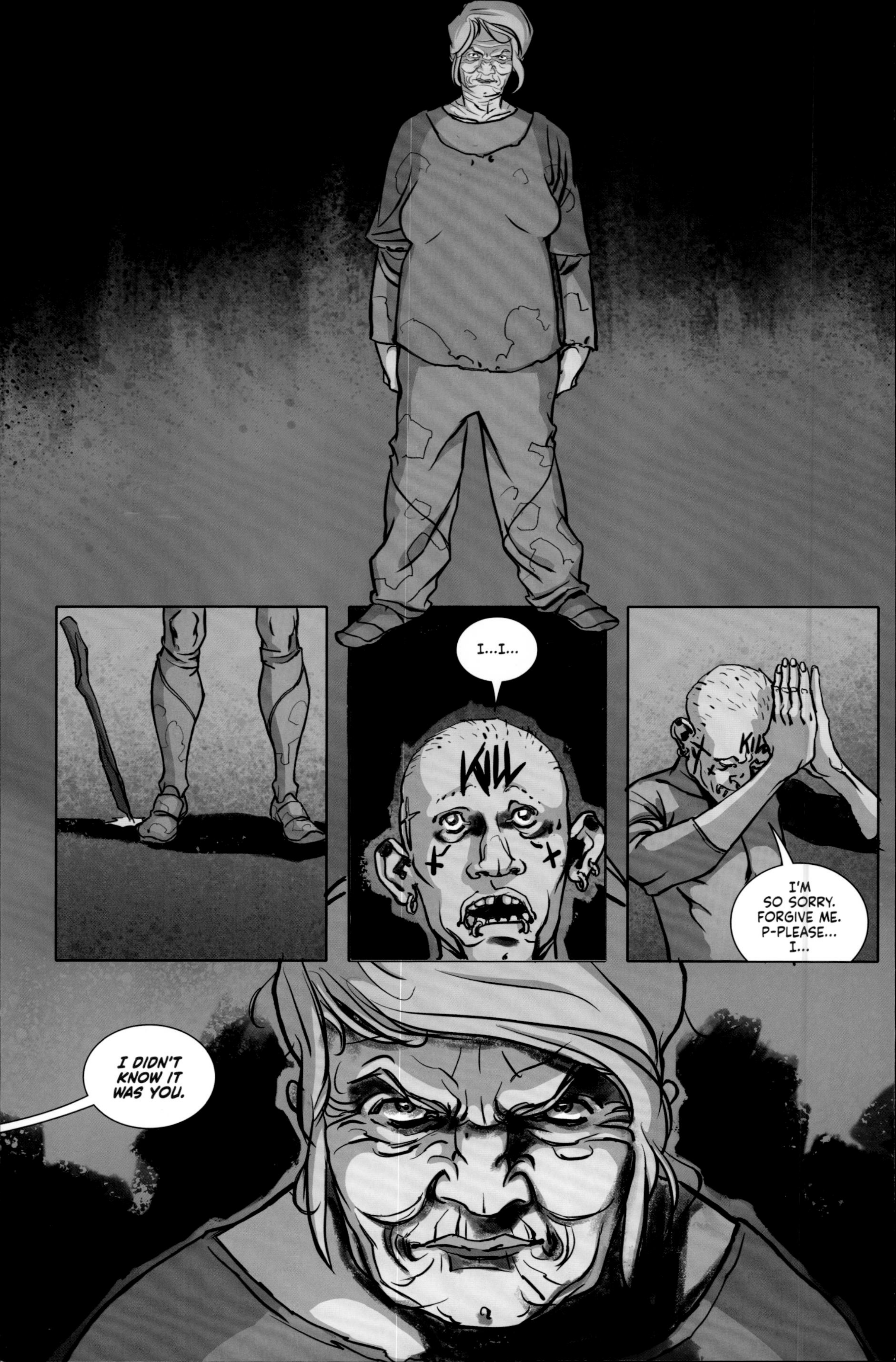
I...I...
I'M SO SORRY. FORGIVE ME. P-PLEASE... I...
I DIDN'T KNOW IT WAS YOU.

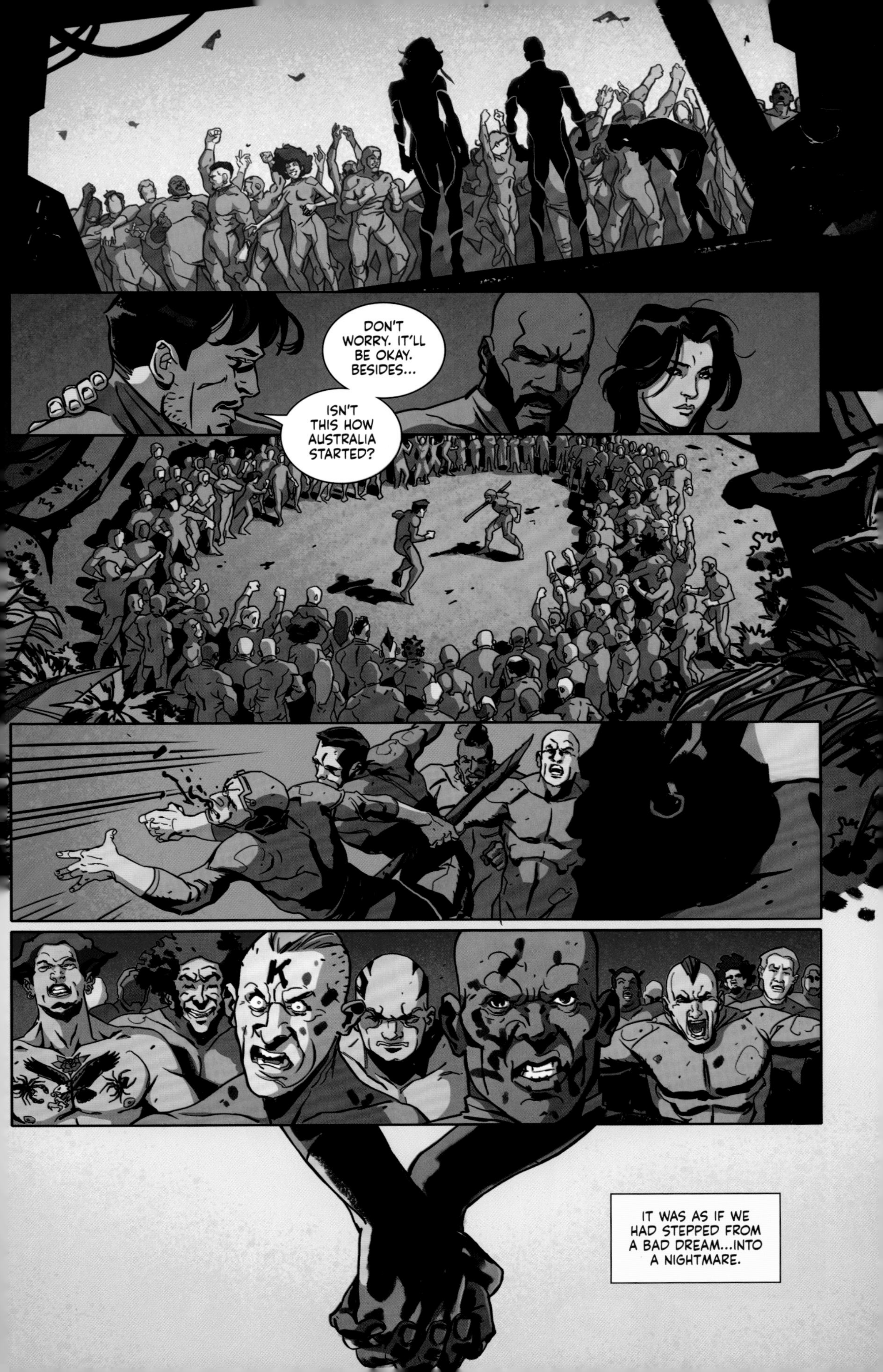
DON'T WORRY. IT'LL BE OKAY. BESIDES...
ISN'T THIS HOW AUSTRALIA STARTED?
K
IT WAS AS IF WE HAD STEPPED FROM A BAD DREAM...INTO A NIGHTMARE.

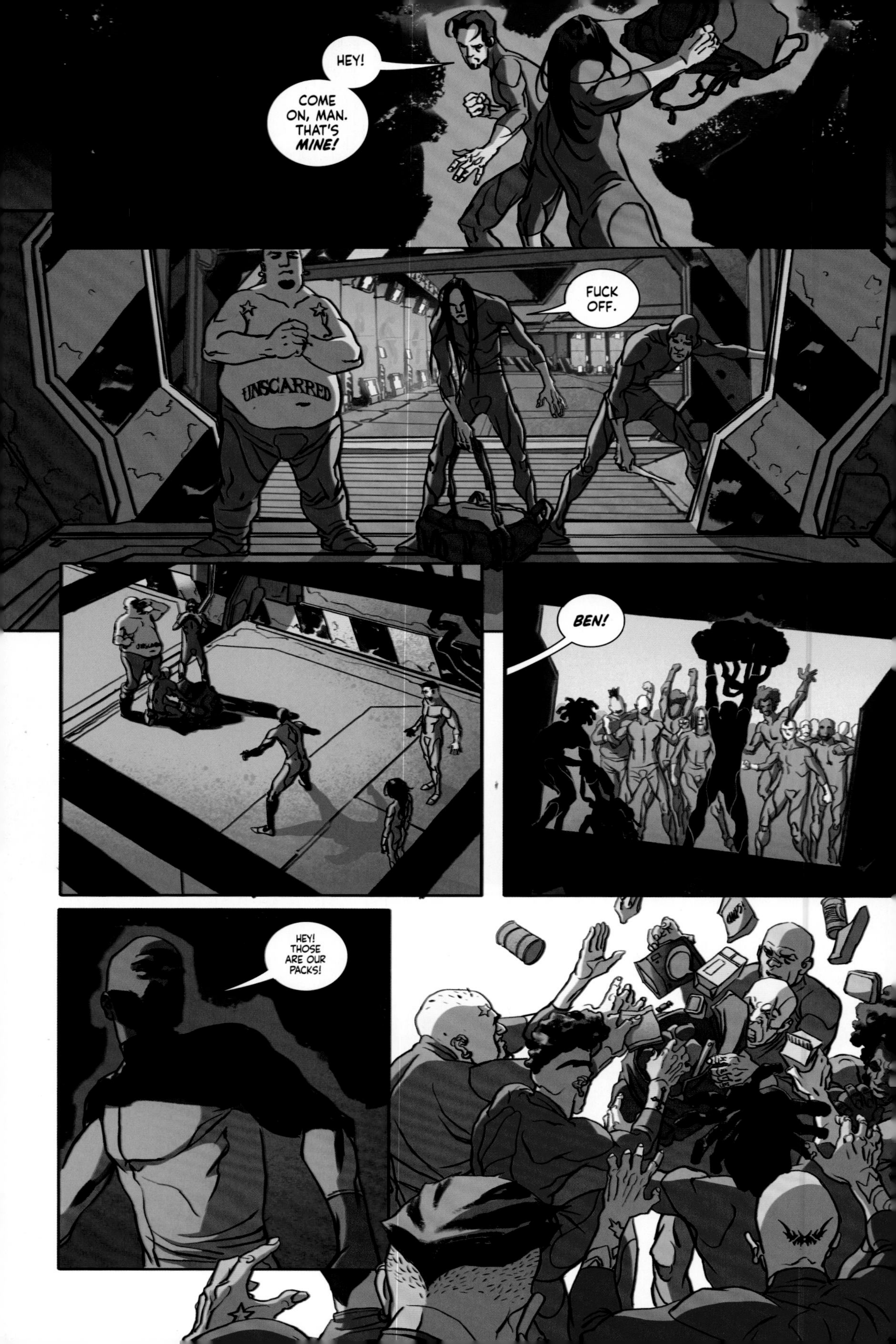
HEY!
COME ON, MAN. THAT'S MINE!
UNSCARRED
FUCK OFF.
BEN!
HEY! THOSE ARE OUR PACKS!

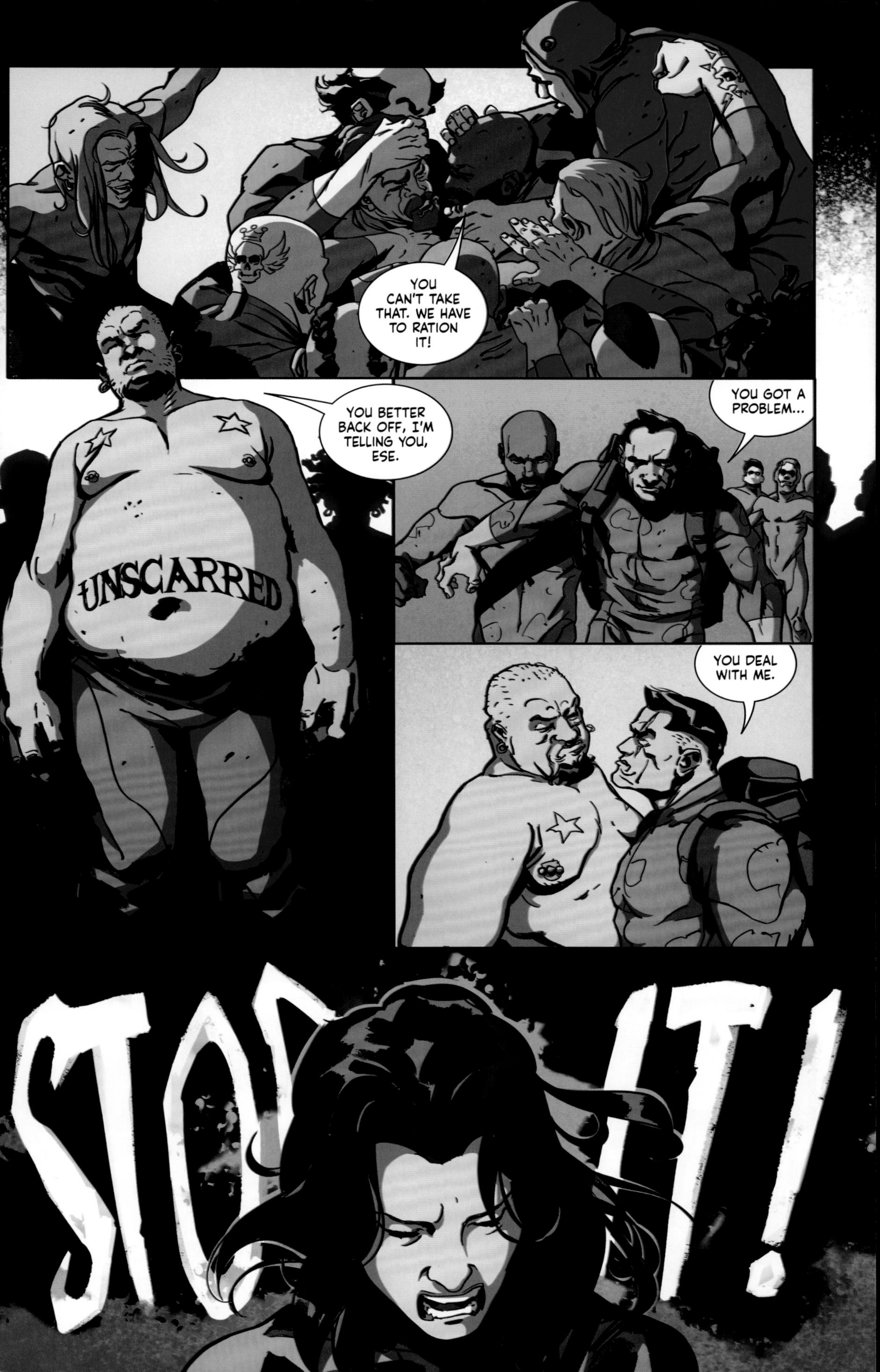

YOU CAN'T TAKE THAT. WE HAVE TO RATION IT!
YOU BETTER BACK OFF, I'M TELLING YOU, ESE.
UNSCARRED
YOU GOT A PROBLEM...
YOU DEAL WITH ME.

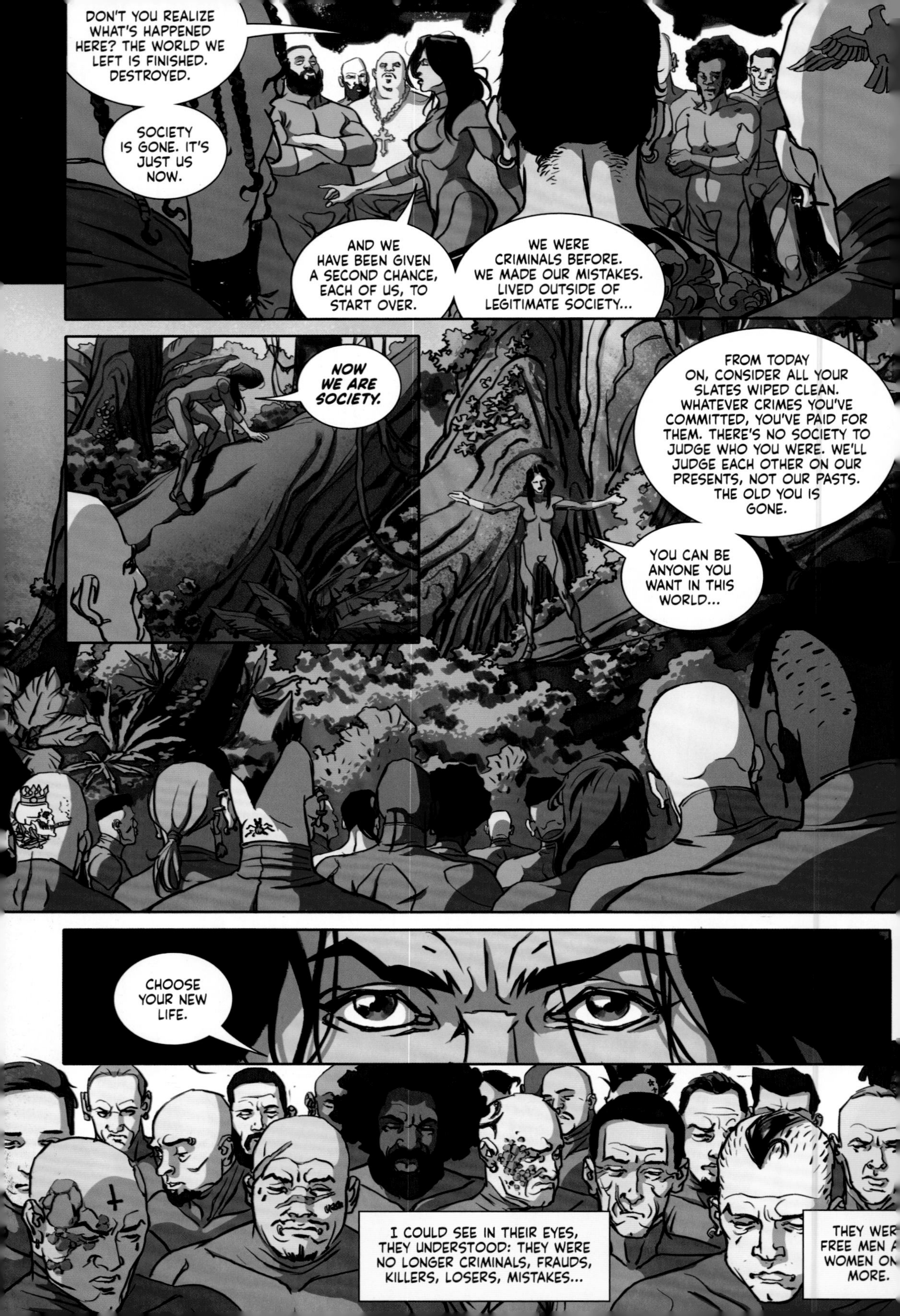
DON'T YOU REALIZE WHAT'S HAPPENED HERE? THE WORLD WE LEFT IS FINISHED. DESTROYED.
SOCIETY IS GONE. IT'S JUST US NOW.
AND WE HAVE BEEN GIVEN A SECOND CHANCE, EACH OF US, TO START OVER.
WE WERE CRIMINALS BEFORE. WE MADE OUR MISTAKES. LIVED OUTSIDE OF LEGITIMATE SOCIETY...
NOW WE ARE SOCIETY.
FROM TODAY ON, CONSIDER ALL YOUR SLATES WIPED CLEAN. WHATEVER CRIMES YOU'VE COMMITTED, YOU'VE PAID FOR THEM. THERE'S NO SOCIETY TO JUDGE WHO YOU WERE. WE'LL JUDGE EACH OTHER ON OUR PRESENTS, NOT OUR PASTS. THE OLD YOU IS GONE.
YOU CAN BE ANYONE YOU WANT IN THIS WORLD...
CHOOSE YOUR NEW LIFE.
I COULD SEE IN THEIR EYES, THEY UNDERSTOOD: THEY WERE NO LONGER CRIMINALS, FRAUDS, KILLERS, LOSERS, MISTAKES...
THEY WER FREE MEN A WOMEN ON MORE.

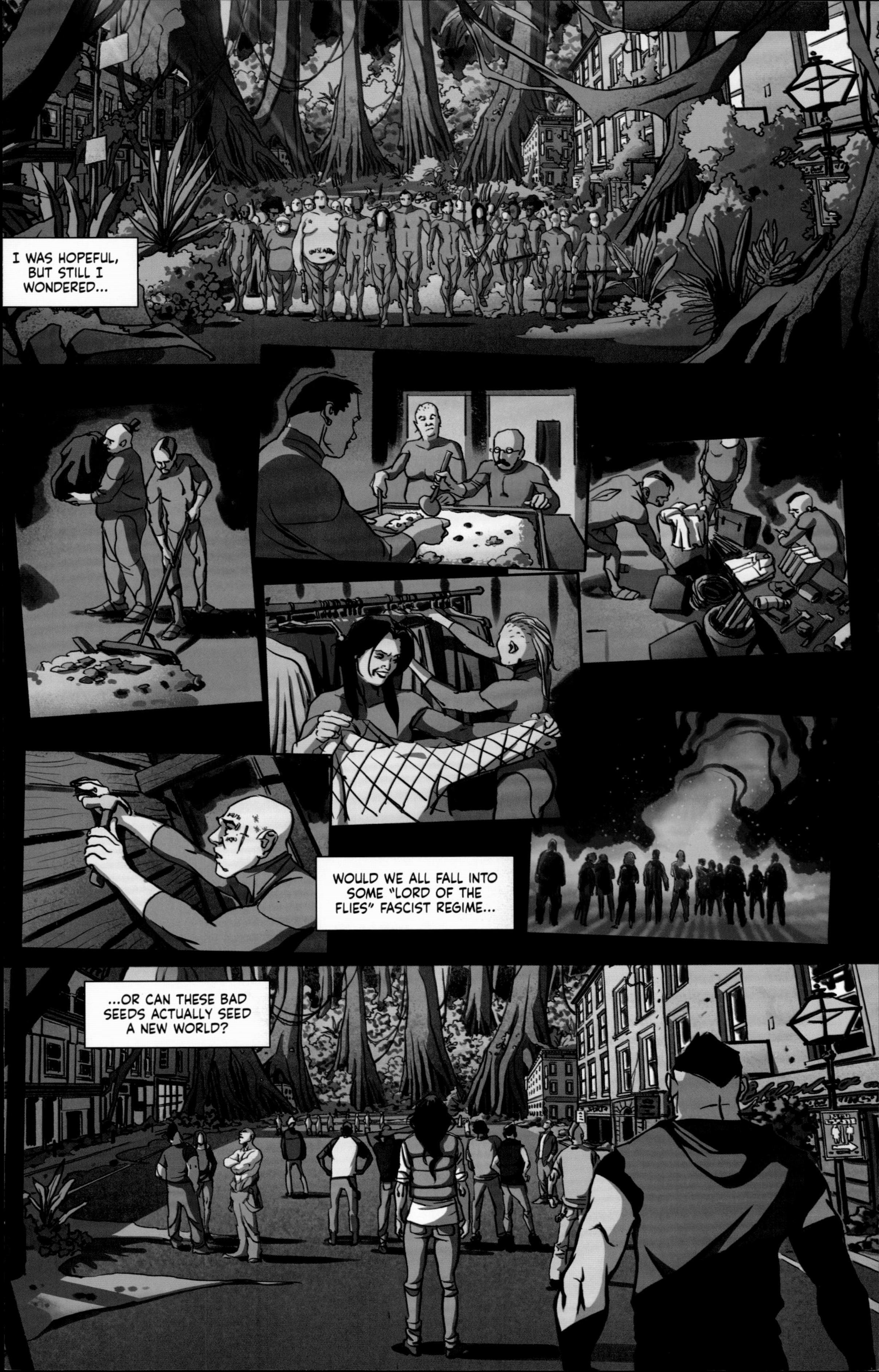
I WAS HOPEFUL, BUT STILL I WONDERED...
WOULD WE ALL FALL INTO SOME "LORD OF THE FLIES" FASCIST REGIME...
...OR CAN THESE BAD SEEDS ACTUALLY SEED A NEW WORLD?

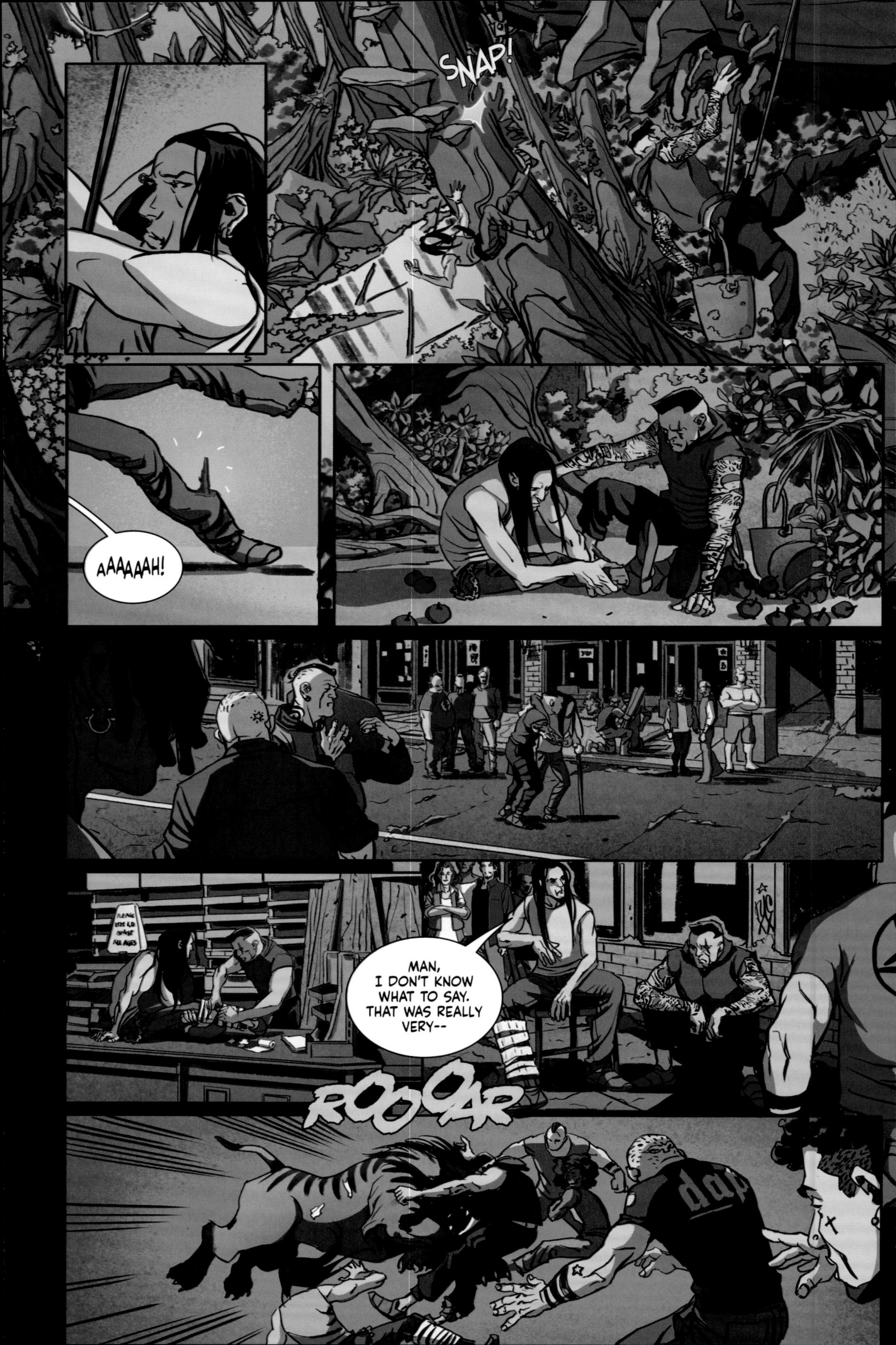
SNAP!
AAAAAAH!
MAN, I DON'T KNOW WHAT TO SAY. THAT WAS REALLY VERY--
ROOOAR

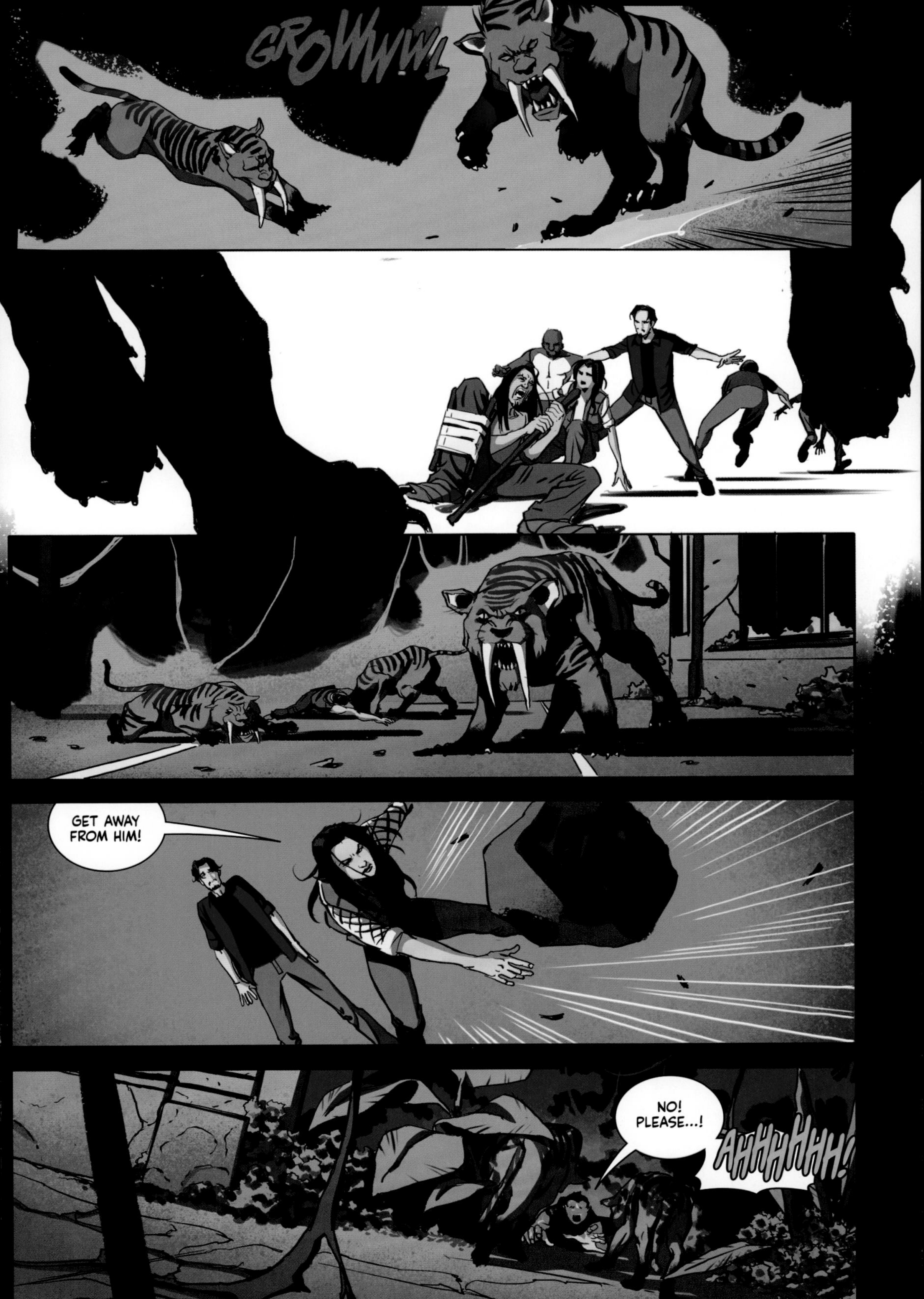
GROWWWL
GET AWAY FROM HIM!
NO! PLEASE...!
AHHHHHH!

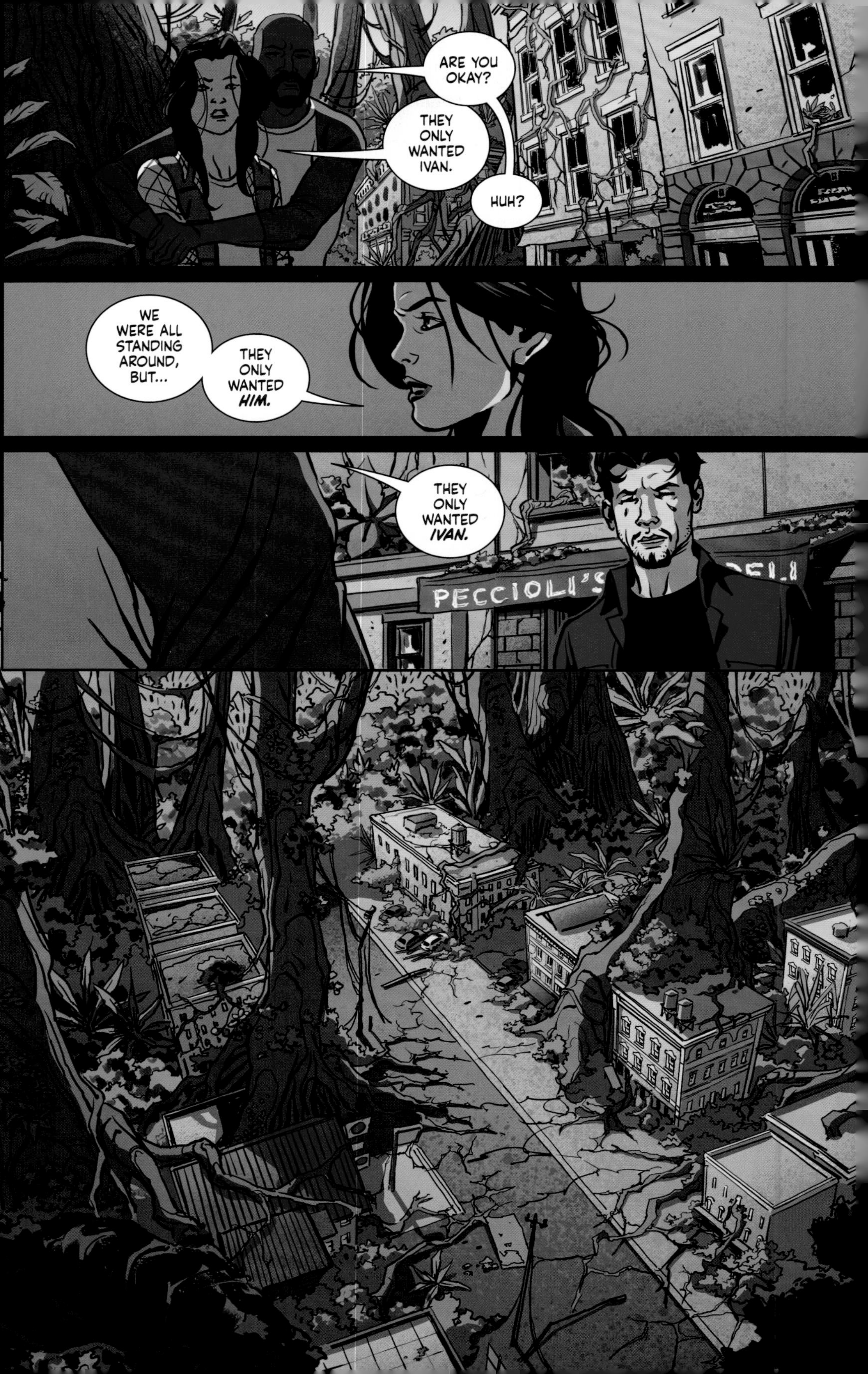
ARE YOU OKAY?
THEY ONLY WANTED IVAN.
HUH?
WE WERE ALL STANDING AROUND, BUT...
THEY ONLY WANTED ***HIM.***
THEY ONLY WANTED ***IVAN.***
PECCIOLI'S

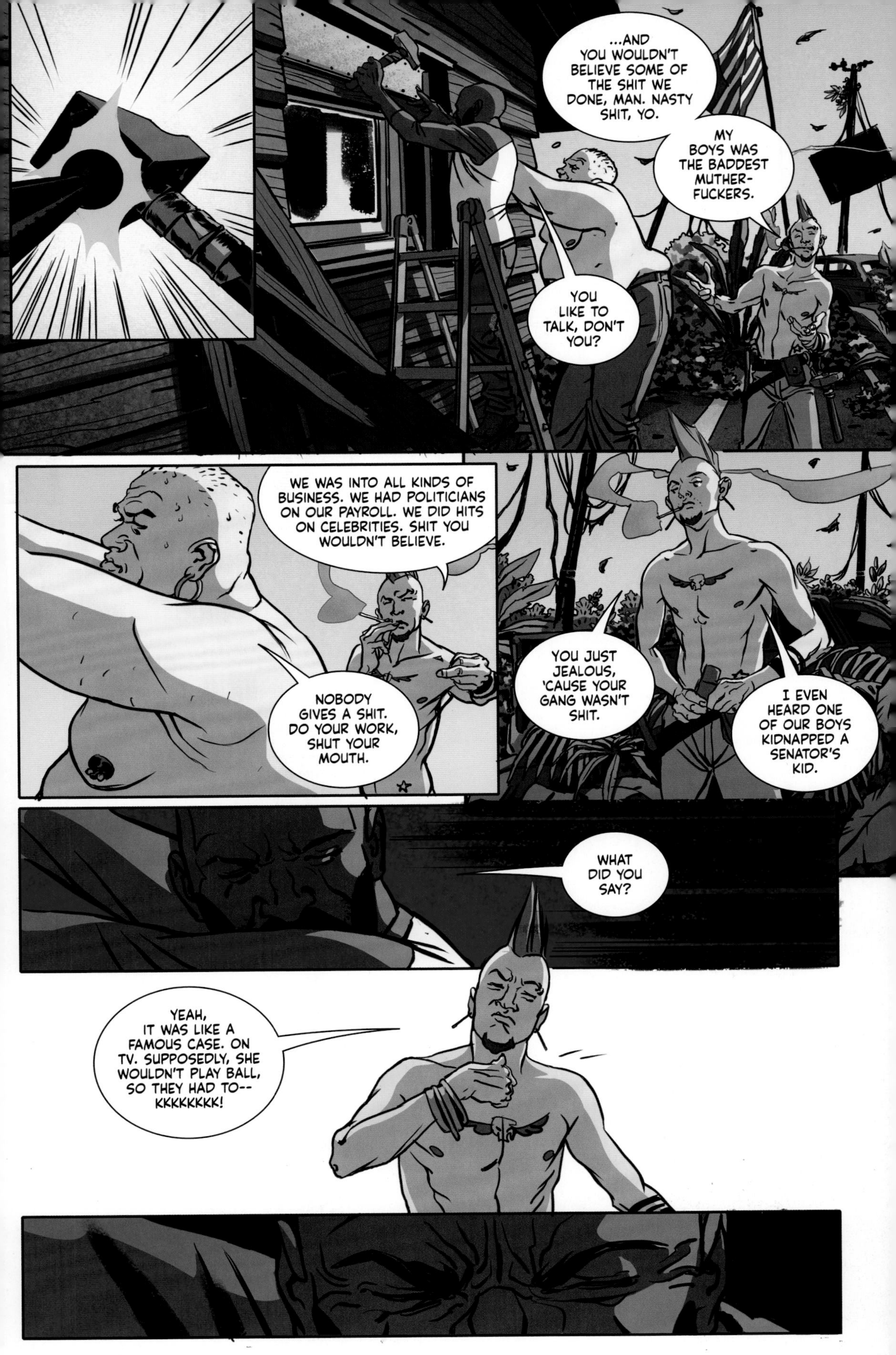
...AND YOU WOULDN'T BELIEVE SOME OF THE SHIT WE DONE, MAN. NASTY SHIT, YO.
MY BOYS WAS THE BADDEST MUTHER-FUCKERS.
YOU LIKE TO TALK, DON'T YOU?
WE WAS INTO ALL KINDS OF BUSINESS. WE HAD POLITICIANS ON OUR PAYROLL. WE DID HITS ON CELEBRITIES. SHIT YOU WOULDN'T BELIEVE.
NOBODY GIVES A SHIT. DO YOUR WORK, SHUT YOUR MOUTH.
YOU JUST JEALOUS, 'CAUSE YOUR GANG WASN'T SHIT.
I EVEN HEARD ONE OF OUR BOYS KIDNAPPED A SENATOR'S KID.
WHAT DID YOU SAY?
YEAH, IT WAS LIKE A FAMOUS CASE. ON TV. SUPPOSEDLY, SHE WOULDN'T PLAY BALL, SO THEY HAD TO-- KKKKKKKK!

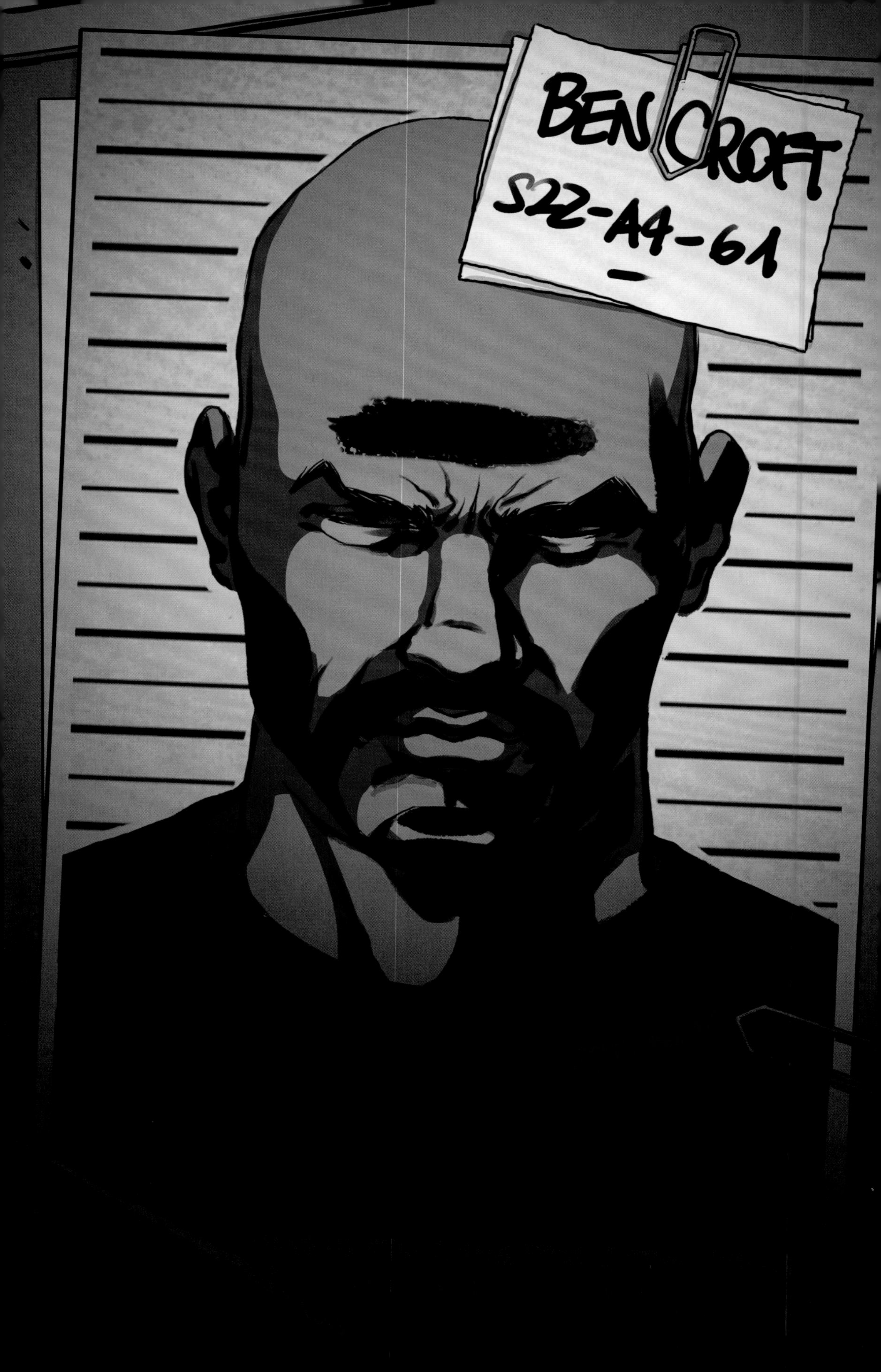
BEN CROFT
S22-A4-61

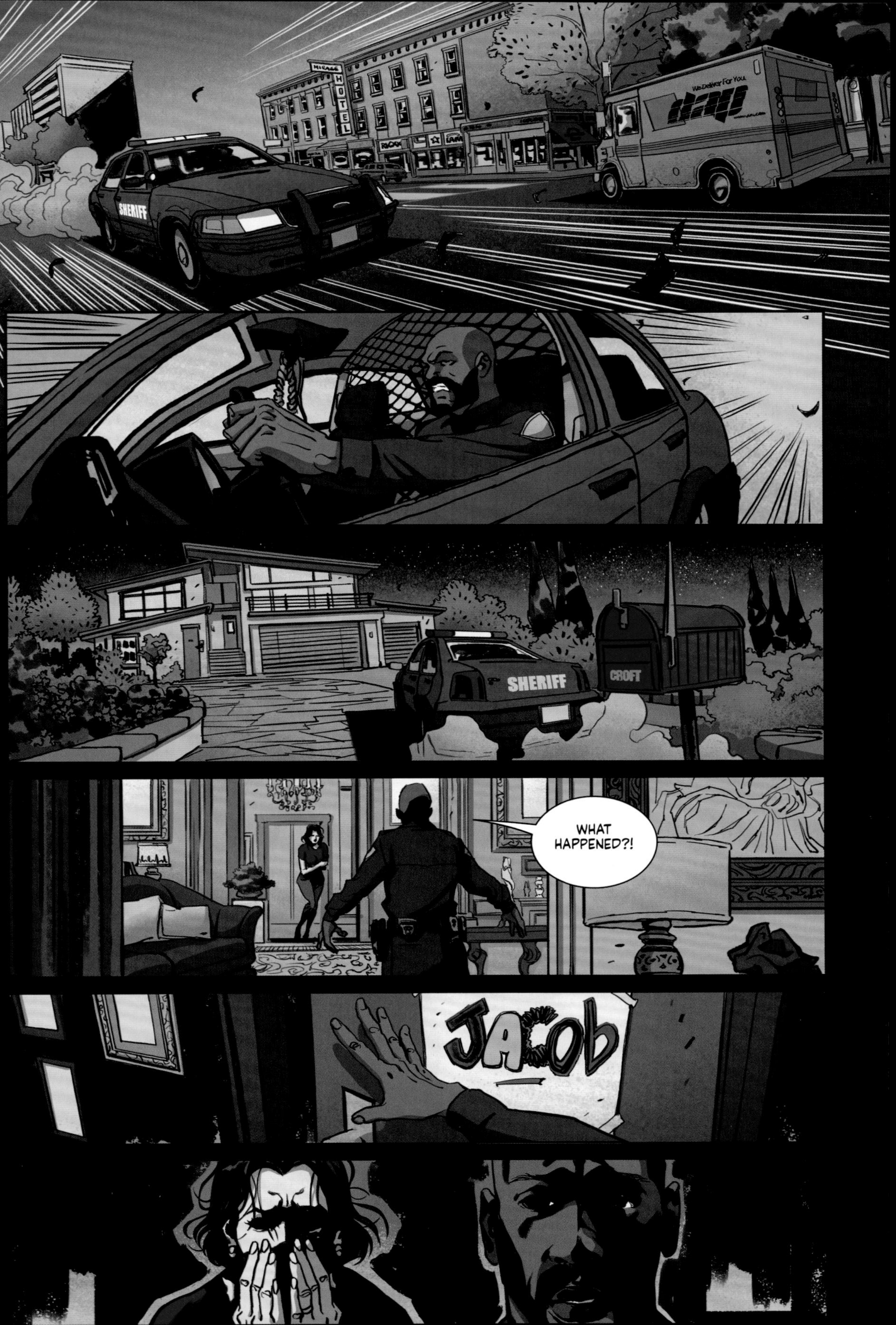
MIRAGE
HOTEL
SHERIFF
We Deliver For You.
SHERIFF
CROFT
WHAT HAPPENED?!
JACOB

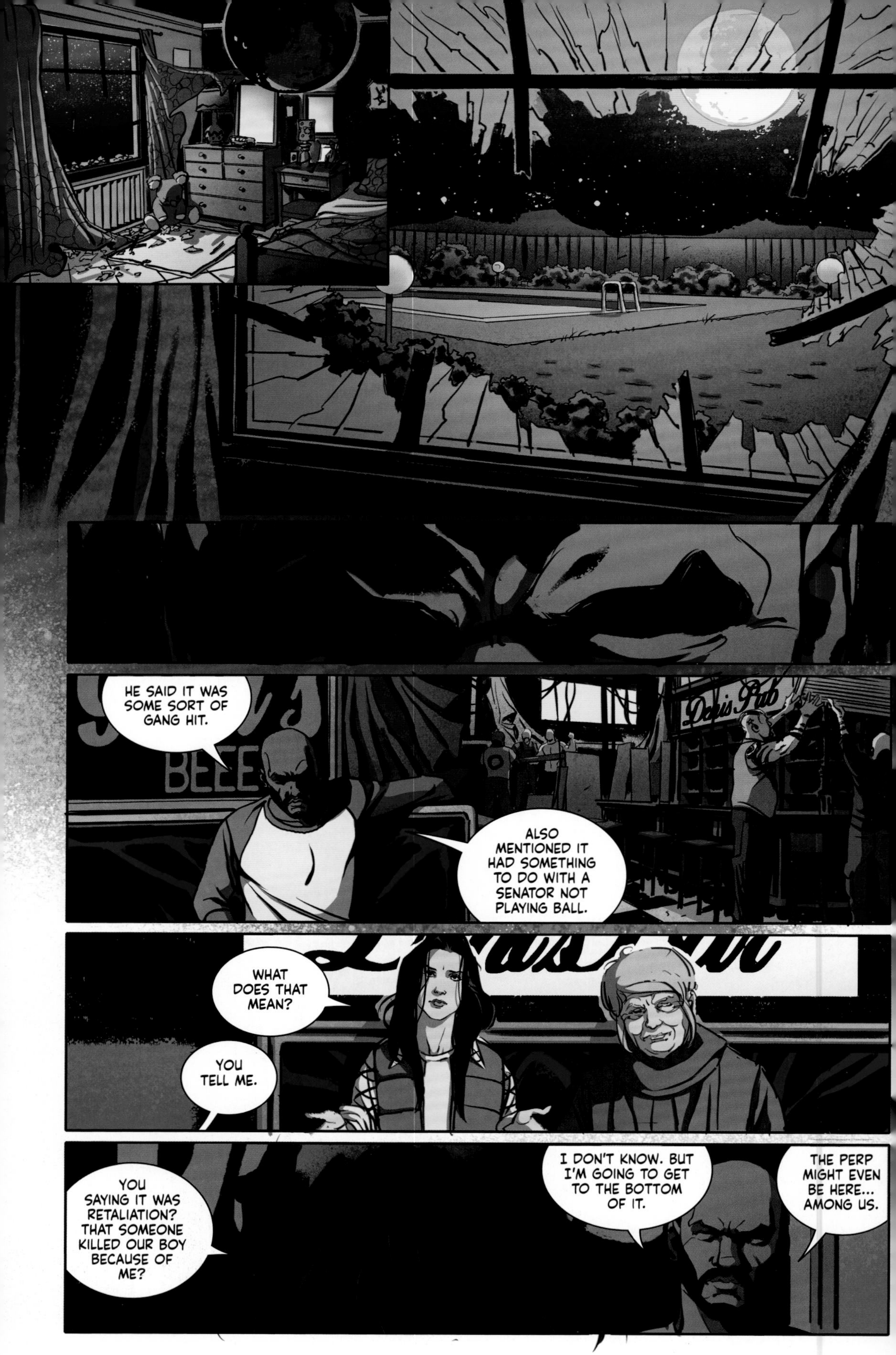

HE SAID IT WAS SOME SORT OF GANG HIT.
ALSO MENTIONED IT HAD SOMETHING TO DO WITH A SENATOR NOT PLAYING BALL.
WHAT DOES THAT MEAN?
YOU TELL ME.
YOU SAYING IT WAS RETALIATION? THAT SOMEONE KILLED OUR BOY BECAUSE OF ME?
I DON'T KNOW. BUT I'M GOING TO GET TO THE BOTTOM OF IT.
THE PERP MIGHT EVEN BE HERE... AMONG US.

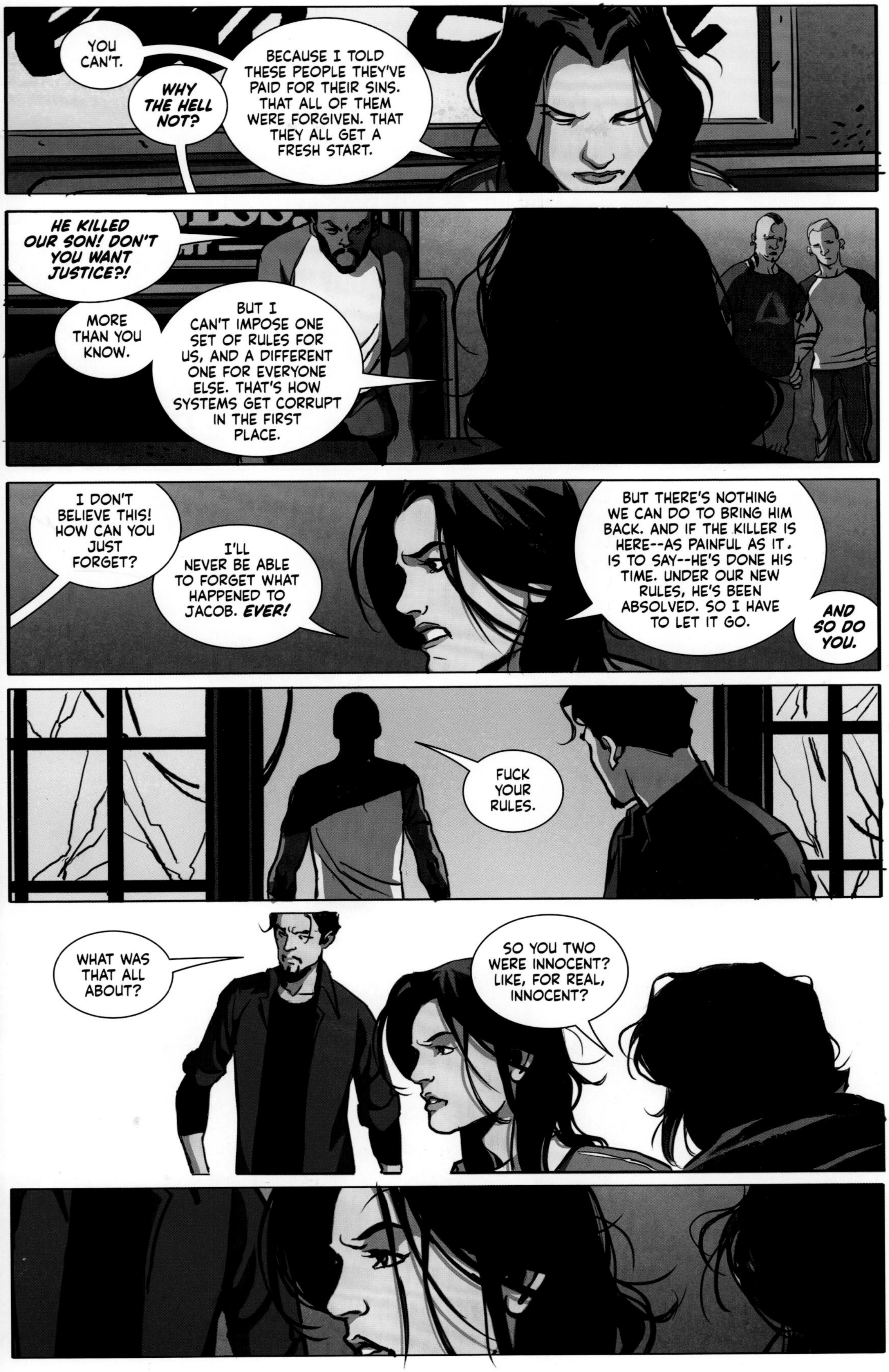
YOU CAN'T.
WHY THE HELL NOT?
BECAUSE I TOLD THESE PEOPLE THEY'VE PAID FOR THEIR SINS. THAT ALL OF THEM WERE FORGIVEN. THAT THEY ALL GET A FRESH START.
HE KILLED OUR SON! DON'T YOU WANT JUSTICE?!
MORE THAN YOU KNOW.
BUT I CAN'T IMPOSE ONE SET OF RULES FOR US, AND A DIFFERENT ONE FOR EVERYONE ELSE. THAT'S HOW SYSTEMS GET CORRUPT IN THE FIRST PLACE.
I DON'T BELIEVE THIS! HOW CAN YOU JUST FORGET?
I'LL NEVER BE ABLE TO FORGET WHAT HAPPENED TO JACOB. EVER!
BUT THERE'S NOTHING WE CAN DO TO BRING HIM BACK. AND IF THE KILLER IS HERE--AS PAINFUL AS IT IS TO SAY--HE'S DONE HIS TIME. UNDER OUR NEW RULES, HE'S BEEN ABSOLVED. SO I HAVE TO LET IT GO.
AND SO DO YOU.
FUCK YOUR RULES.
WHAT WAS THAT ALL ABOUT?
SO YOU TWO WERE INNOCENT? LIKE, FOR REAL, INNOCENT?

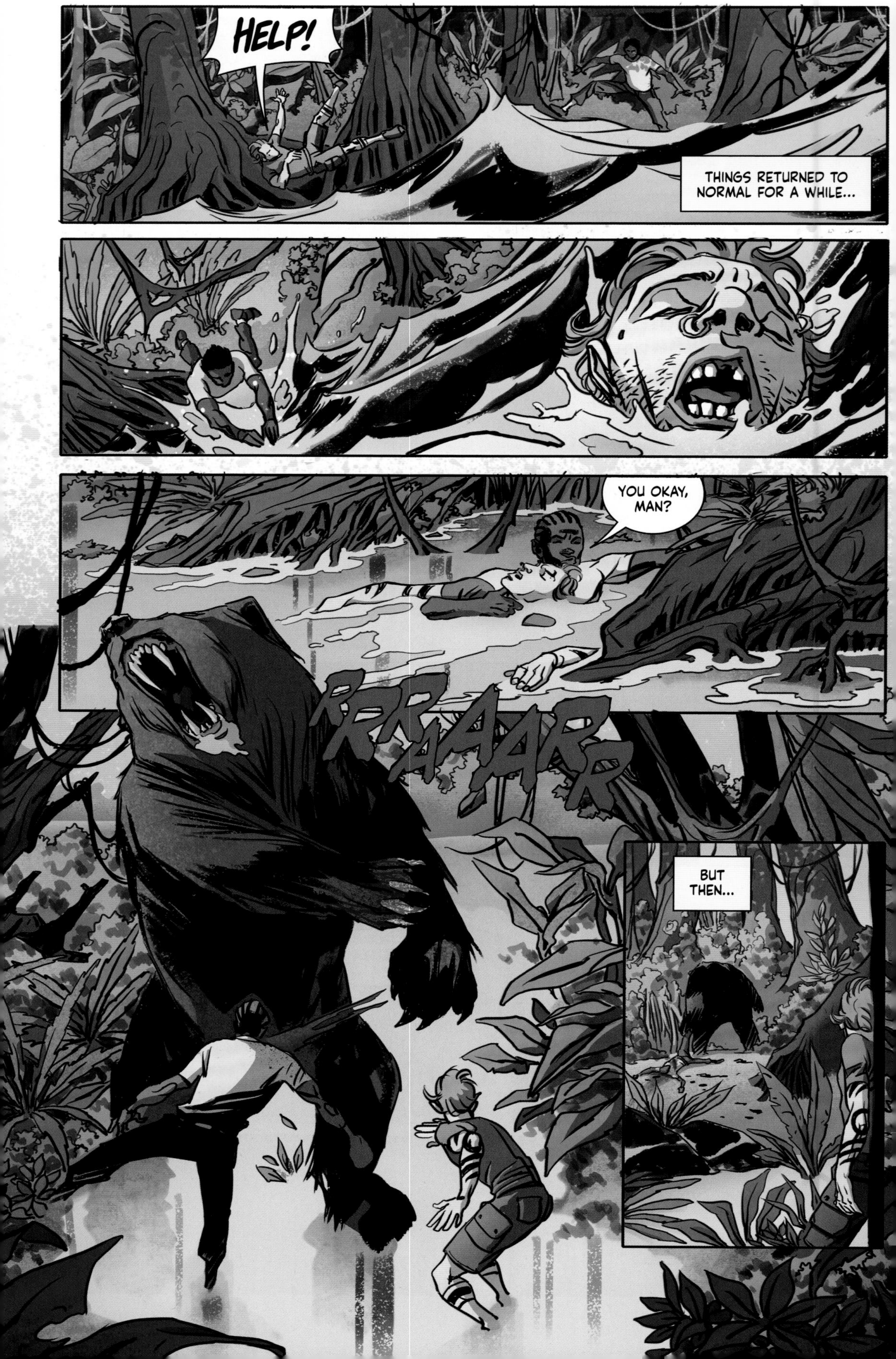
HELP!
THINGS RETURNED TO NORMAL FOR A WHILE...
YOU OKAY, MAN?
RRRAAARR
BUT THEN...

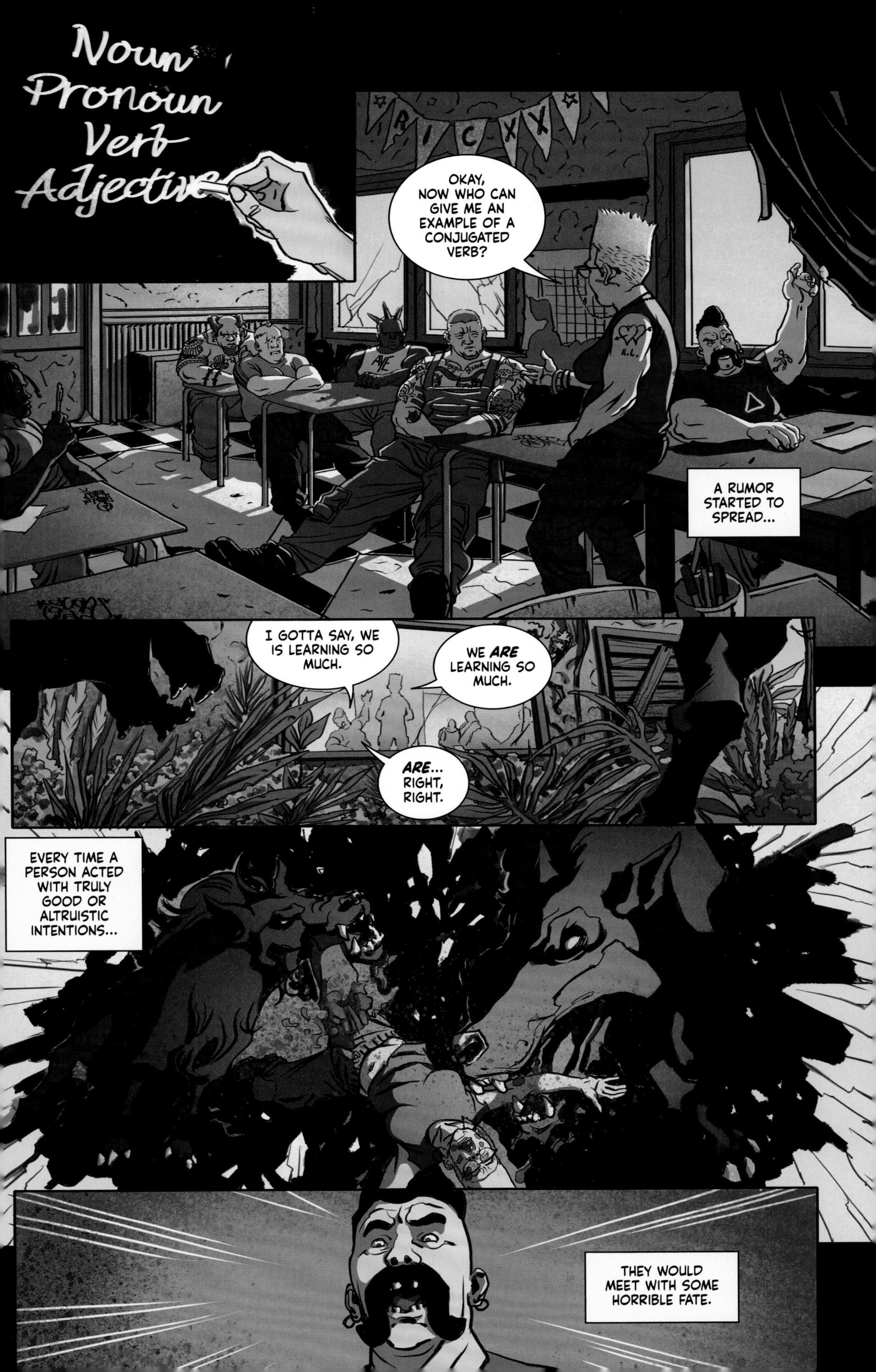
Noun
Pronoun
Verb
Adjective
OKAY, NOW WHO CAN GIVE ME AN EXAMPLE OF A CONJUGATED VERB?
A RUMOR STARTED TO SPREAD...
I GOTTA SAY, WE IS LEARNING SO MUCH.
WE ARE LEARNING SO MUCH.
ARE... RIGHT, RIGHT.
EVERY TIME A PERSON ACTED WITH TRULY GOOD OR ALTRUISTIC INTENTIONS...
THEY WOULD MEET WITH SOME HORRIBLE FATE.

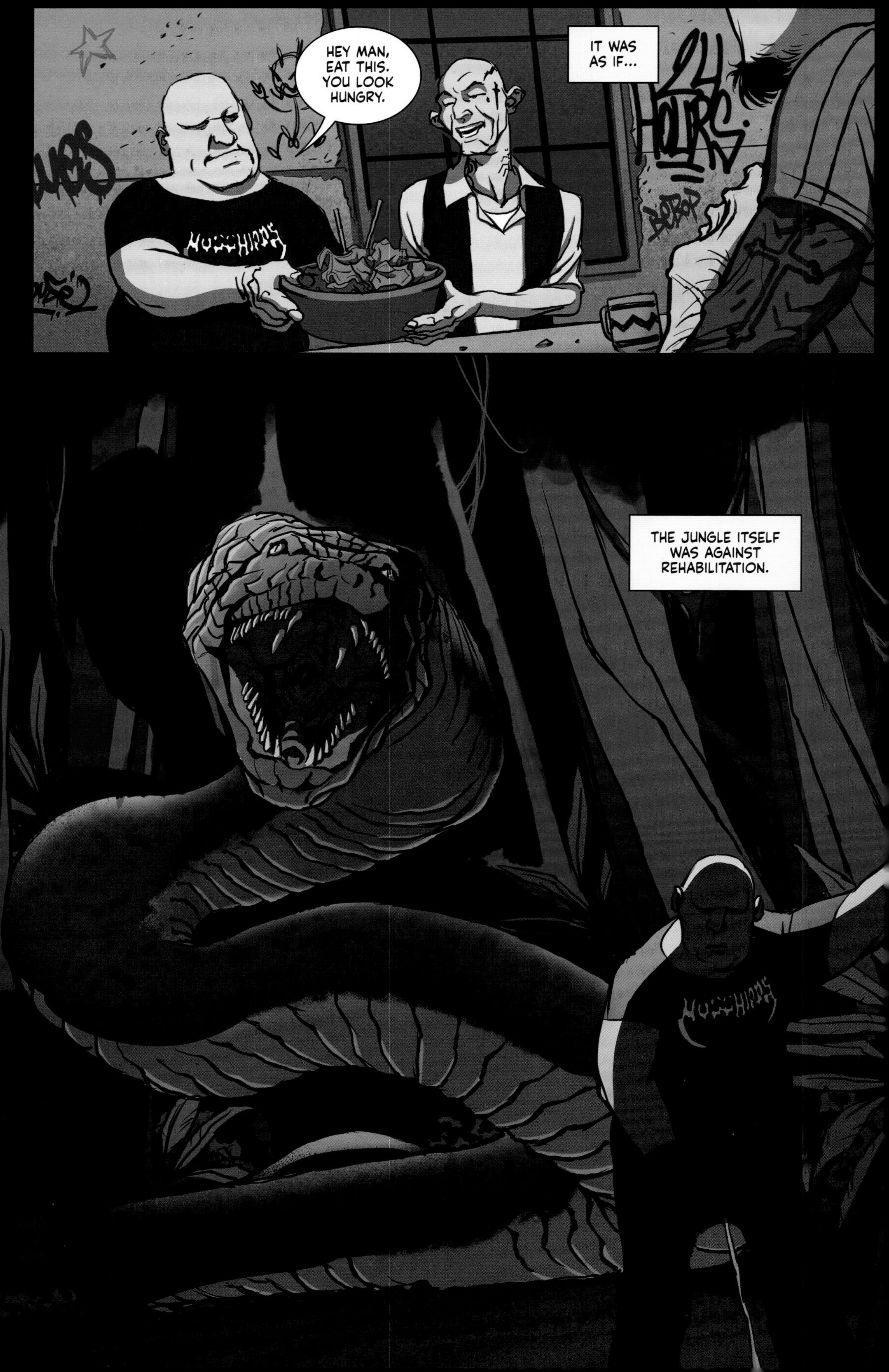
HEY MAN, EAT THIS. YOU LOOK HUNGRY.
IT WAS AS IF...
THE JUNGLE ITSELF WAS AGAINST REHABILITATION.

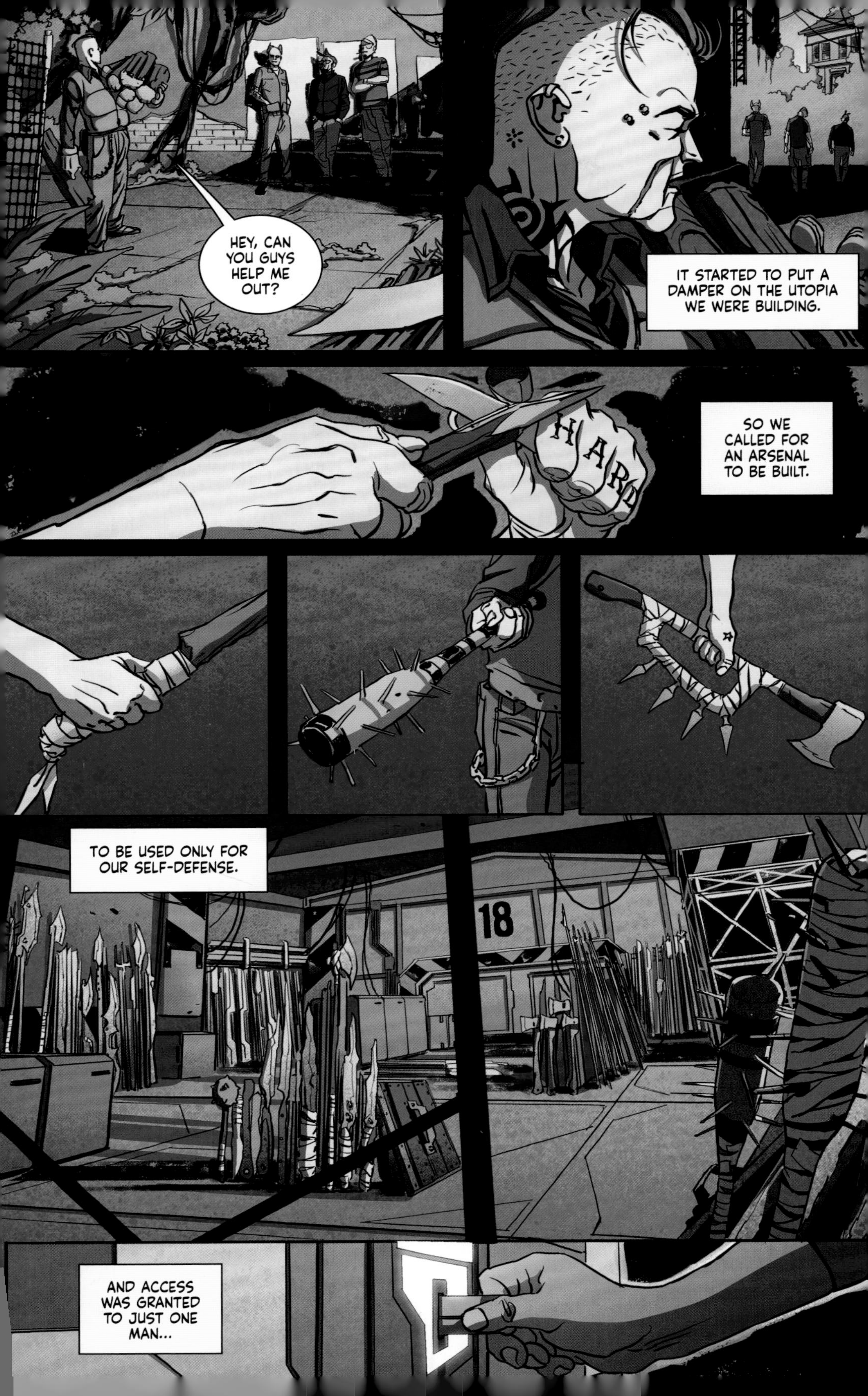
HEY, CAN YOU GUYS HELP ME OUT?
IT STARTED TO PUT A DAMPER ON THE UTOPIA WE WERE BUILDING.
SO WE CALLED FOR AN ARSENAL TO BE BUILT.
TO BE USED ONLY FOR OUR SELF-DEFENSE.
18
AND ACCESS WAS GRANTED TO JUST ONE MAN...

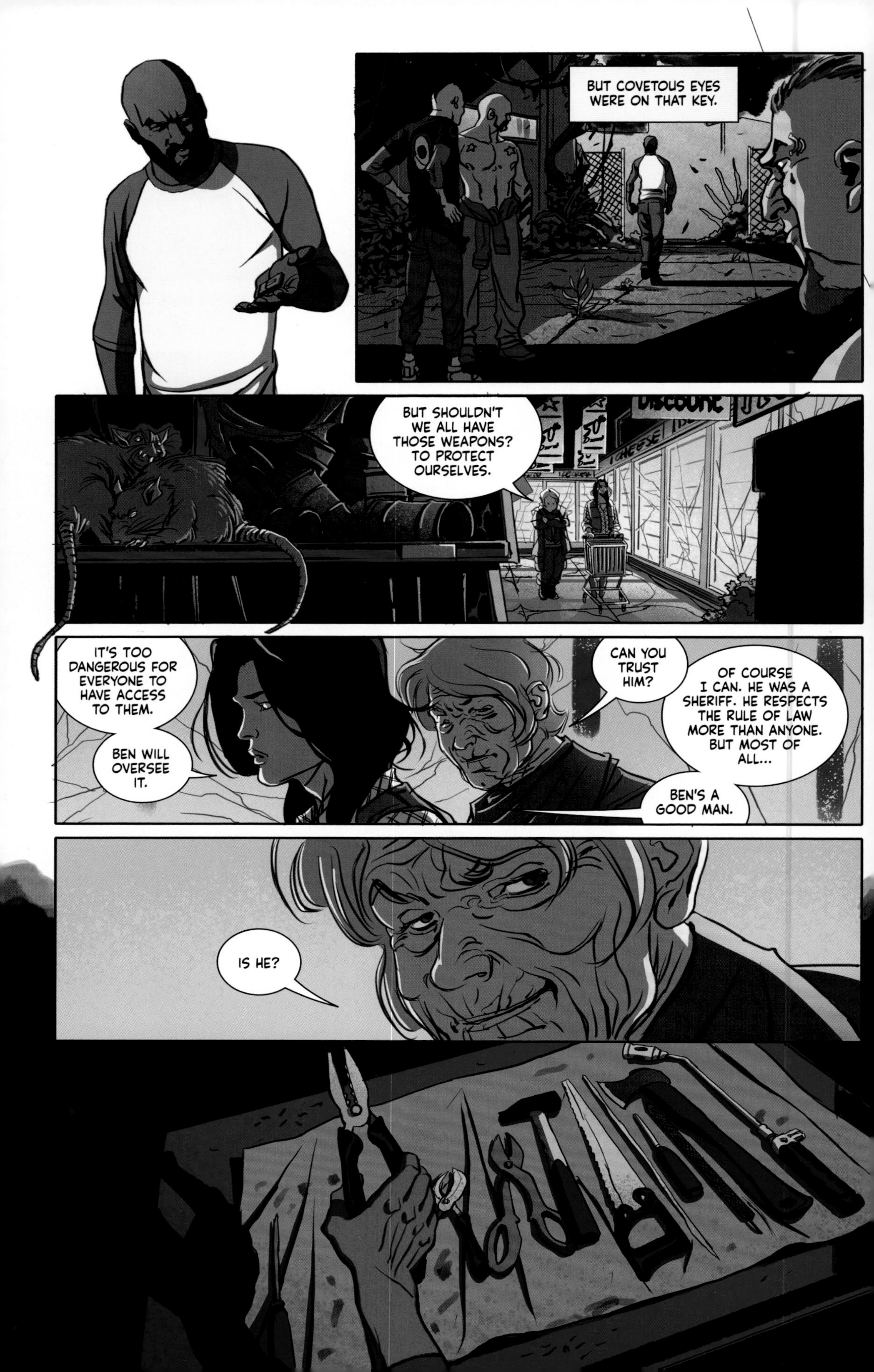

BUT COVETOUS EYES WERE ON THAT KEY.
BUT SHOULDN'T WE ALL HAVE THOSE WEAPONS? TO PROTECT OURSELVES.
DISCOUNT
CHEESE
IT'S TOO DANGEROUS FOR EVERYONE TO HAVE ACCESS TO THEM.
BEN WILL OVERSEE IT.
CAN YOU TRUST HIM?
OF COURSE I CAN. HE WAS A SHERIFF. HE RESPECTS THE RULE OF LAW MORE THAN ANYONE. BUT MOST OF ALL...
BEN'S A GOOD MAN.
IS HE?

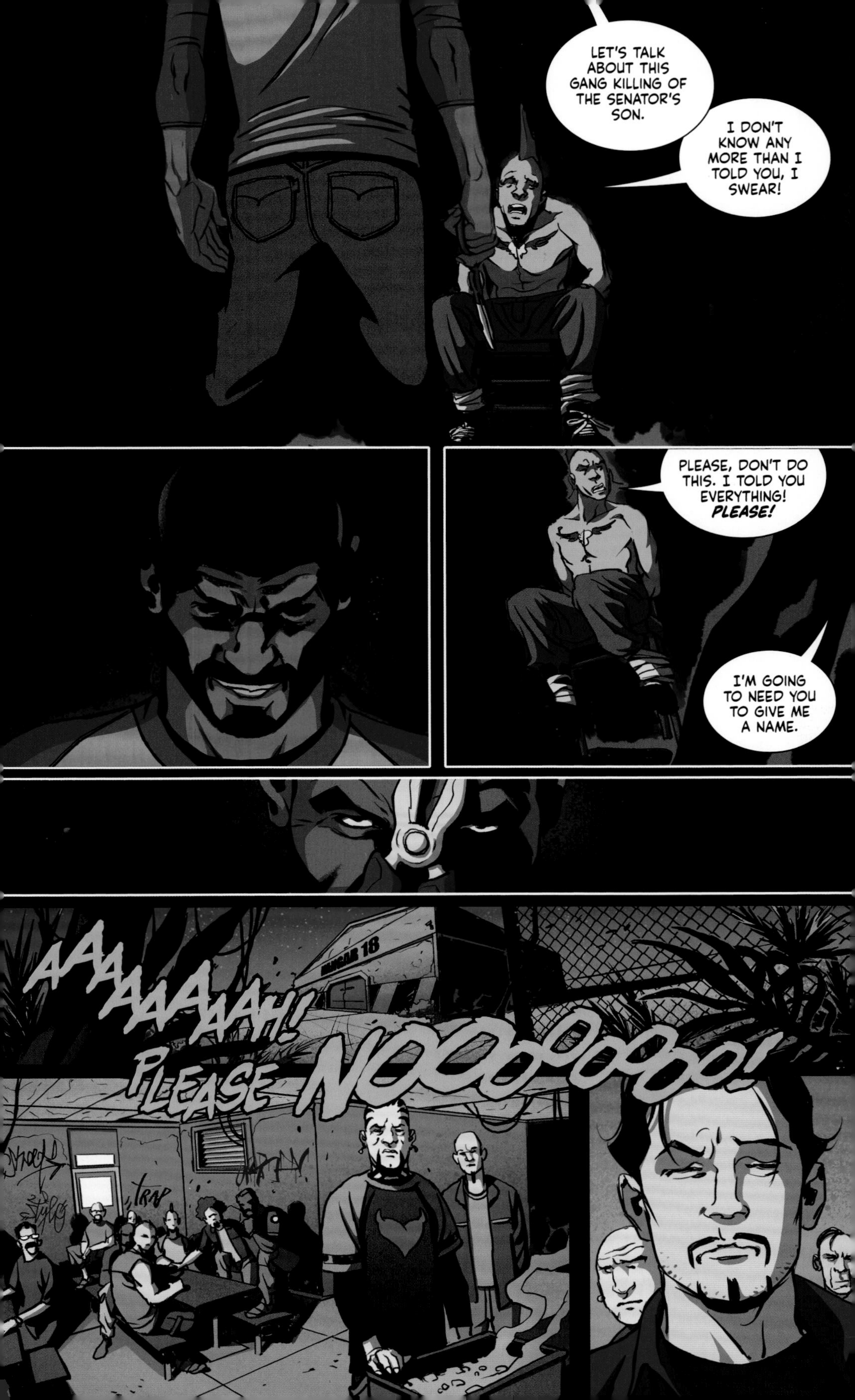
LET'S TALK ABOUT THIS GANG KILLING OF THE SENATOR'S SON.
I DON'T KNOW ANY MORE THAN I TOLD YOU, I SWEAR!
PLEASE, DON'T DO THIS. I TOLD YOU EVERYTHING! *PLEASE!*
I'M GOING TO NEED YOU TO GIVE ME A NAME.
HANGAR 18
AAAAAAAH!
PLEASE NOOOOOOOO!

IV

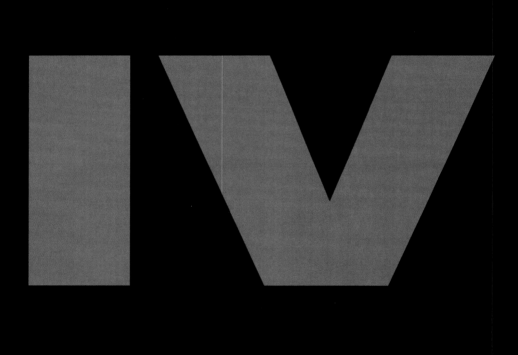

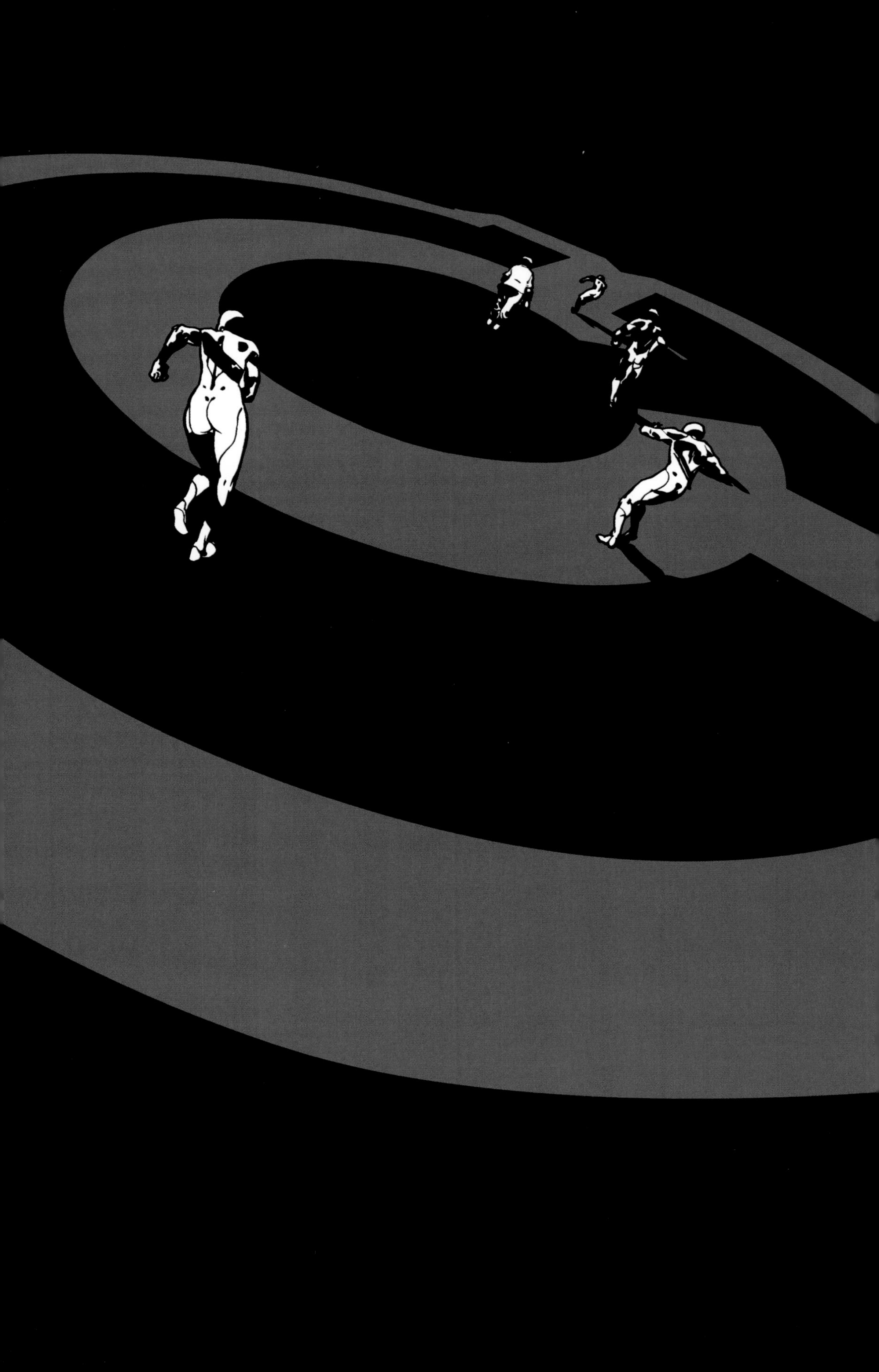

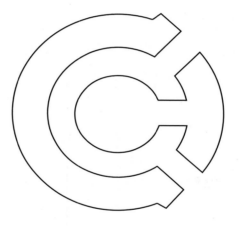

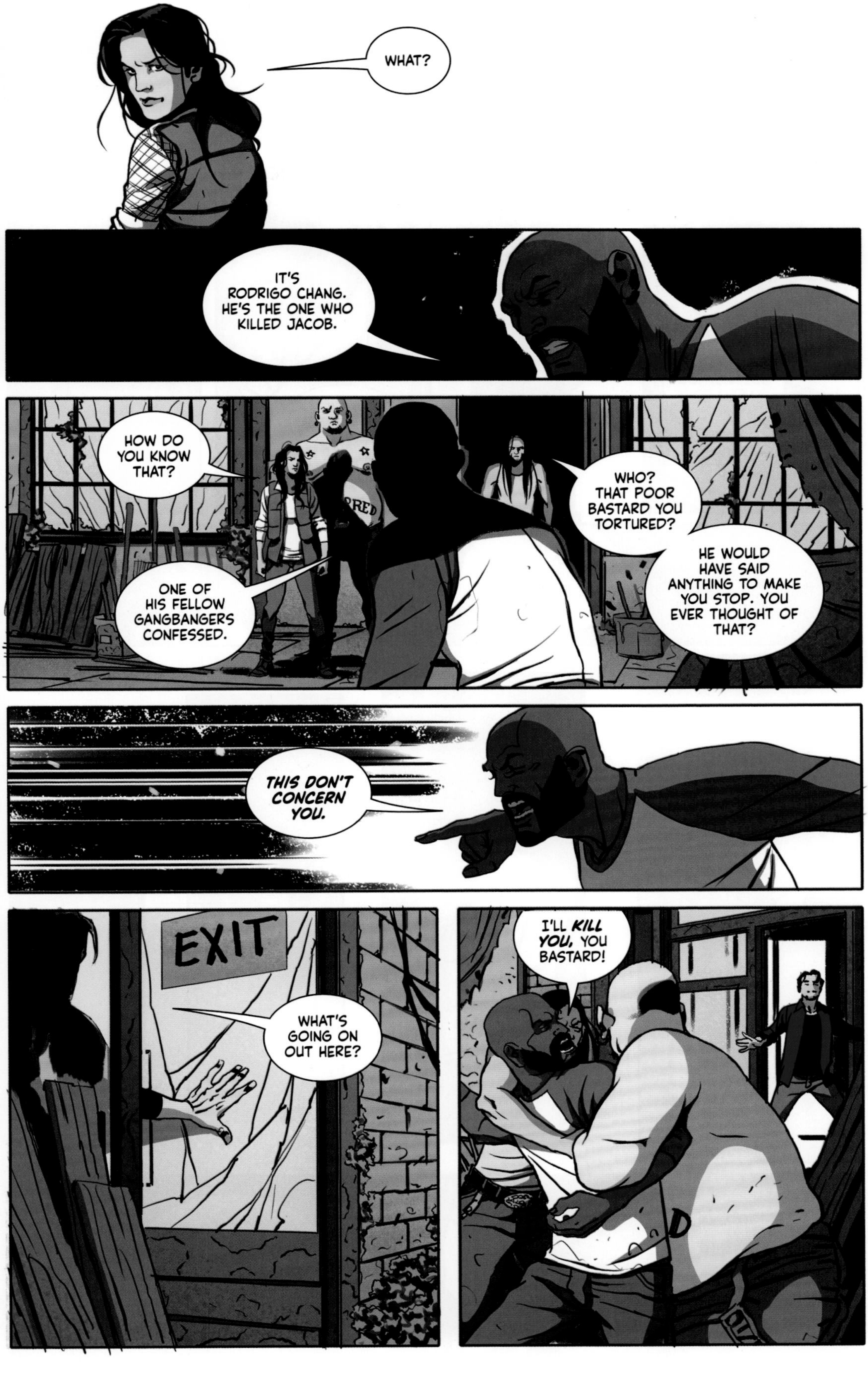
WHAT?
IT'S RODRIGO CHANG. HE'S THE ONE WHO KILLED JACOB.
HOW DO YOU KNOW THAT?
ONE OF HIS FELLOW GANGBANGERS CONFESSED.
WHO? THAT POOR BASTARD YOU TORTURED?
HE WOULD HAVE SAID ANYTHING TO MAKE YOU STOP. YOU EVER THOUGHT OF THAT?
THIS DON'T CONCERN YOU.
EXIT
WHAT'S GOING ON OUT HERE?
I'LL ***KILL YOU,*** YOU BASTARD!

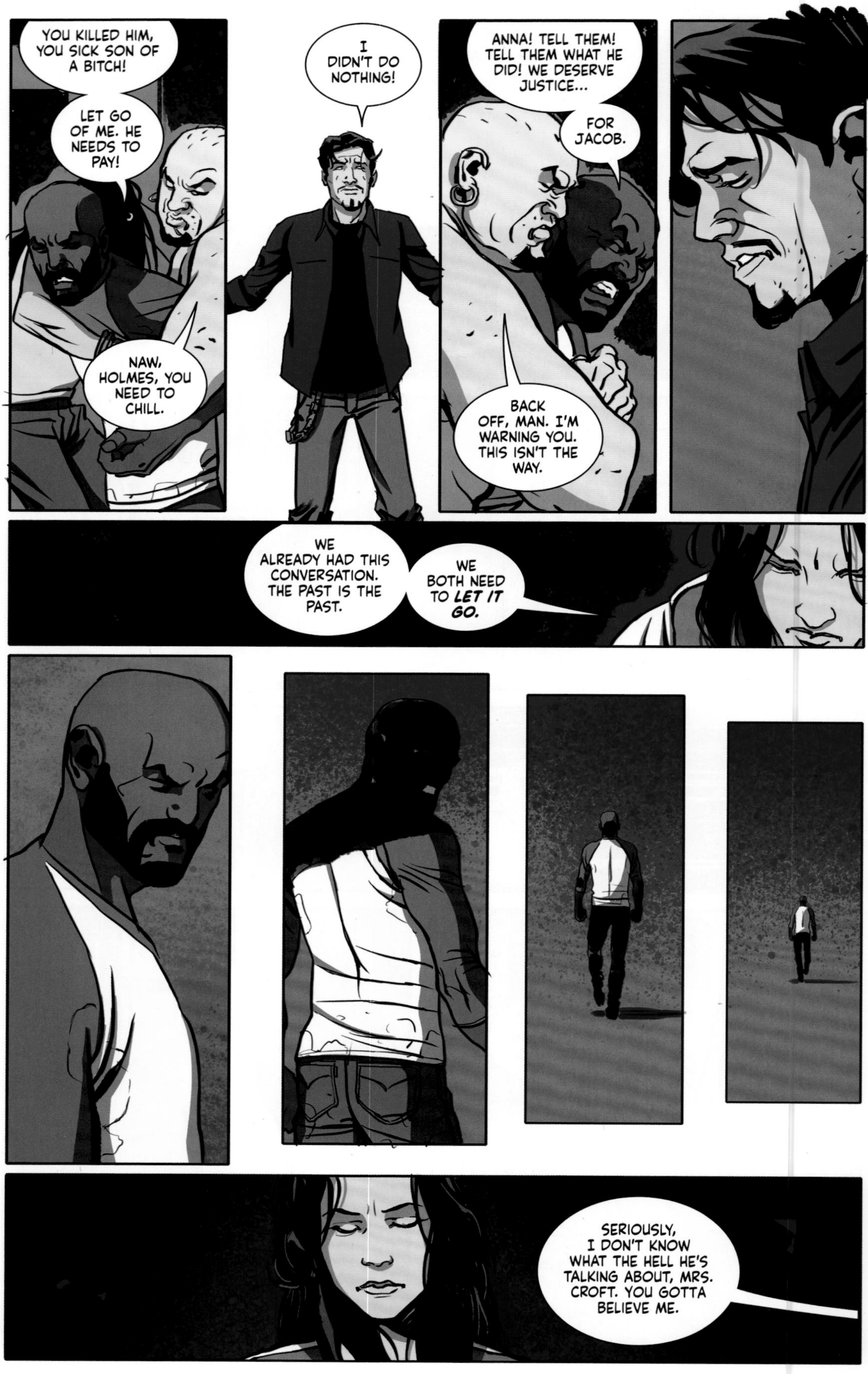
YOU KILLED HIM, YOU SICK SON OF A BITCH!
LET GO OF ME. HE NEEDS TO PAY!
NAW, HOLMES, YOU NEED TO CHILL.
I DIDN'T DO NOTHING!
ANNA! TELL THEM! TELL THEM WHAT HE DID! WE DESERVE JUSTICE...
FOR JACOB.
BACK OFF, MAN. I'M WARNING YOU. THIS ISN'T THE WAY.
WE ALREADY HAD THIS CONVERSATION. THE PAST IS THE PAST.
WE BOTH NEED TO LET IT GO.
SERIOUSLY, I DON'T KNOW WHAT THE HELL HE'S TALKING ABOUT, MRS. CROFT. YOU GOTTA BELIEVE ME.

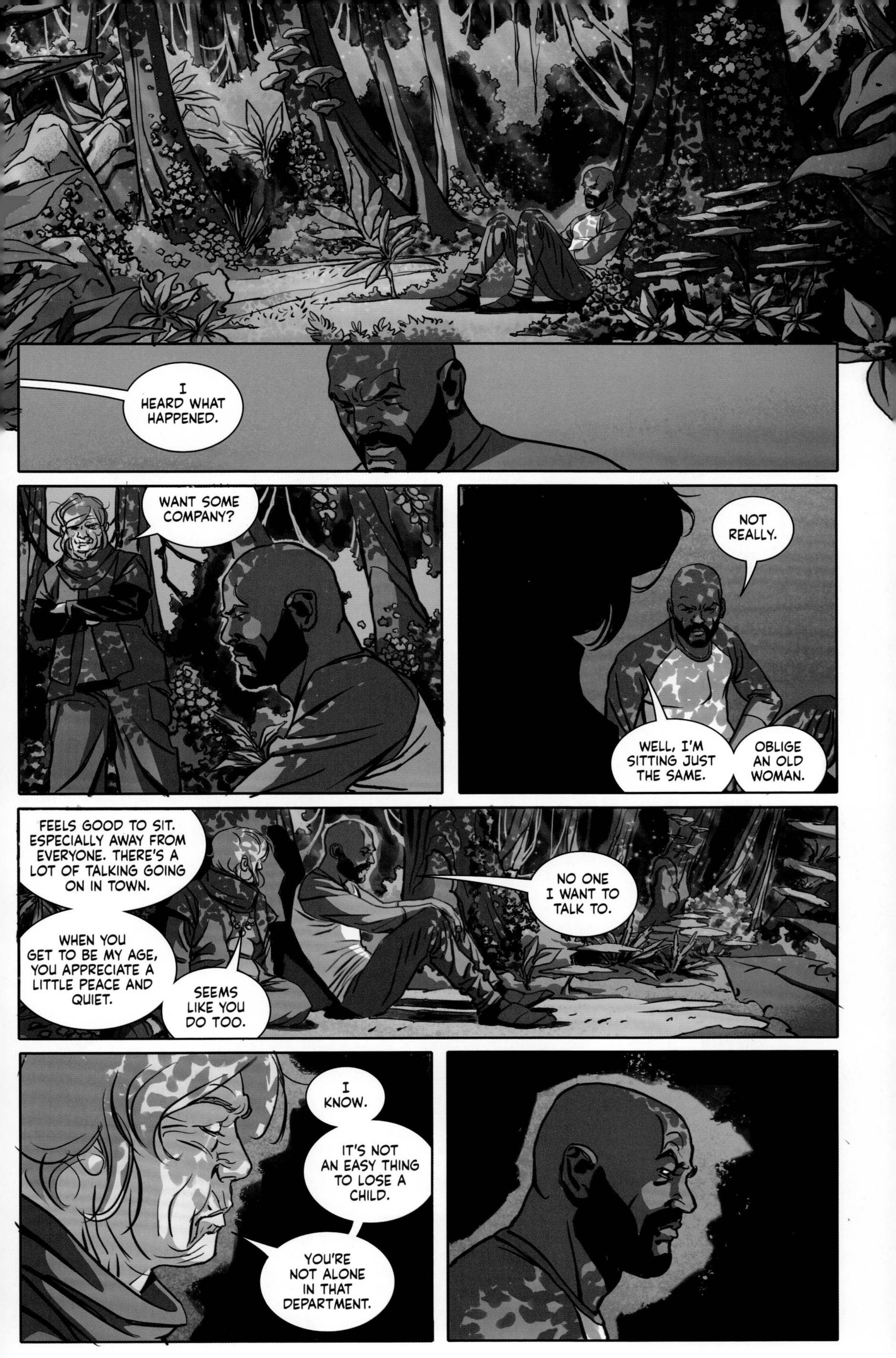
I HEARD WHAT HAPPENED.
WANT SOME COMPANY?
NOT REALLY.
WELL, I'M SITTING JUST THE SAME.
OBLIGE AN OLD WOMAN.
FEELS GOOD TO SIT. ESPECIALLY AWAY FROM EVERYONE. THERE'S A LOT OF TALKING GOING ON IN TOWN.
WHEN YOU GET TO BE MY AGE, YOU APPRECIATE A LITTLE PEACE AND QUIET.
SEEMS LIKE YOU DO TOO.
NO ONE I WANT TO TALK TO.
I KNOW.
IT'S NOT AN EASY THING TO LOSE A CHILD.
YOU'RE NOT ALONE IN THAT DEPARTMENT.

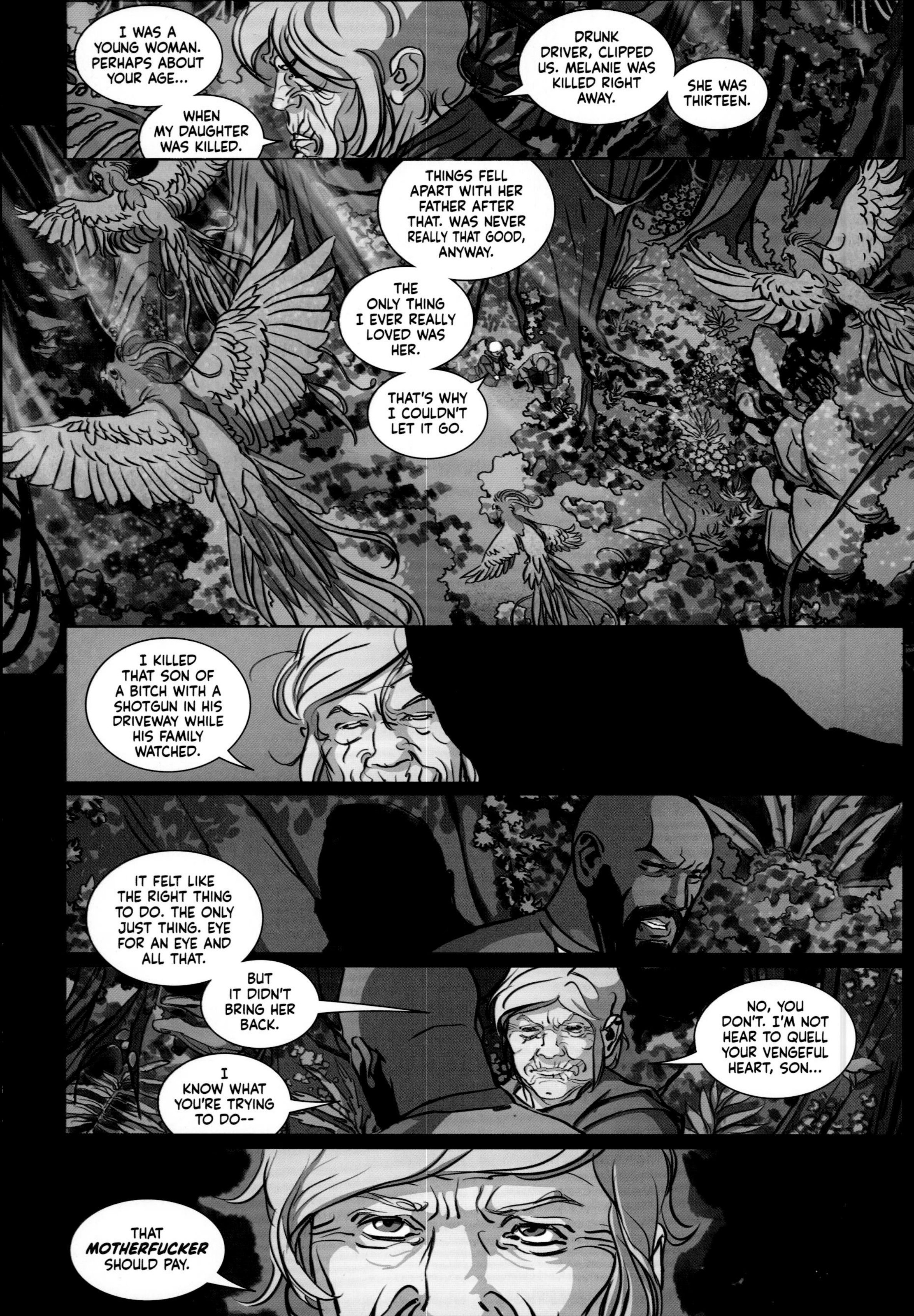
I WAS A YOUNG WOMAN. PERHAPS ABOUT YOUR AGE...
WHEN MY DAUGHTER WAS KILLED.
DRUNK DRIVER, CLIPPED US. MELANIE WAS KILLED RIGHT AWAY.
SHE WAS THIRTEEN.
THINGS FELL APART WITH HER FATHER AFTER THAT. WAS NEVER REALLY THAT GOOD, ANYWAY.
THE ONLY THING I EVER REALLY LOVED WAS HER.
THAT'S WHY I COULDN'T LET IT GO.
I KILLED THAT SON OF A BITCH WITH A SHOTGUN IN HIS DRIVEWAY WHILE HIS FAMILY WATCHED.
IT FELT LIKE THE RIGHT THING TO DO. THE ONLY JUST THING. EYE FOR AN EYE AND ALL THAT.
BUT IT DIDN'T BRING HER BACK.
I KNOW WHAT YOU'RE TRYING TO DO--
NO, YOU DON'T. I'M NOT HEAR TO QUELL YOUR VENGEFUL HEART, SON...
THAT ***MOTHERFUCKER*** SHOULD PAY.

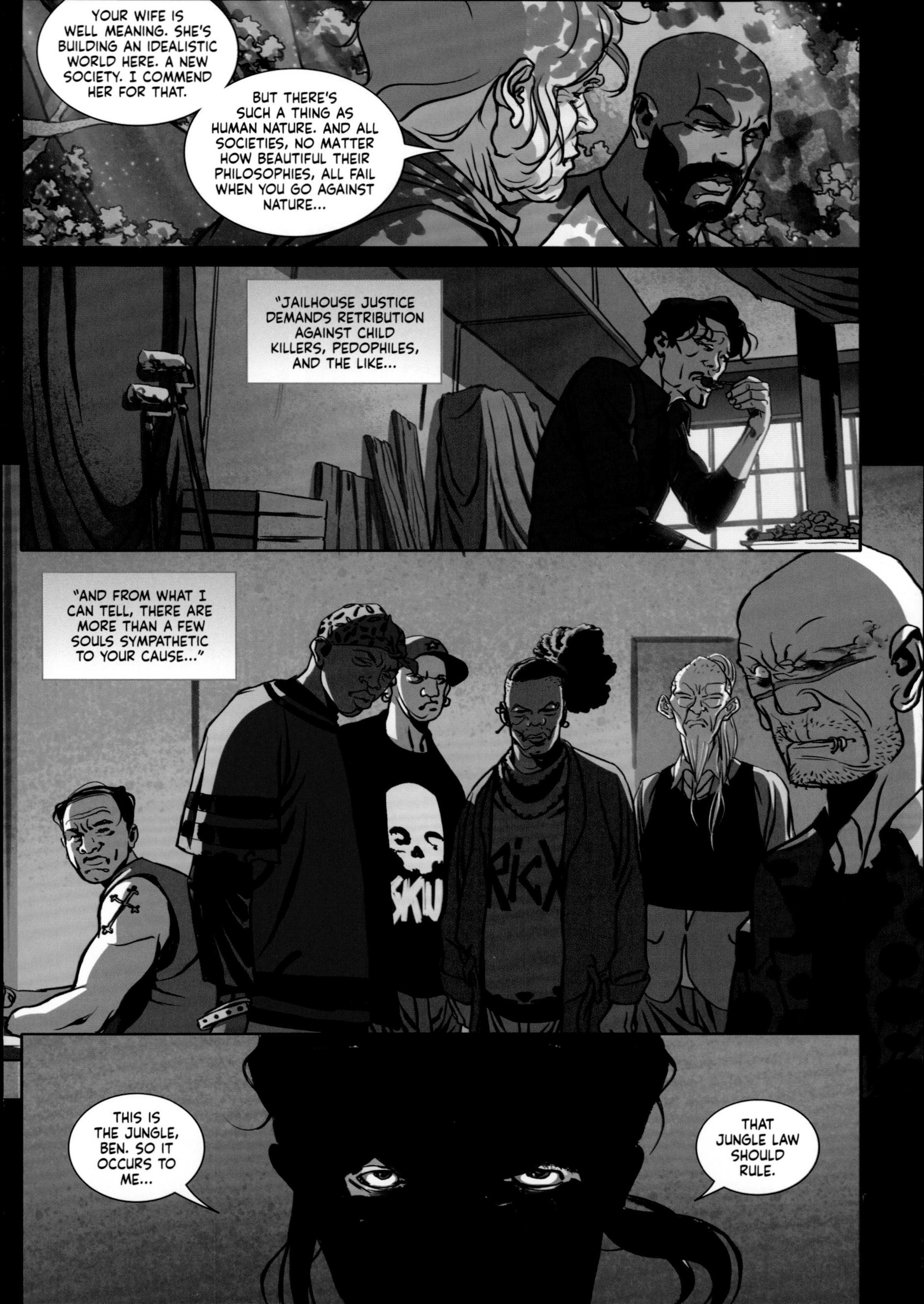
YOUR WIFE IS WELL MEANING. SHE'S BUILDING AN IDEALISTIC WORLD HERE. A NEW SOCIETY. I COMMEND HER FOR THAT.
BUT THERE'S SUCH A THING AS HUMAN NATURE. AND ALL SOCIETIES, NO MATTER HOW BEAUTIFUL THEIR PHILOSOPHIES, ALL FAIL WHEN YOU GO AGAINST NATURE...
"JAILHOUSE JUSTICE DEMANDS RETRIBUTION AGAINST CHILD KILLERS, PEDOPHILES, AND THE LIKE...
"AND FROM WHAT I CAN TELL, THERE ARE MORE THAN A FEW SOULS SYMPATHETIC TO YOUR CAUSE..."
SKU
RICK
THIS IS THE JUNGLE, BEN. SO IT OCCURS TO ME...
THAT JUNGLE LAW SHOULD RULE.

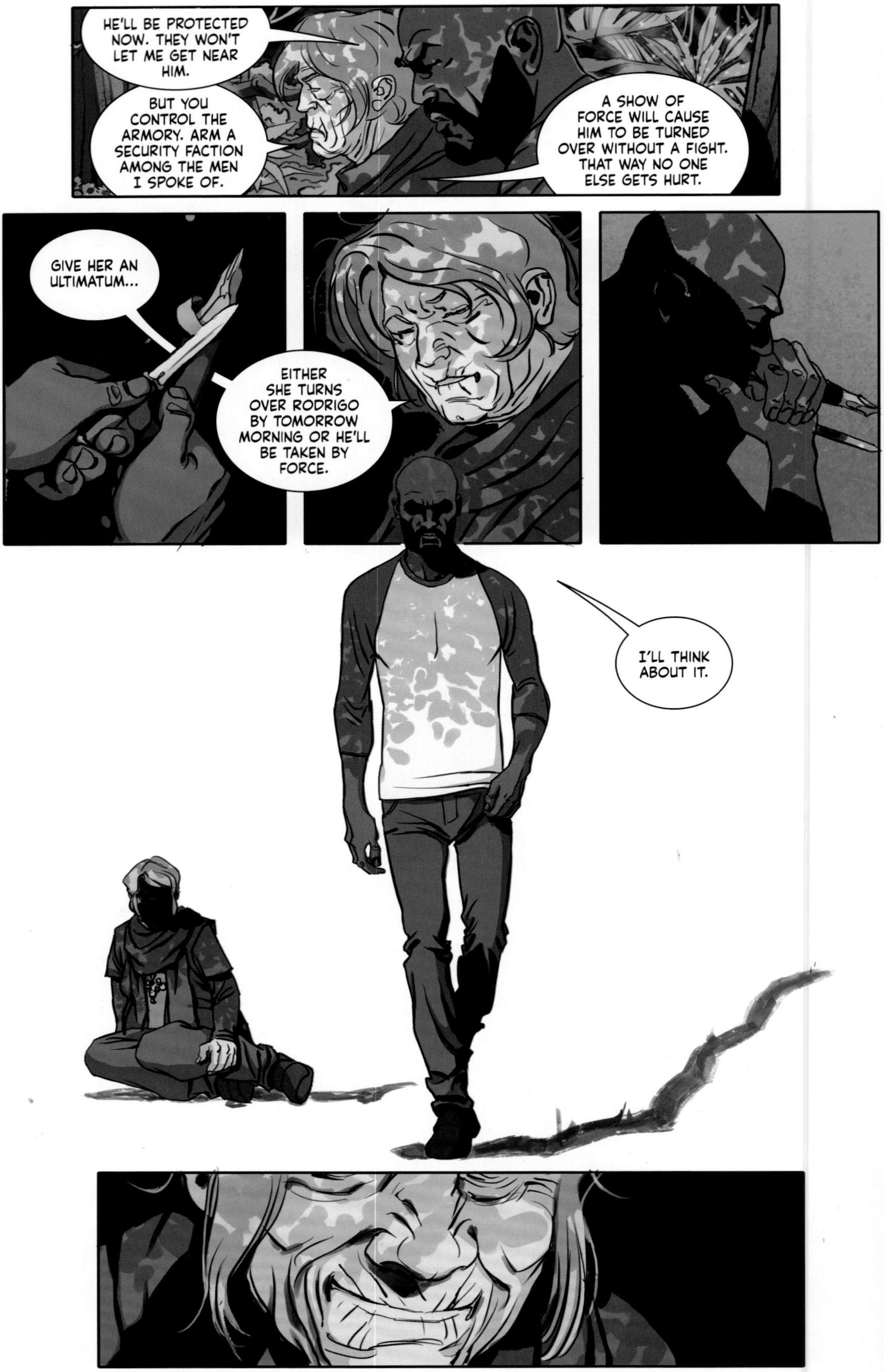
HE'LL BE PROTECTED NOW. THEY WON'T LET ME GET NEAR HIM.
BUT YOU CONTROL THE ARMORY. ARM A SECURITY FACTION AMONG THE MEN I SPOKE OF.
A SHOW OF FORCE WILL CAUSE HIM TO BE TURNED OVER WITHOUT A FIGHT. THAT WAY NO ONE ELSE GETS HURT.
GIVE HER AN ULTIMATUM...
EITHER SHE TURNS OVER RODRIGO BY TOMORROW MORNING OR HE'LL BE TAKEN BY FORCE.
I'LL THINK ABOUT IT.

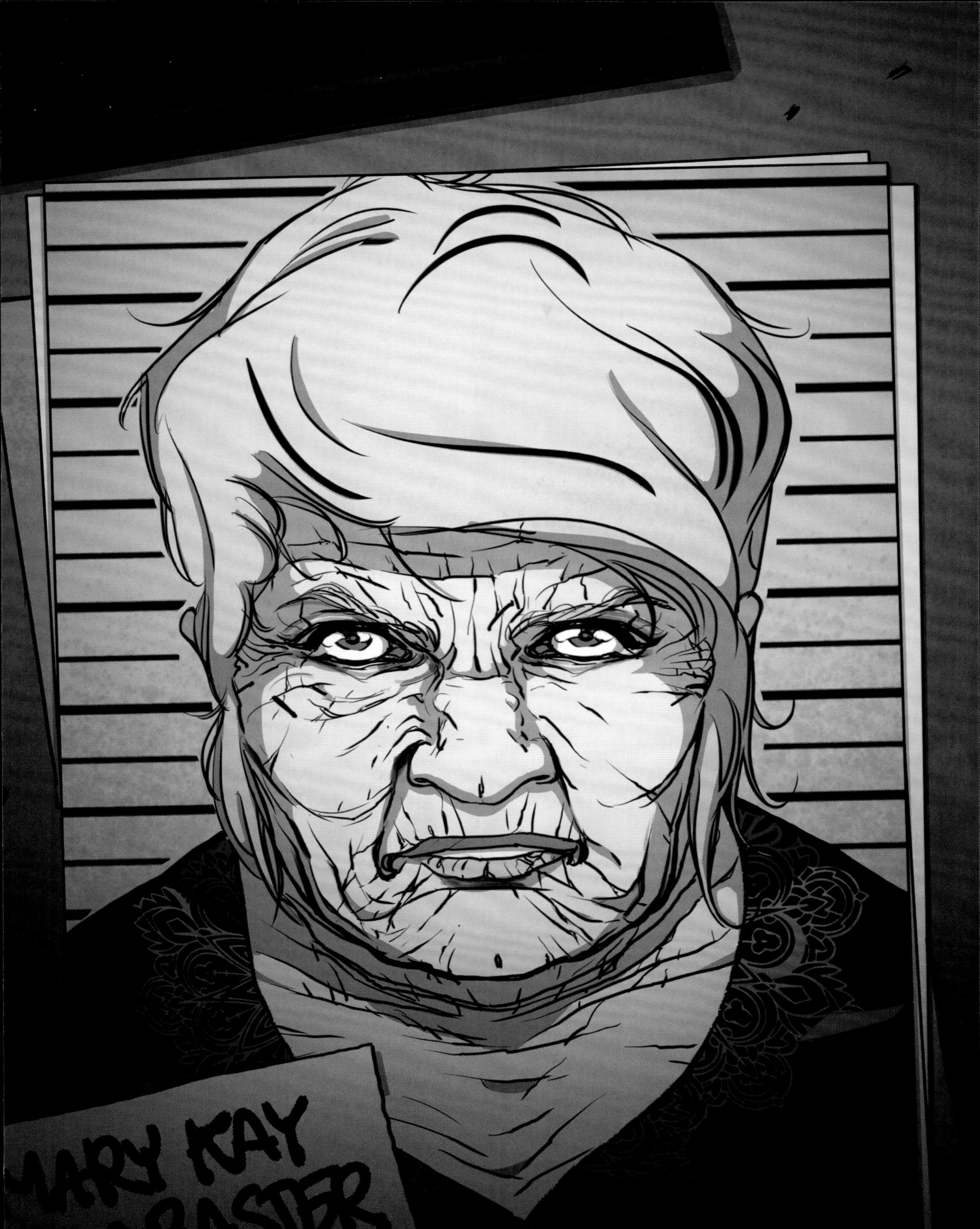
MARY KAY

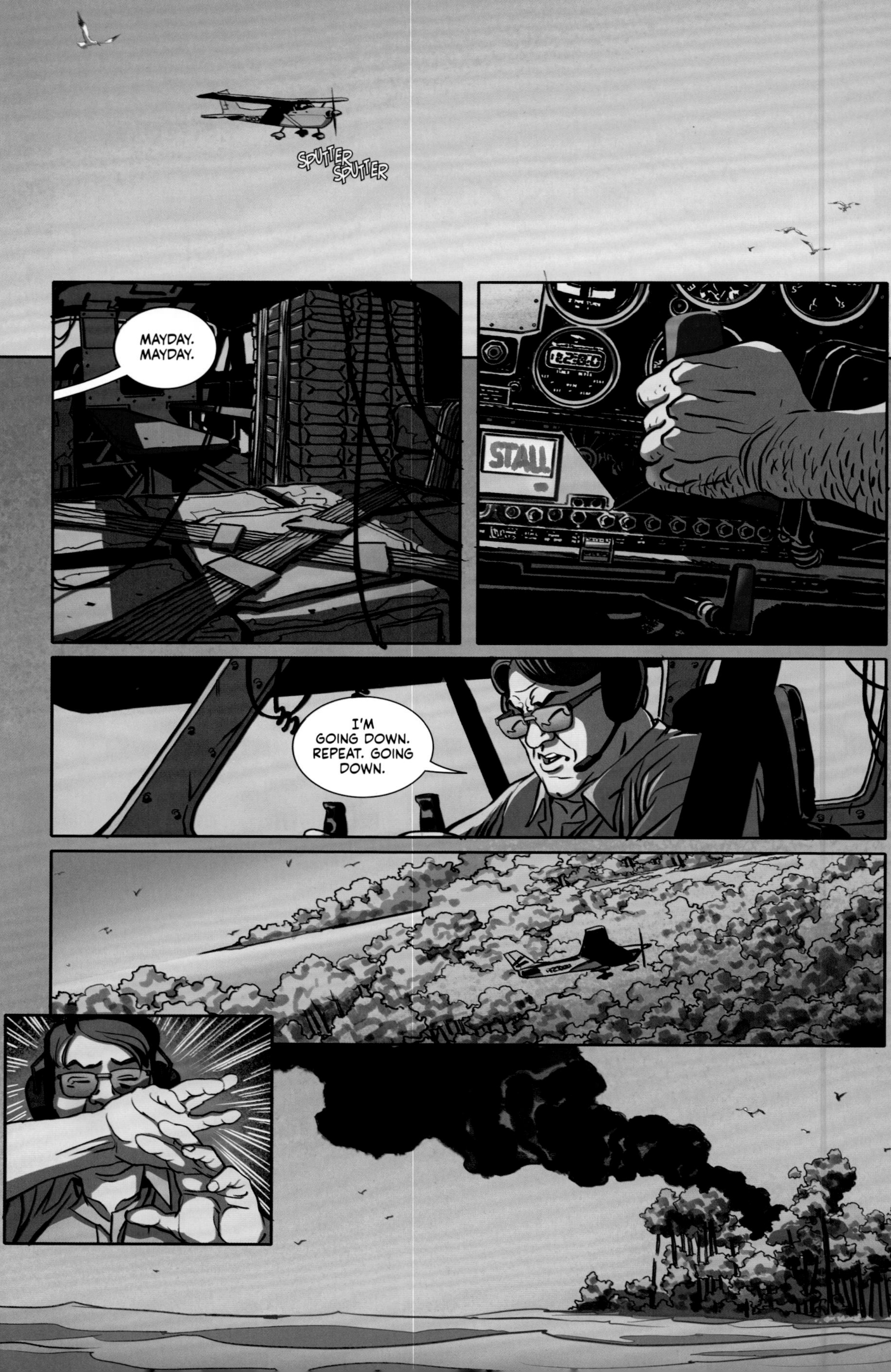
SPUTTER SPUTTER
MAYDAY. MAYDAY.
STALL
I'M GOING DOWN. REPEAT. GOING DOWN.

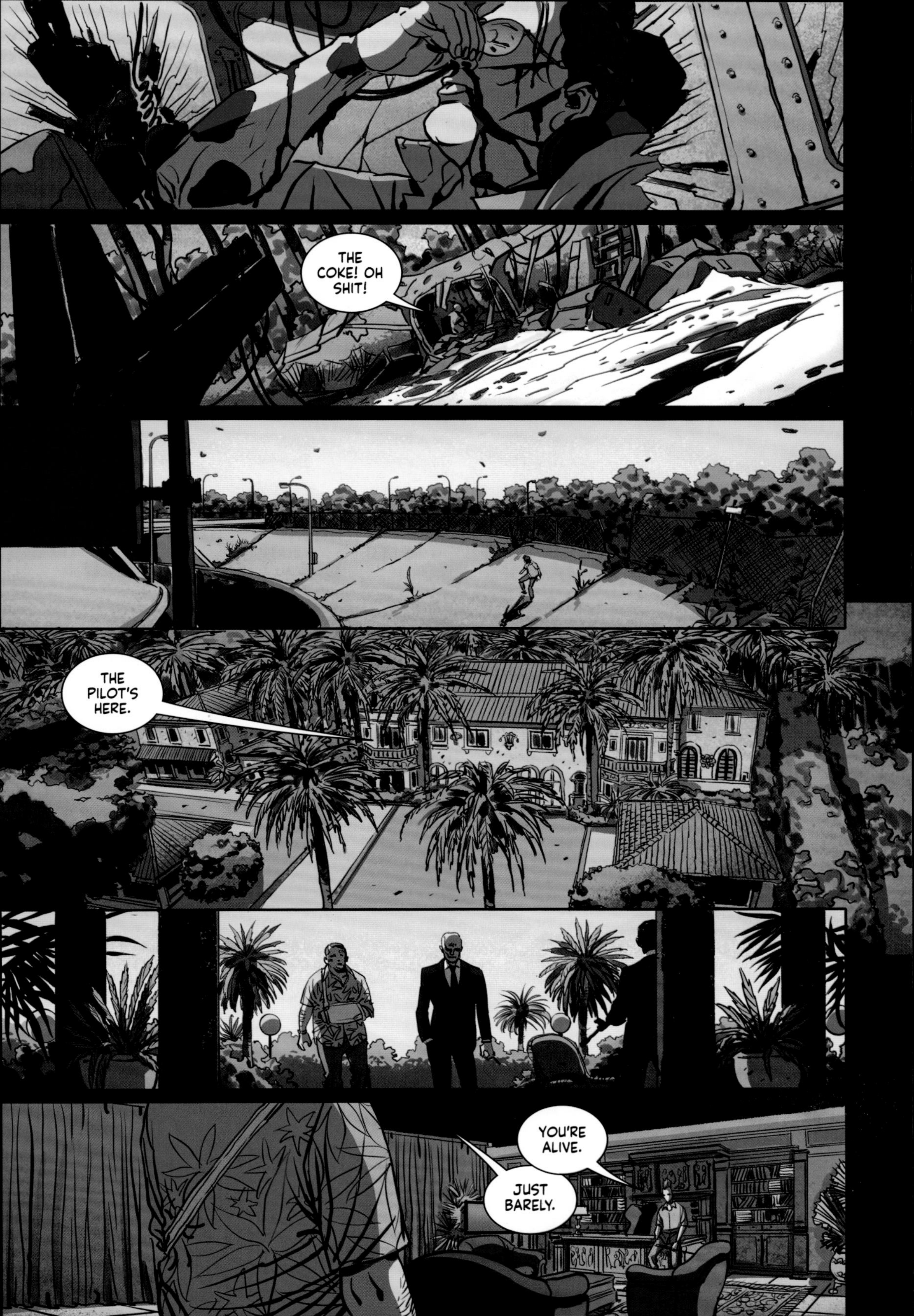
THE COKE! OH SHIT!
THE PILOT'S HERE.
YOU'RE ALIVE.
JUST BARELY.

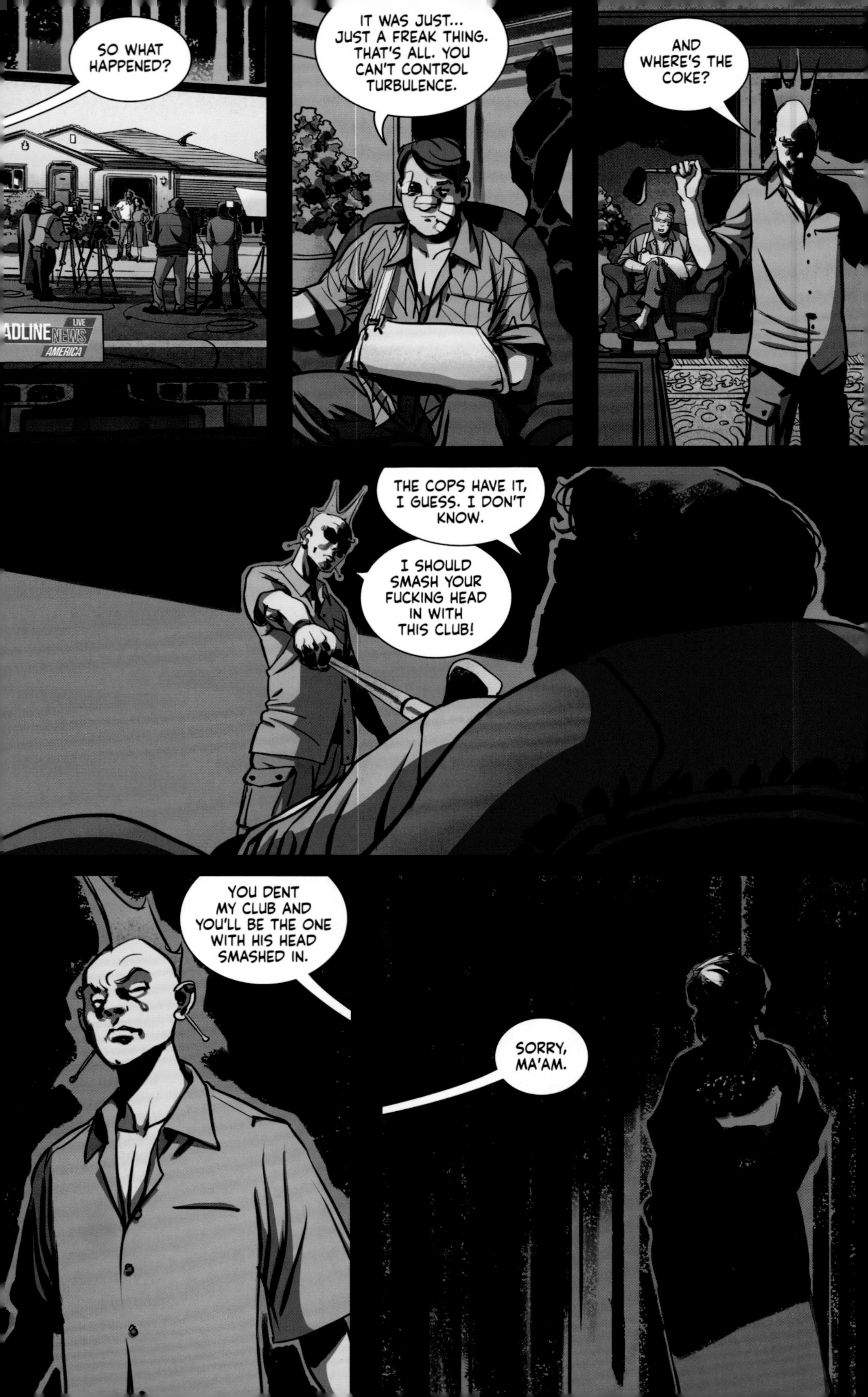
SO WHAT HAPPENED?
ADLINE NEWS LIVE AMERICA
IT WAS JUST... JUST A FREAK THING. THAT'S ALL. YOU CAN'T CONTROL TURBULENCE.
AND WHERE'S THE COKE?
THE COPS HAVE IT, I GUESS. I DON'T KNOW.
I SHOULD SMASH YOUR FUCKING HEAD IN WITH THIS CLUB!
YOU DENT MY CLUB AND YOU'LL BE THE ONE WITH HIS HEAD SMASHED IN.
SORRY, MA'AM.

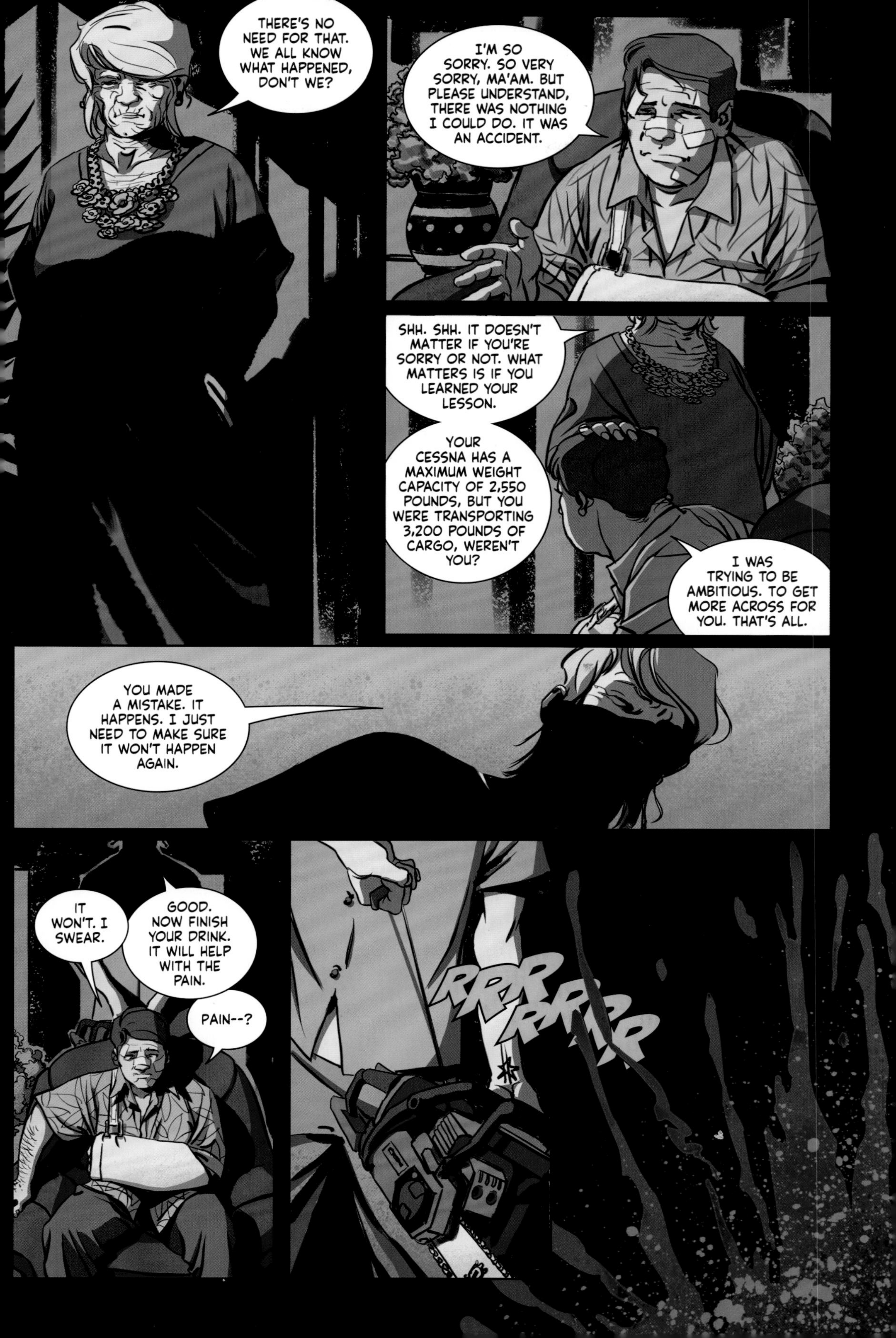
THERE'S NO NEED FOR THAT. WE ALL KNOW WHAT HAPPENED, DON'T WE?
I'M SO SORRY. SO VERY SORRY, MA'AM. BUT PLEASE UNDERSTAND, THERE WAS NOTHING I COULD DO. IT WAS AN ACCIDENT.
SHH. SHH. IT DOESN'T MATTER IF YOU'RE SORRY OR NOT. WHAT MATTERS IS IF YOU LEARNED YOUR LESSON.
YOUR CESSNA HAS A MAXIMUM WEIGHT CAPACITY OF 2,550 POUNDS, BUT YOU WERE TRANSPORTING 3,200 POUNDS OF CARGO, WEREN'T YOU?
I WAS TRYING TO BE AMBITIOUS. TO GET MORE ACROSS FOR YOU. THAT'S ALL.
YOU MADE A MISTAKE. IT HAPPENS. I JUST NEED TO MAKE SURE IT WON'T HAPPEN AGAIN.
IT WON'T. I SWEAR.
GOOD. NOW FINISH YOUR DRINK. IT WILL HELP WITH THE PAIN.
PAIN--?
RRRR RRRR

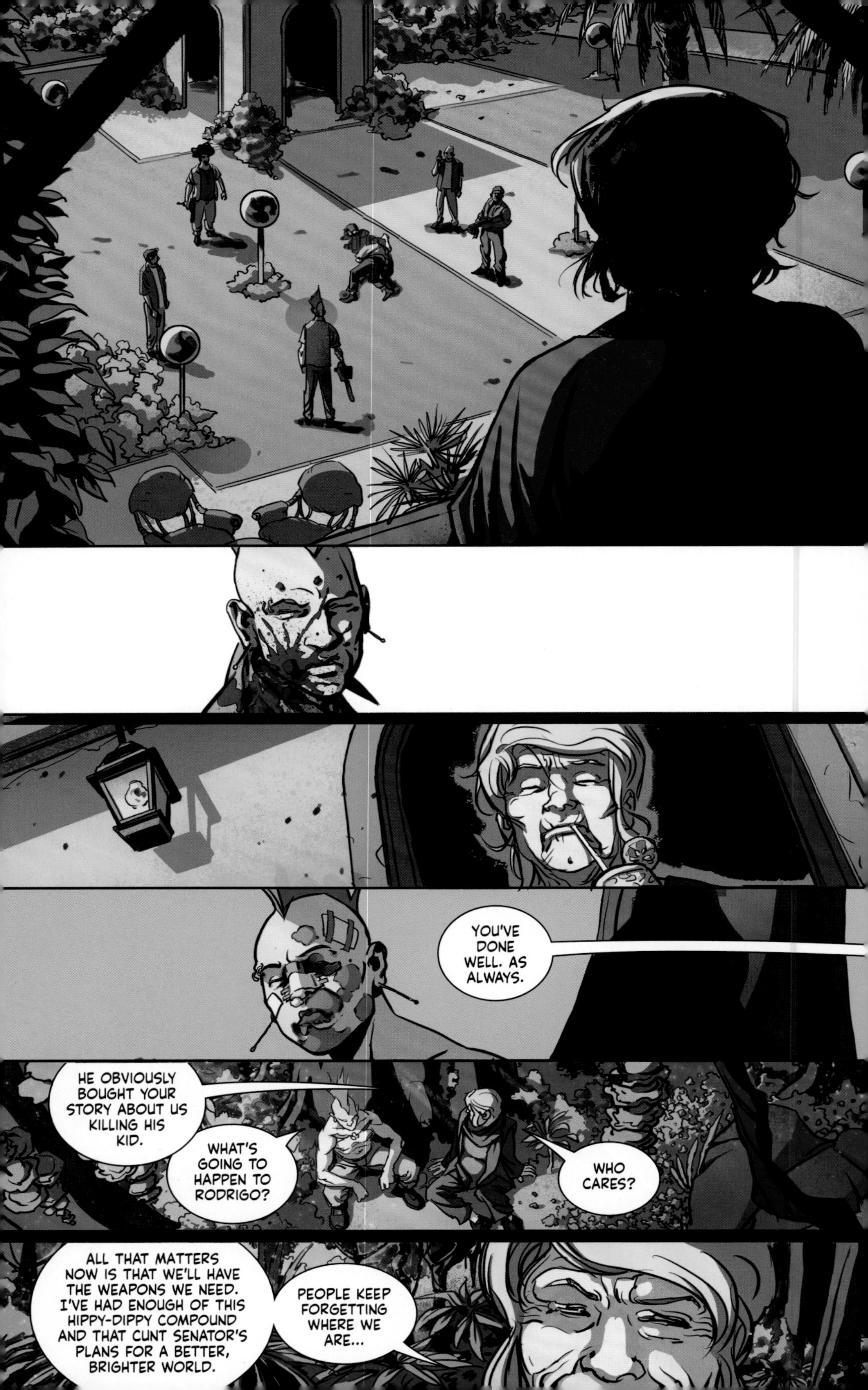

YOU'VE DONE WELL. AS ALWAYS.
HE OBVIOUSLY BOUGHT YOUR STORY ABOUT US KILLING HIS KID.
WHAT'S GOING TO HAPPEN TO RODRIGO?
WHO CARES?
ALL THAT MATTERS NOW IS THAT WE'LL HAVE THE WEAPONS WE NEED. I'VE HAD ENOUGH OF THIS HIPPY-DIPPY COMPOUND AND THAT CUNT SENATOR'S PLANS FOR A BETTER, BRIGHTER WORLD.
PEOPLE KEEP FORGETTING WHERE WE ARE...

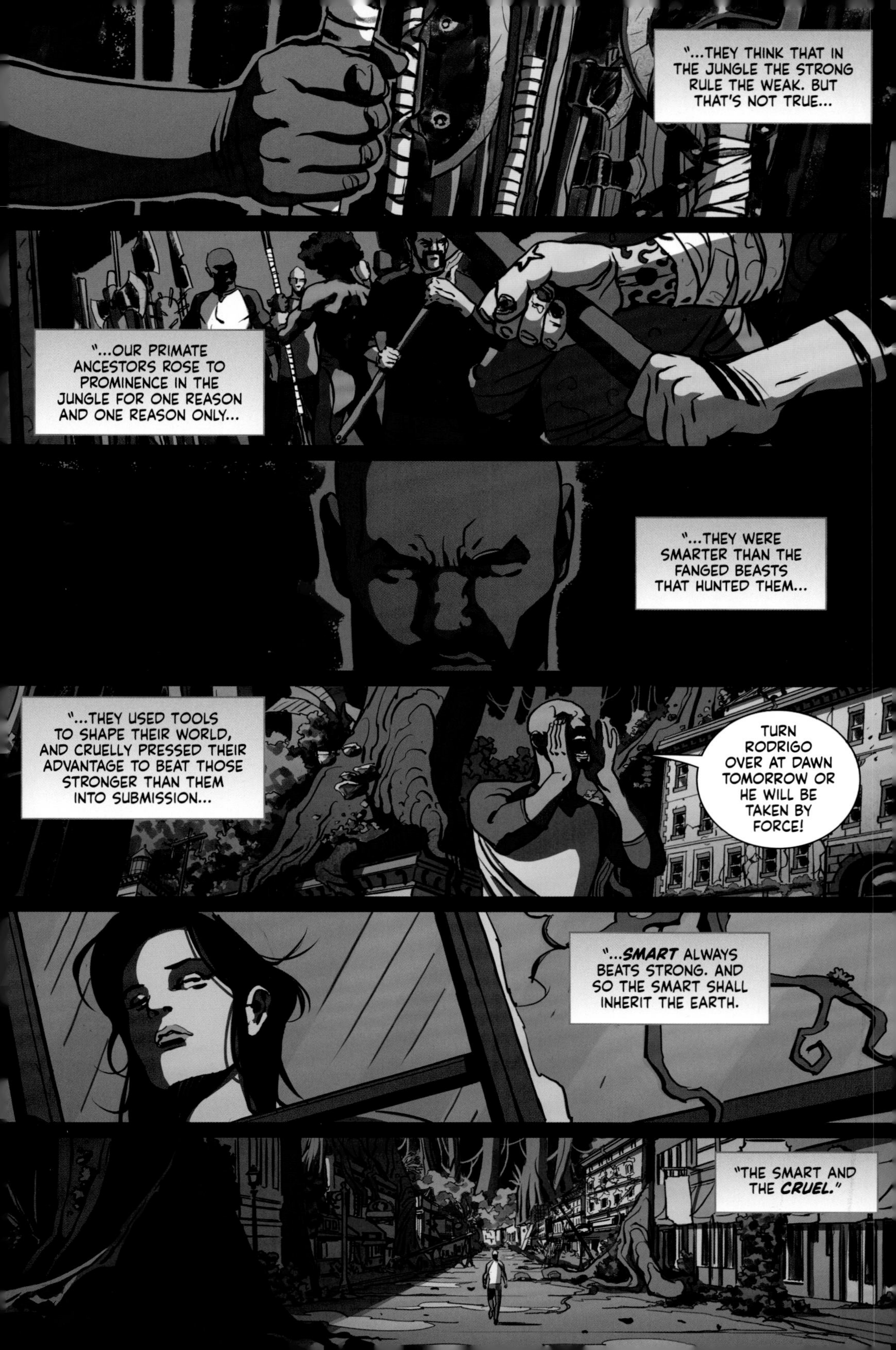
"...THEY THINK THAT IN THE JUNGLE THE STRONG RULE THE WEAK. BUT THAT'S NOT TRUE...
"...OUR PRIMATE ANCESTORS ROSE TO PROMINENCE IN THE JUNGLE FOR ONE REASON AND ONE REASON ONLY...
"...THEY WERE SMARTER THAN THE FANGED BEASTS THAT HUNTED THEM...
"...THEY USED TOOLS TO SHAPE THEIR WORLD, AND CRUELLY PRESSED THEIR ADVANTAGE TO BEAT THOSE STRONGER THAN THEM INTO SUBMISSION...
TURN RODRIGO OVER AT DAWN TOMORROW OR HE WILL BE TAKEN BY FORCE!
"...*SMART* ALWAYS BEATS STRONG. AND SO THE SMART SHALL INHERIT THE EARTH.
"THE SMART AND THE *CRUEL.*"

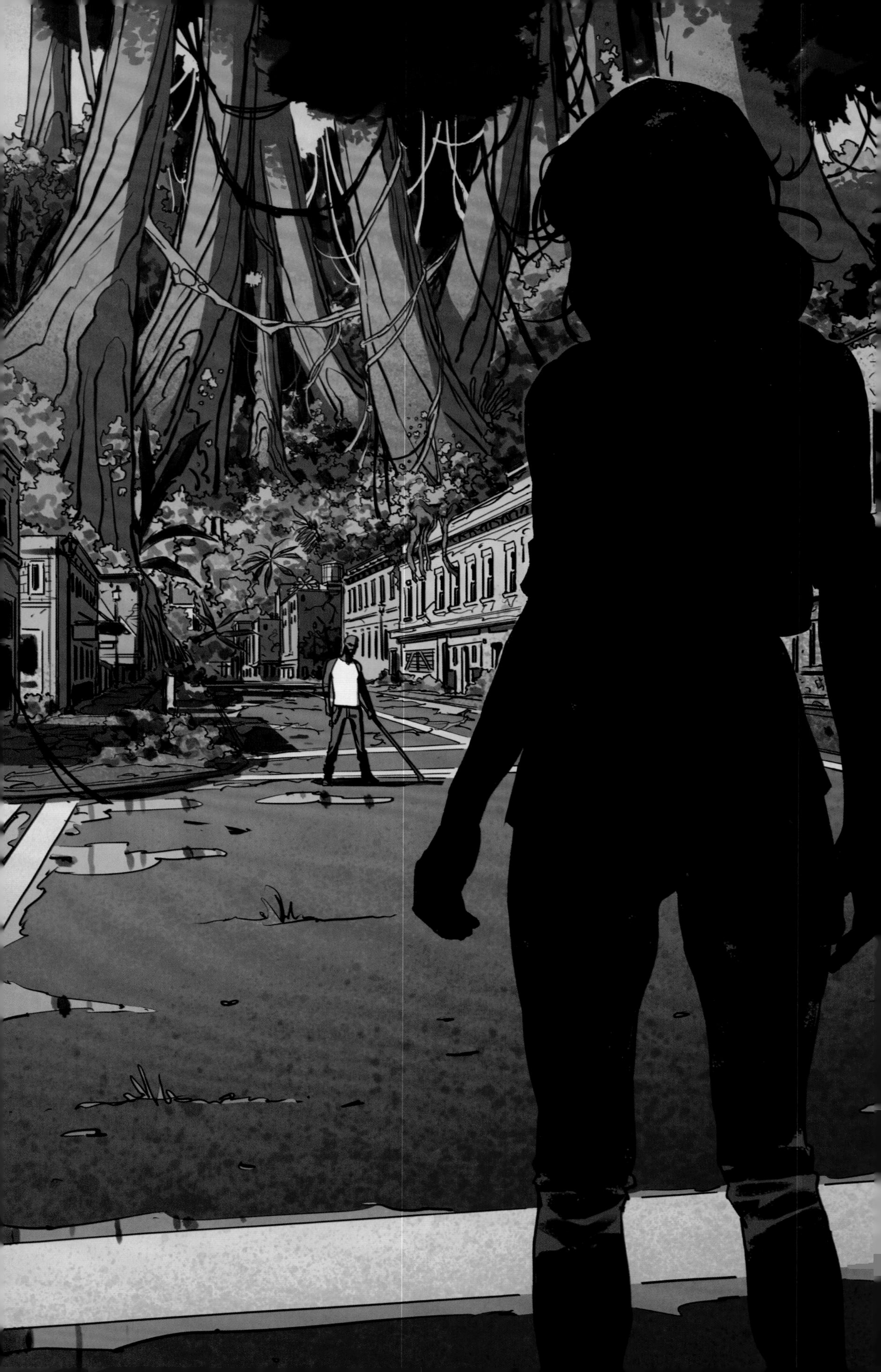

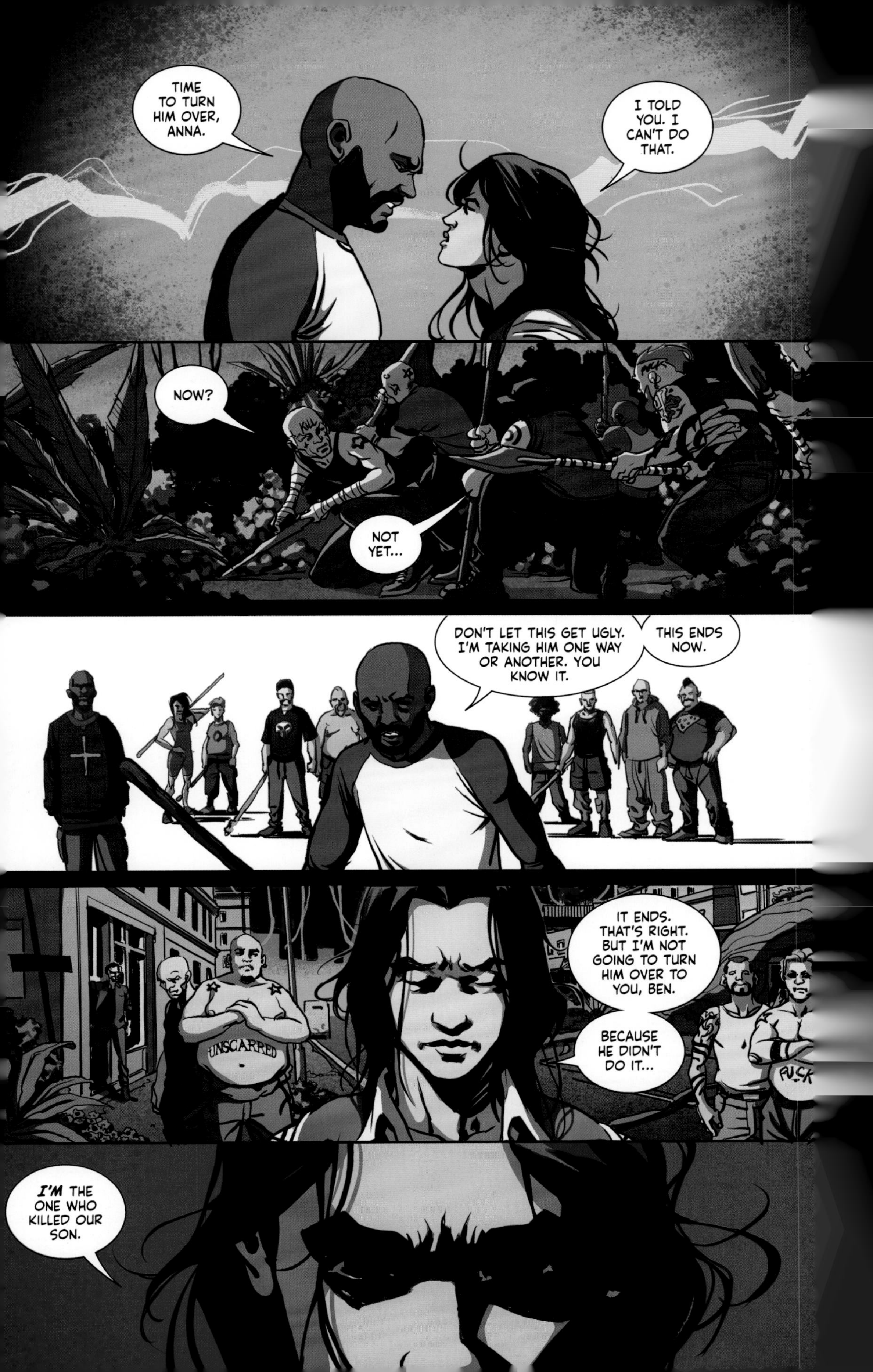
TIME TO TURN HIM OVER, ANNA.
I TOLD YOU. I CAN'T DO THAT.
NOW?
NOT YET...
DON'T LET THIS GET UGLY. I'M TAKING HIM ONE WAY OR ANOTHER. YOU KNOW IT.
THIS ENDS NOW.
UNSCARRED
IT ENDS. THAT'S RIGHT. BUT I'M NOT GOING TO TURN HIM OVER TO YOU, BEN.
BECAUSE HE DIDN'T DO IT...
I'M THE ONE WHO KILLED OUR SON.

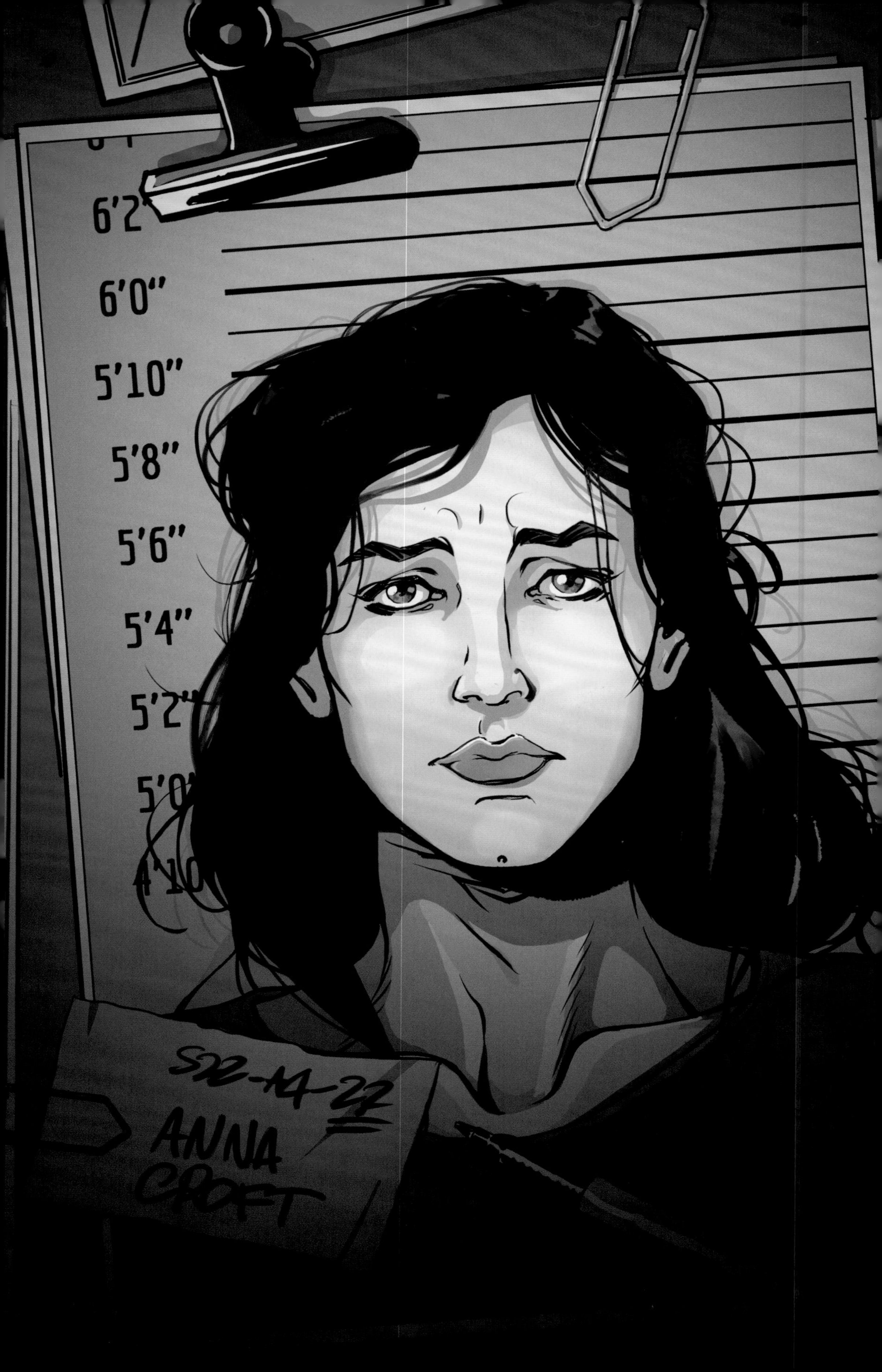
6'2"
6'0"
5'10"
5'8"
5'6"
5'4"
5'2"
S22-11-22
ANNA
CROFT

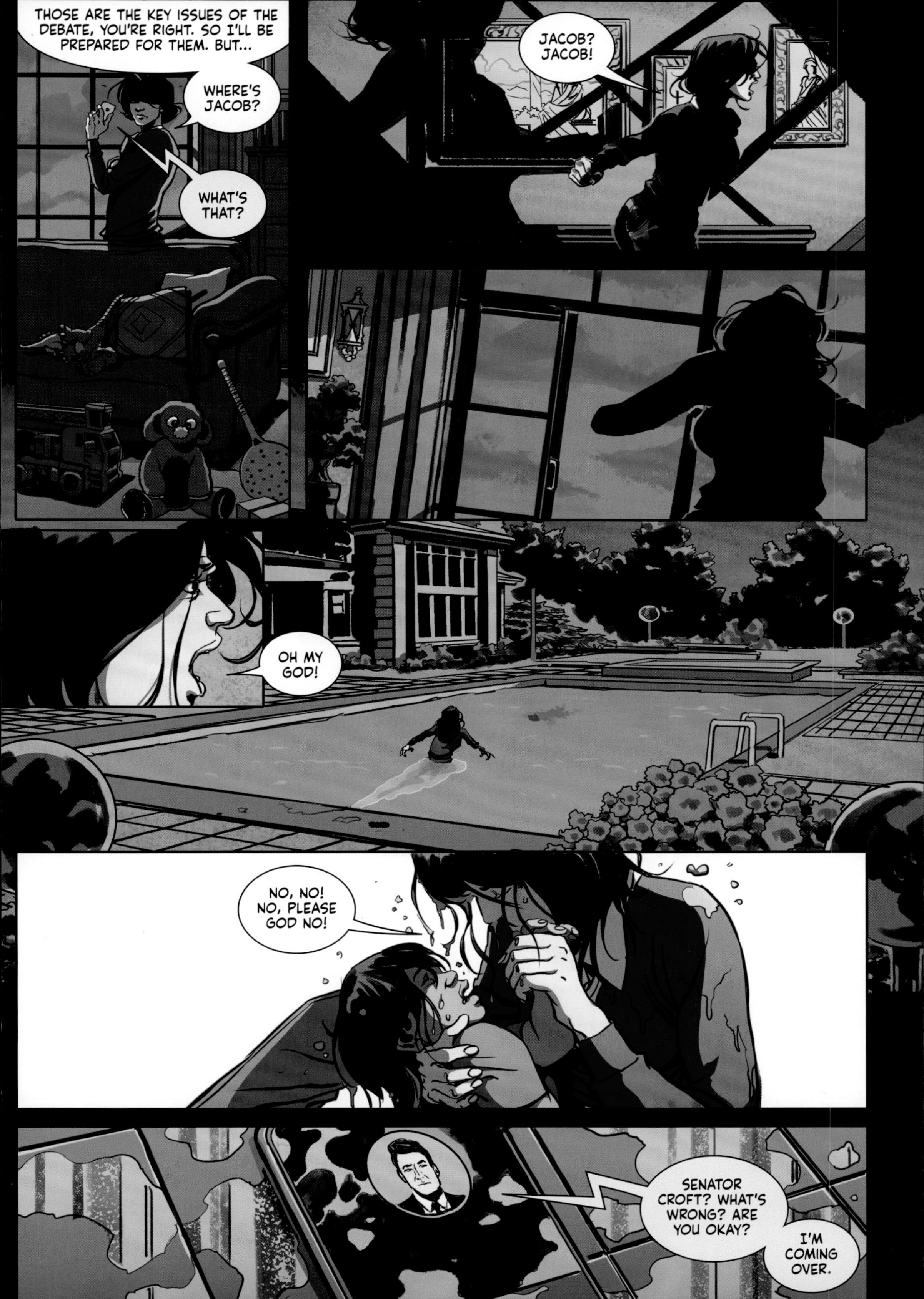
THOSE ARE THE KEY ISSUES OF THE DEBATE, YOU'RE RIGHT. SO I'LL BE PREPARED FOR THEM. BUT...
WHERE'S JACOB?
WHAT'S THAT?
JACOB? JACOB!
OH MY GOD!
NO, NO! NO, PLEASE GOD NO!
SENATOR CROFT? WHAT'S WRONG? ARE YOU OKAY?
I'M COMING OVER.

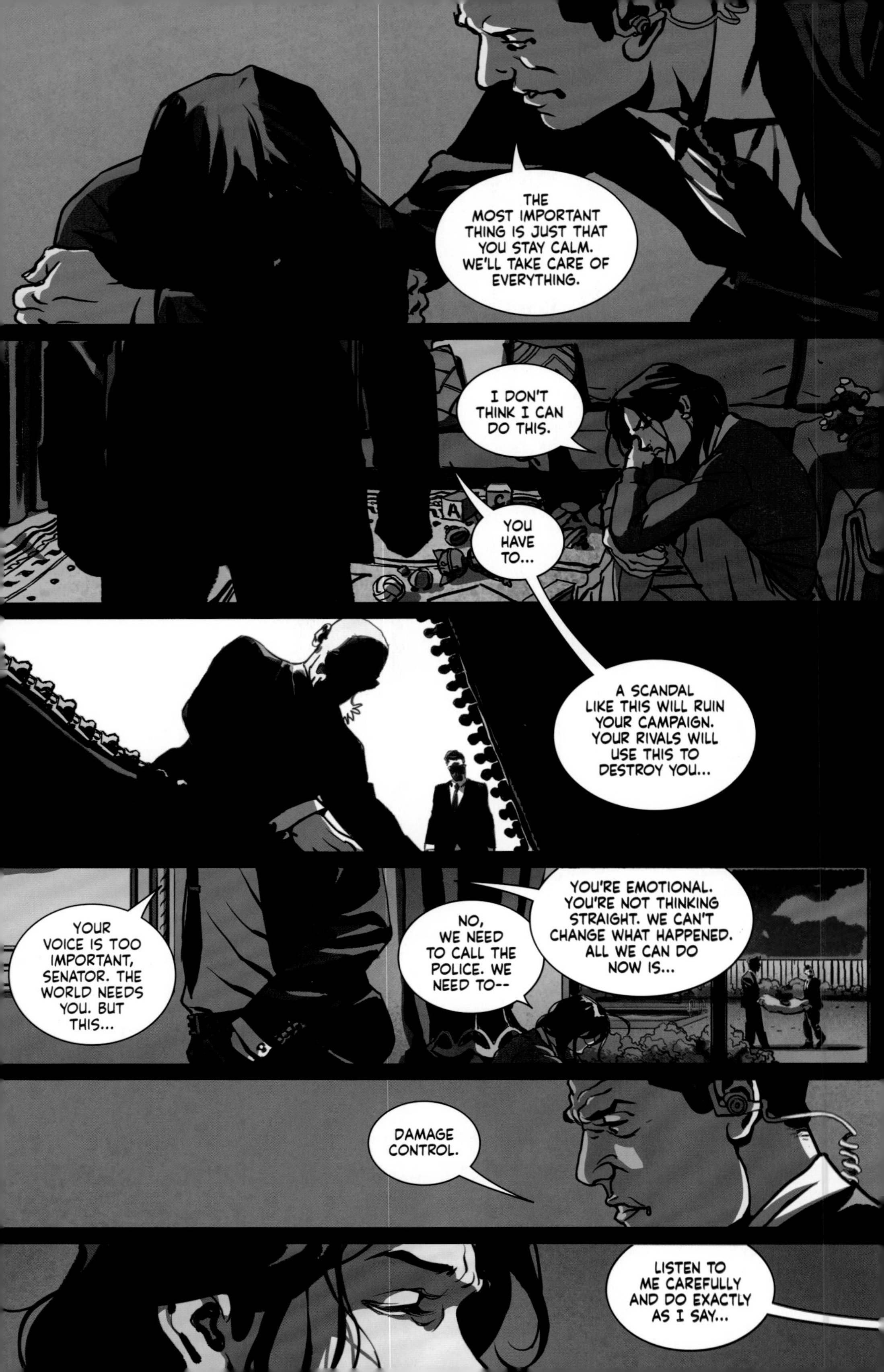
THE MOST IMPORTANT THING IS JUST THAT YOU STAY CALM. WE'LL TAKE CARE OF EVERYTHING.
I DON'T THINK I CAN DO THIS.
YOU HAVE TO...
A SCANDAL LIKE THIS WILL RUIN YOUR CAMPAIGN. YOUR RIVALS WILL USE THIS TO DESTROY YOU...
YOUR VOICE IS TOO IMPORTANT, SENATOR. THE WORLD NEEDS YOU. BUT THIS...
NO, WE NEED TO CALL THE POLICE. WE NEED TO--
YOU'RE EMOTIONAL. YOU'RE NOT THINKING STRAIGHT. WE CAN'T CHANGE WHAT HAPPENED. ALL WE CAN DO NOW IS...
DAMAGE CONTROL.
LISTEN TO ME CAREFULLY AND DO EXACTLY AS I SAY...

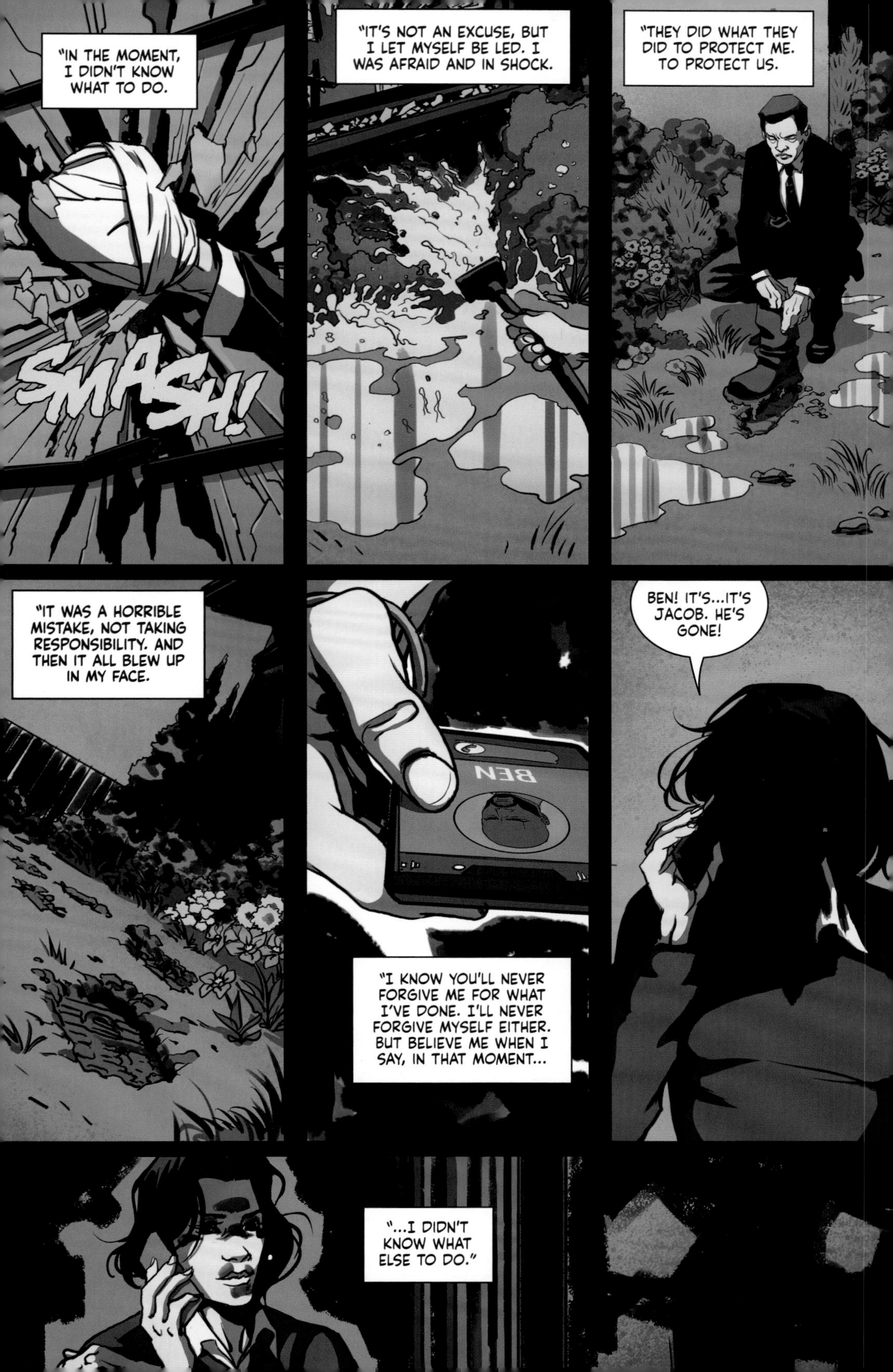
"IN THE MOMENT, I DIDN'T KNOW WHAT TO DO.
SMASH!
"IT'S NOT AN EXCUSE, BUT I LET MYSELF BE LED. I WAS AFRAID AND IN SHOCK.
"THEY DID WHAT THEY DID TO PROTECT ME. TO PROTECT US.
"IT WAS A HORRIBLE MISTAKE, NOT TAKING RESPONSIBILITY. AND THEN IT ALL BLEW UP IN MY FACE.
BEN
"I KNOW YOU'LL NEVER FORGIVE ME FOR WHAT I'VE DONE. I'LL NEVER FORGIVE MYSELF EITHER. BUT BELIEVE ME WHEN I SAY, IN THAT MOMENT...
BEN! IT'S...IT'S JACOB. HE'S GONE!
"...I DIDN'T KNOW WHAT ELSE TO DO."

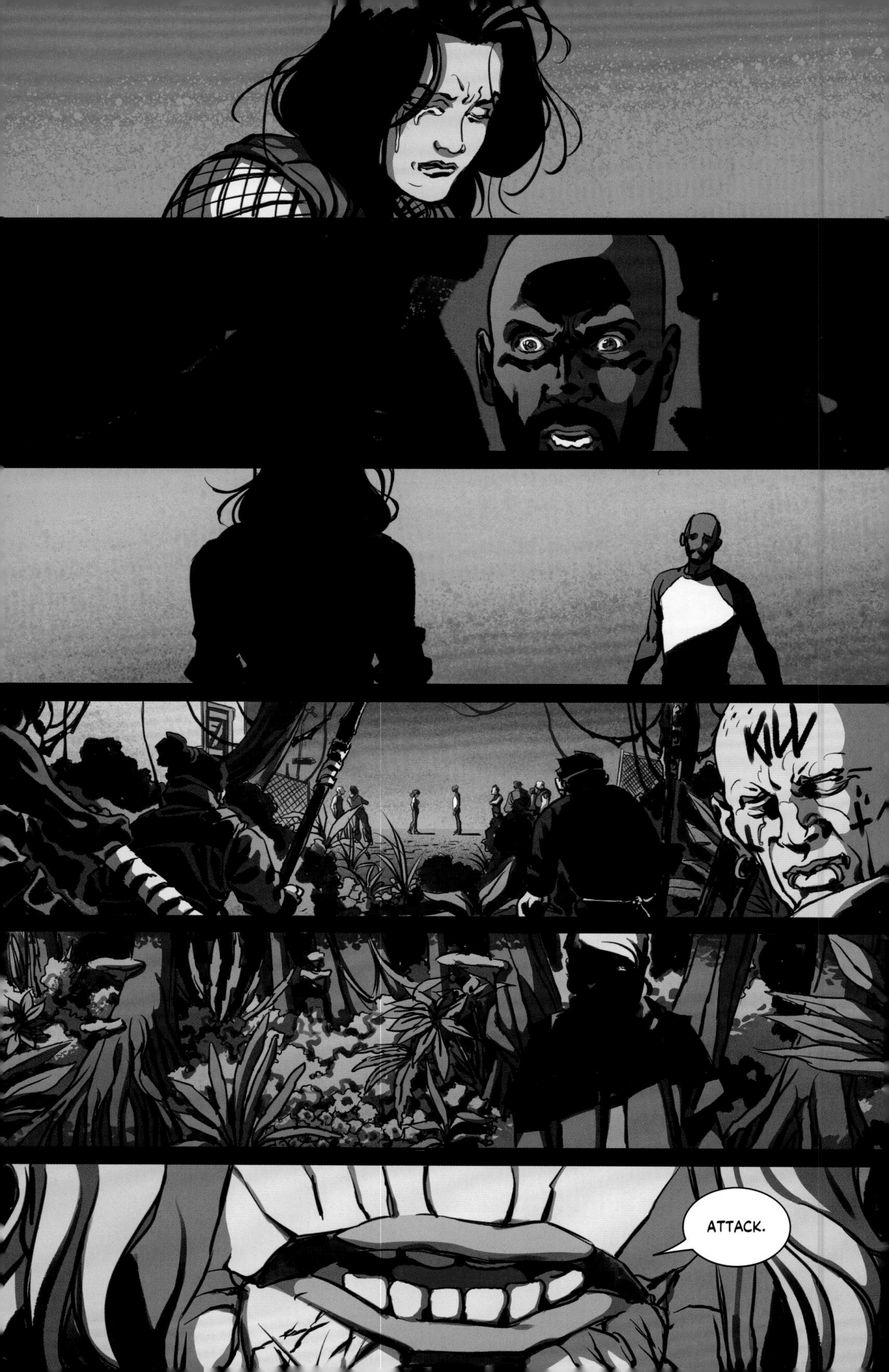
ATTACK.

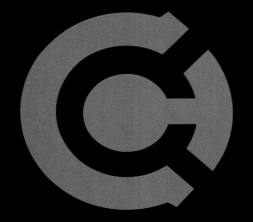

V

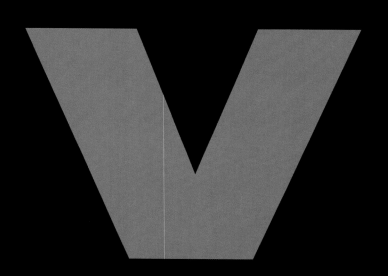

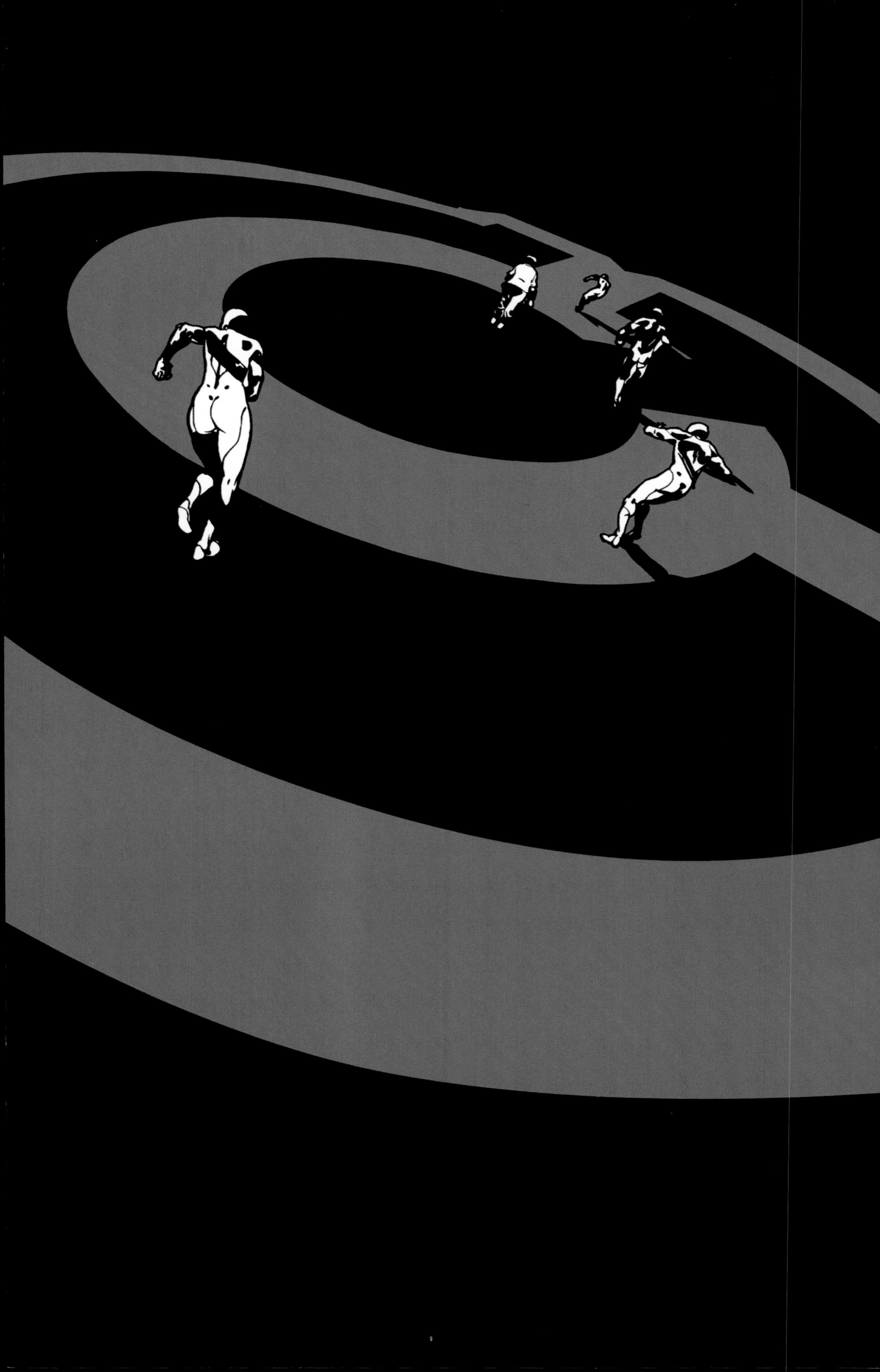

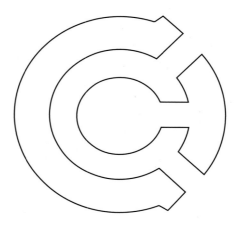

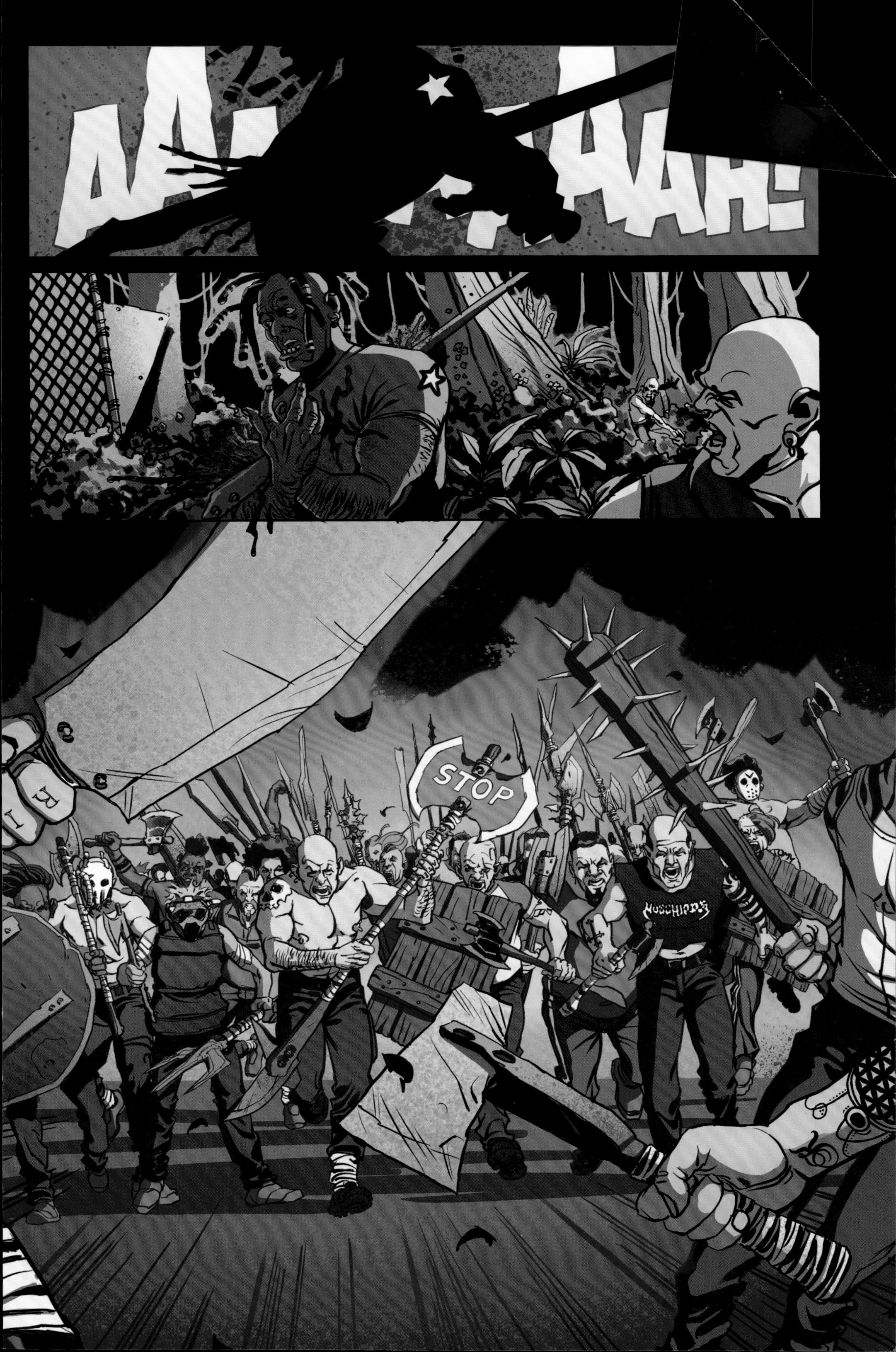
STOP

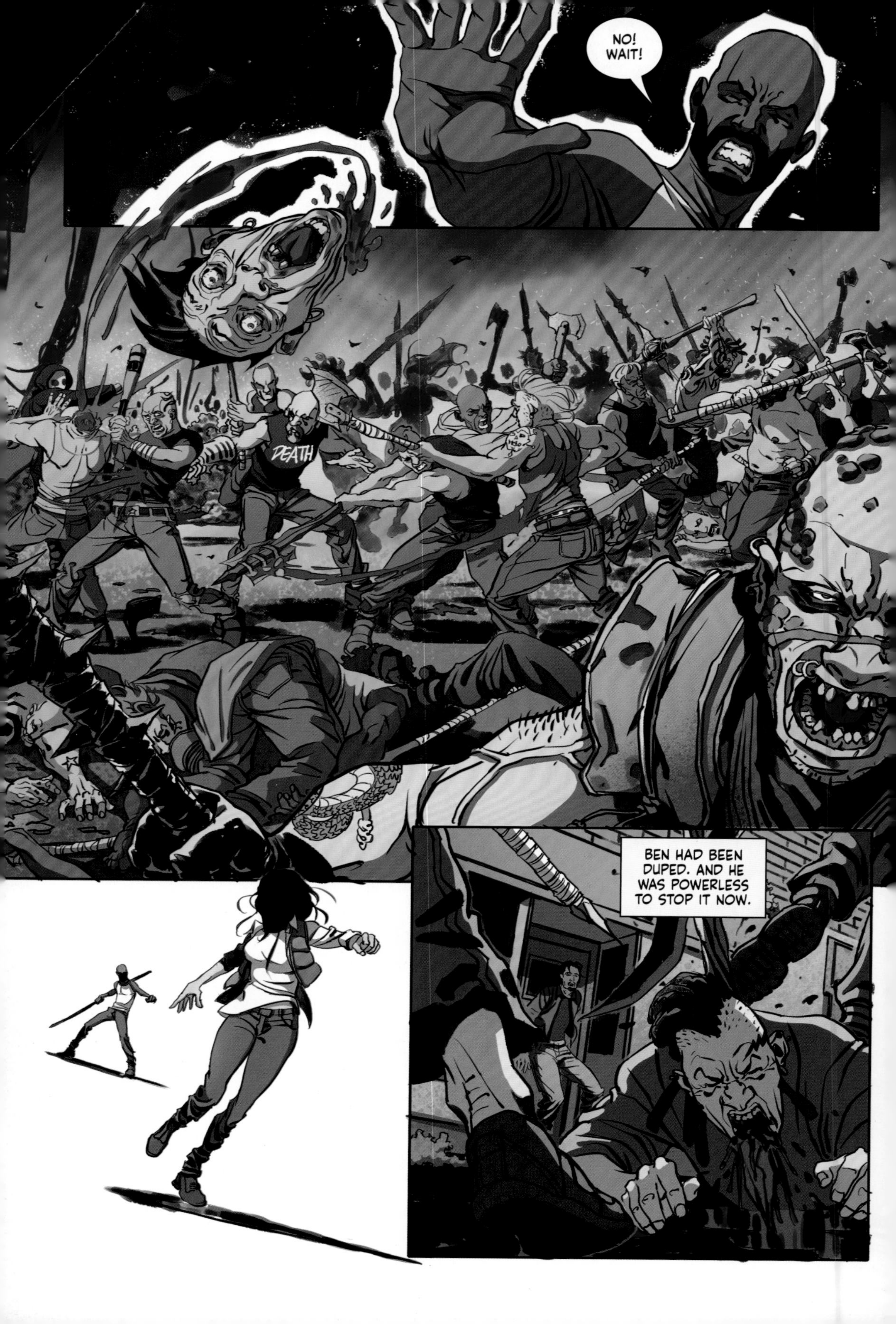
NO! WAIT!
DEATH
BEN HAD BEEN DUPED. AND HE WAS POWERLESS TO STOP IT NOW.

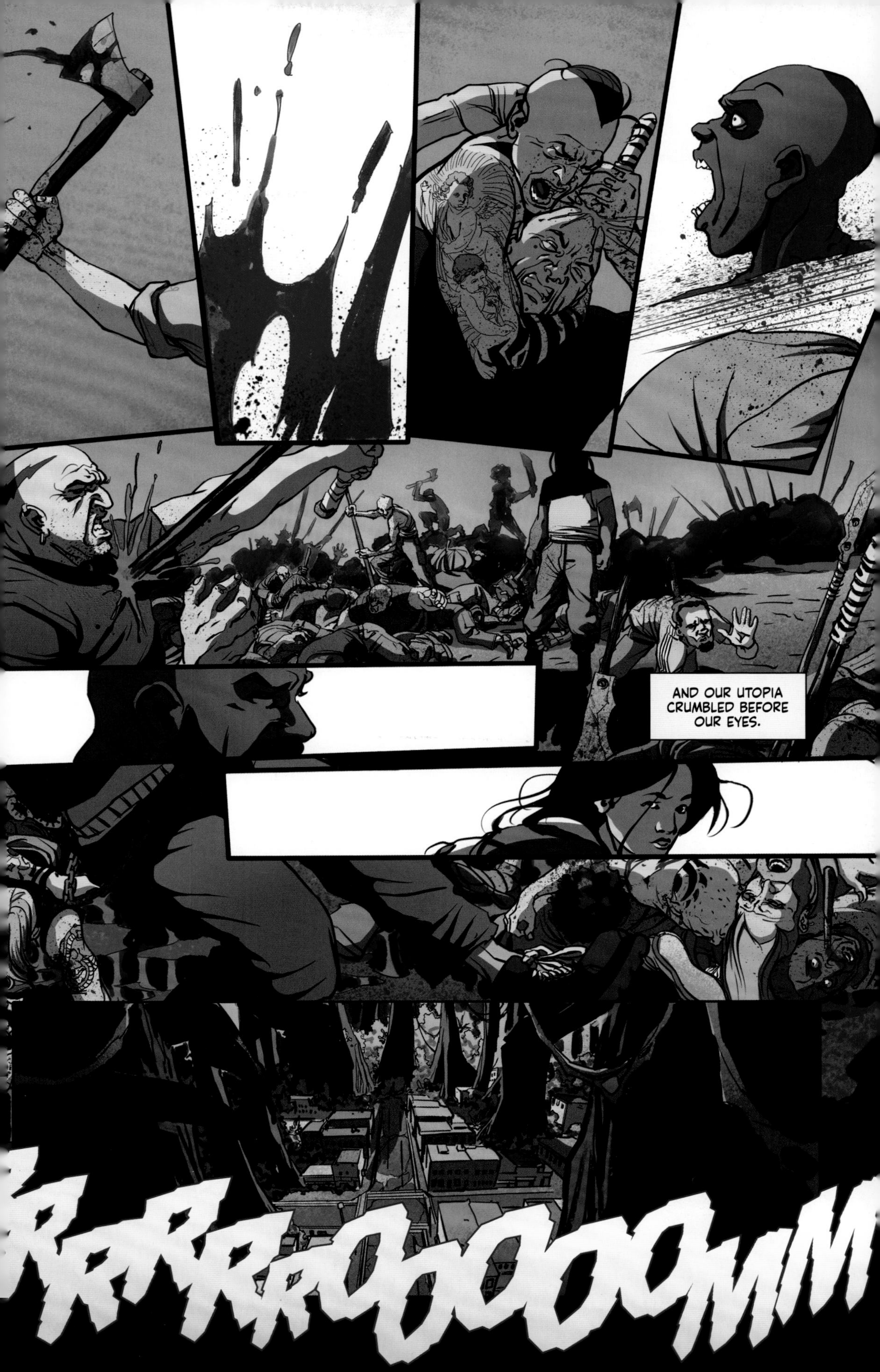
AND OUR UTOPIA CRUMBLED BEFORE OUR EYES.
RRRROOOOOMM

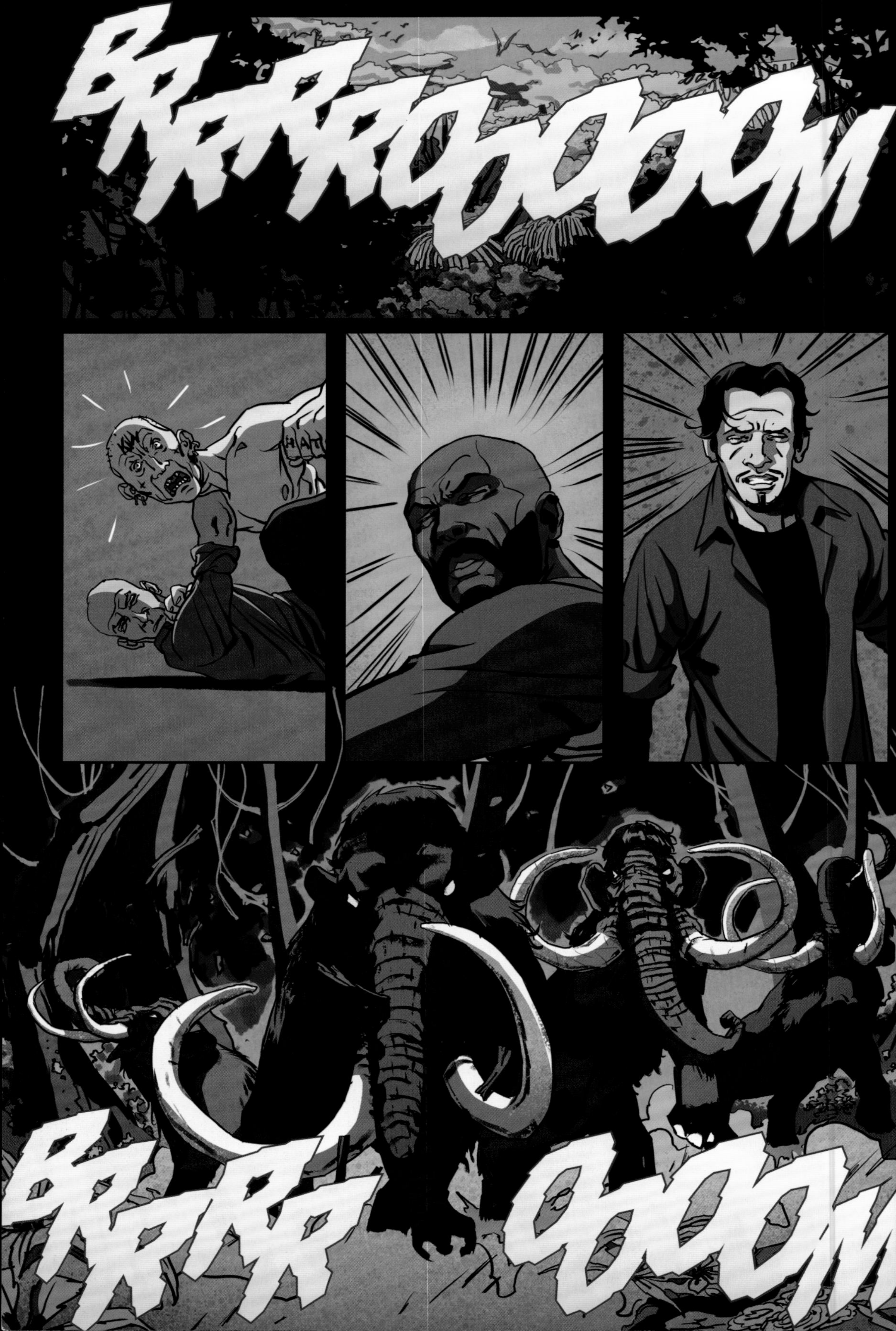
BRRROOOOM
BRRROOOOM

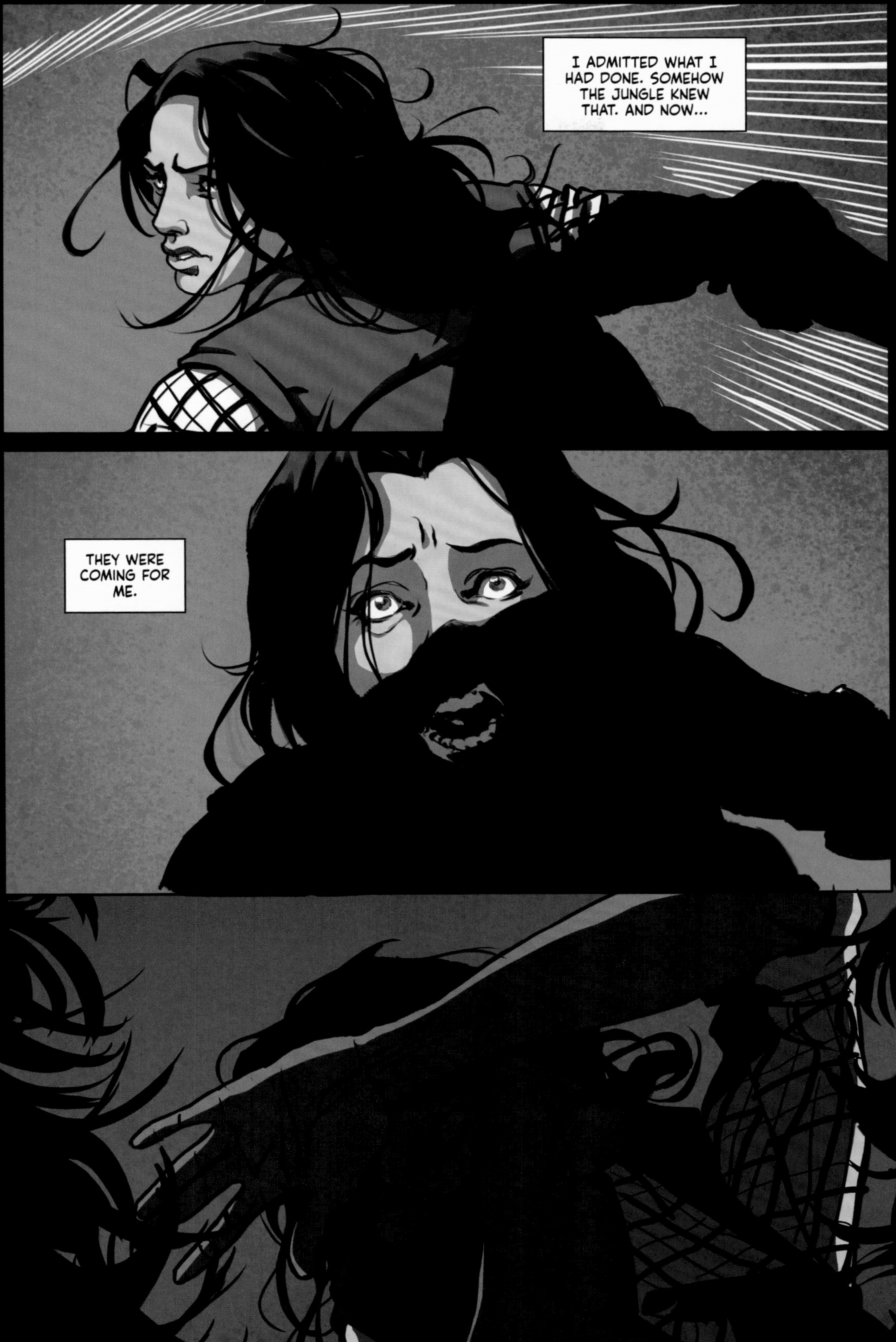
I ADMITTED WHAT I HAD DONE. SOMEHOW THE JUNGLE KNEW THAT. AND NOW...
THEY WERE COMING FOR ME.

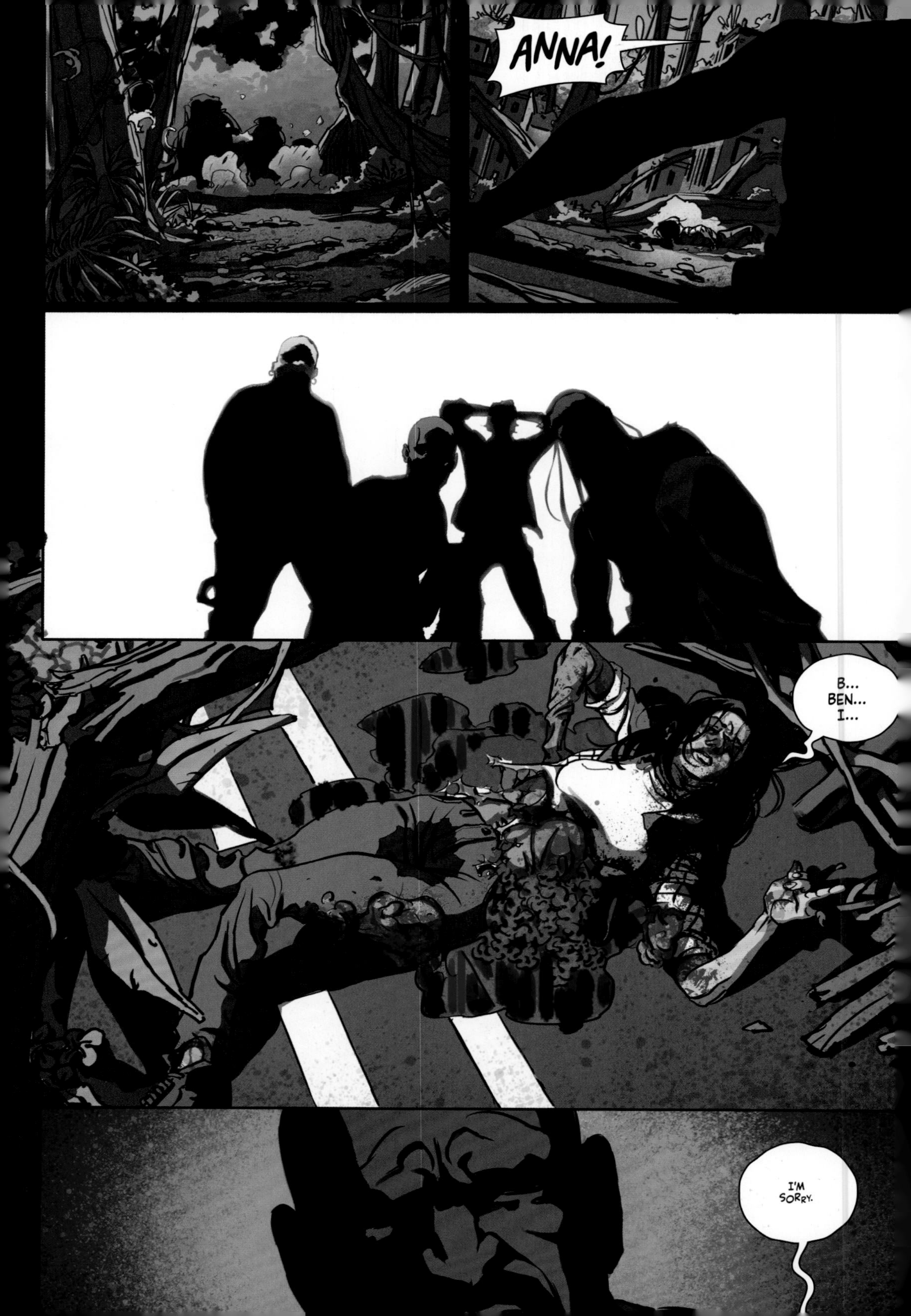
ANNA!
B... BEN... I...
I'M SORRY.

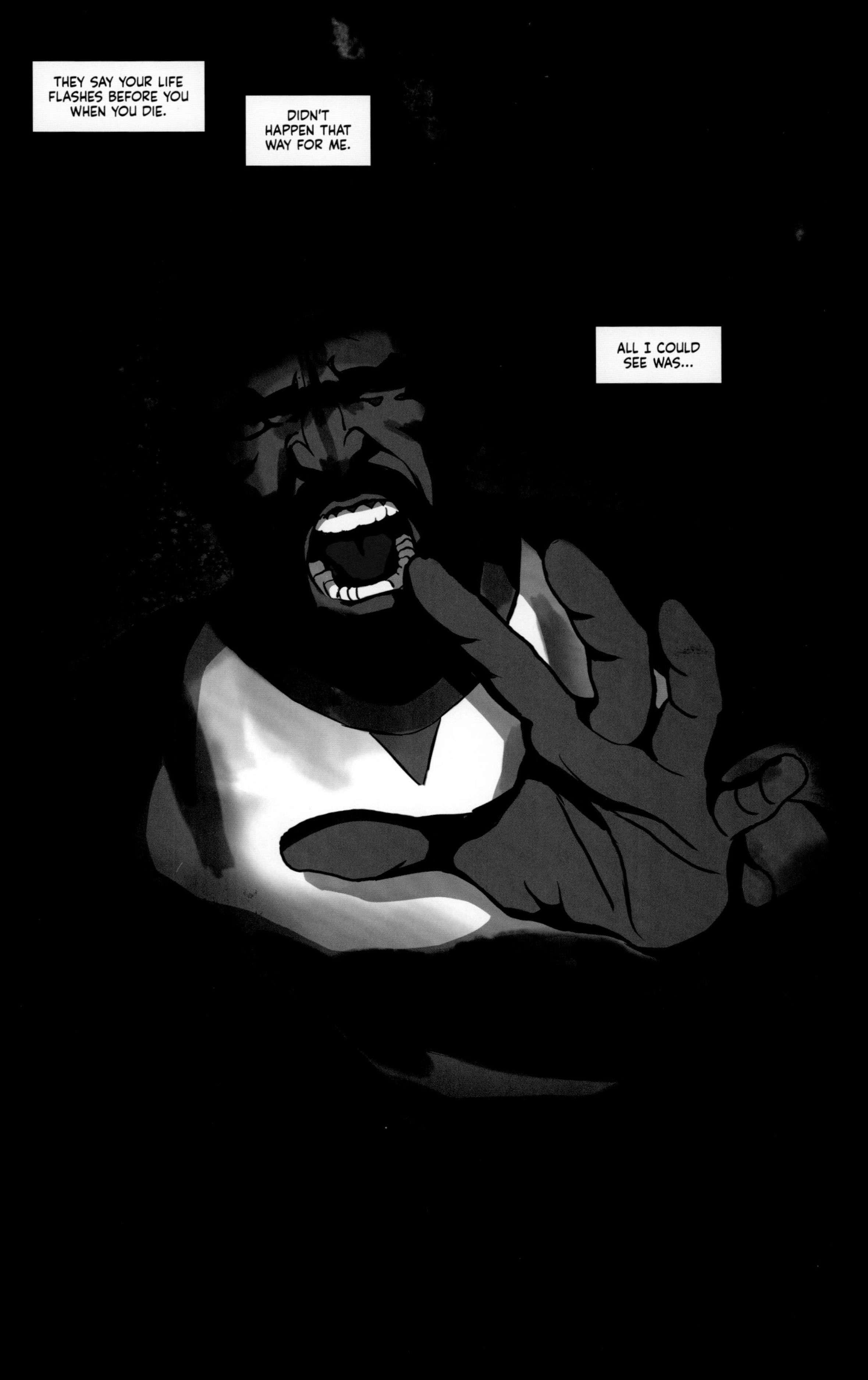
THEY SAY YOUR LIFE FLASHES BEFORE YOU WHEN YOU DIE.
DIDN'T HAPPEN THAT WAY FOR ME.
ALL I COULD SEE WAS...

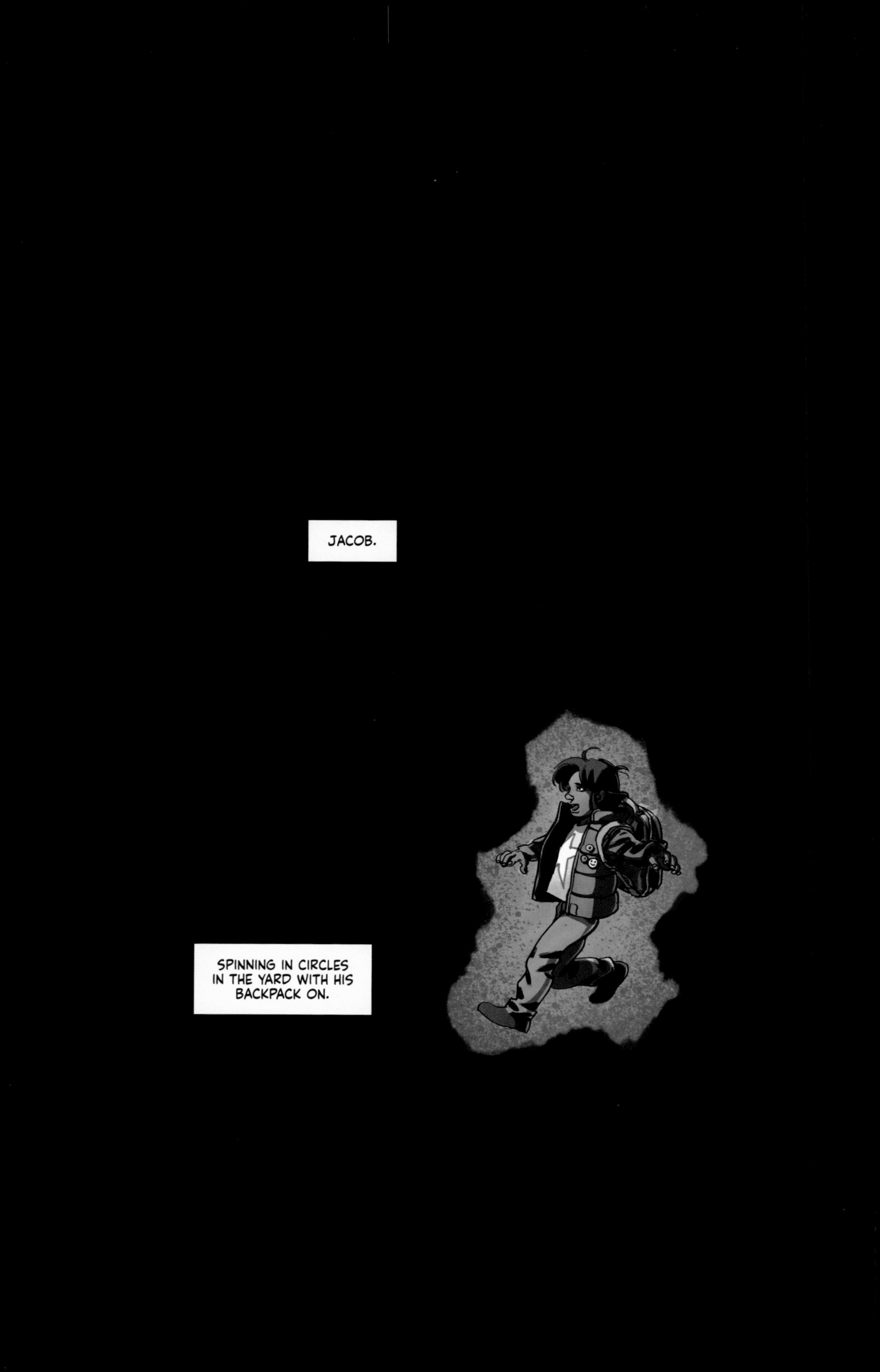
JACOB.
SPINNING IN CIRCLES IN THE YARD WITH HIS BACKPACK ON.

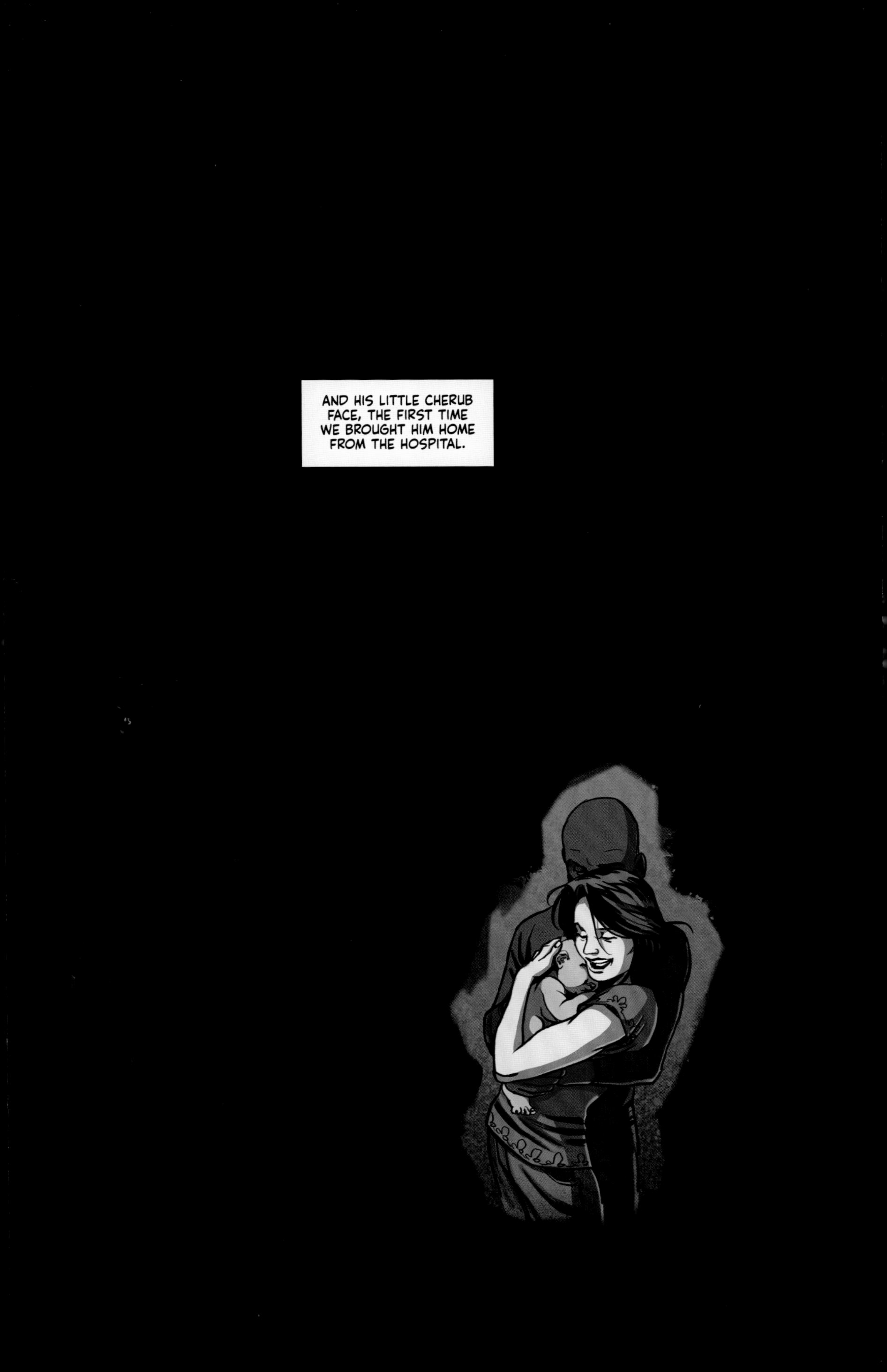
AND HIS LITTLE CHERUB FACE, THE FIRST TIME WE BROUGHT HIM HOME FROM THE HOSPITAL.

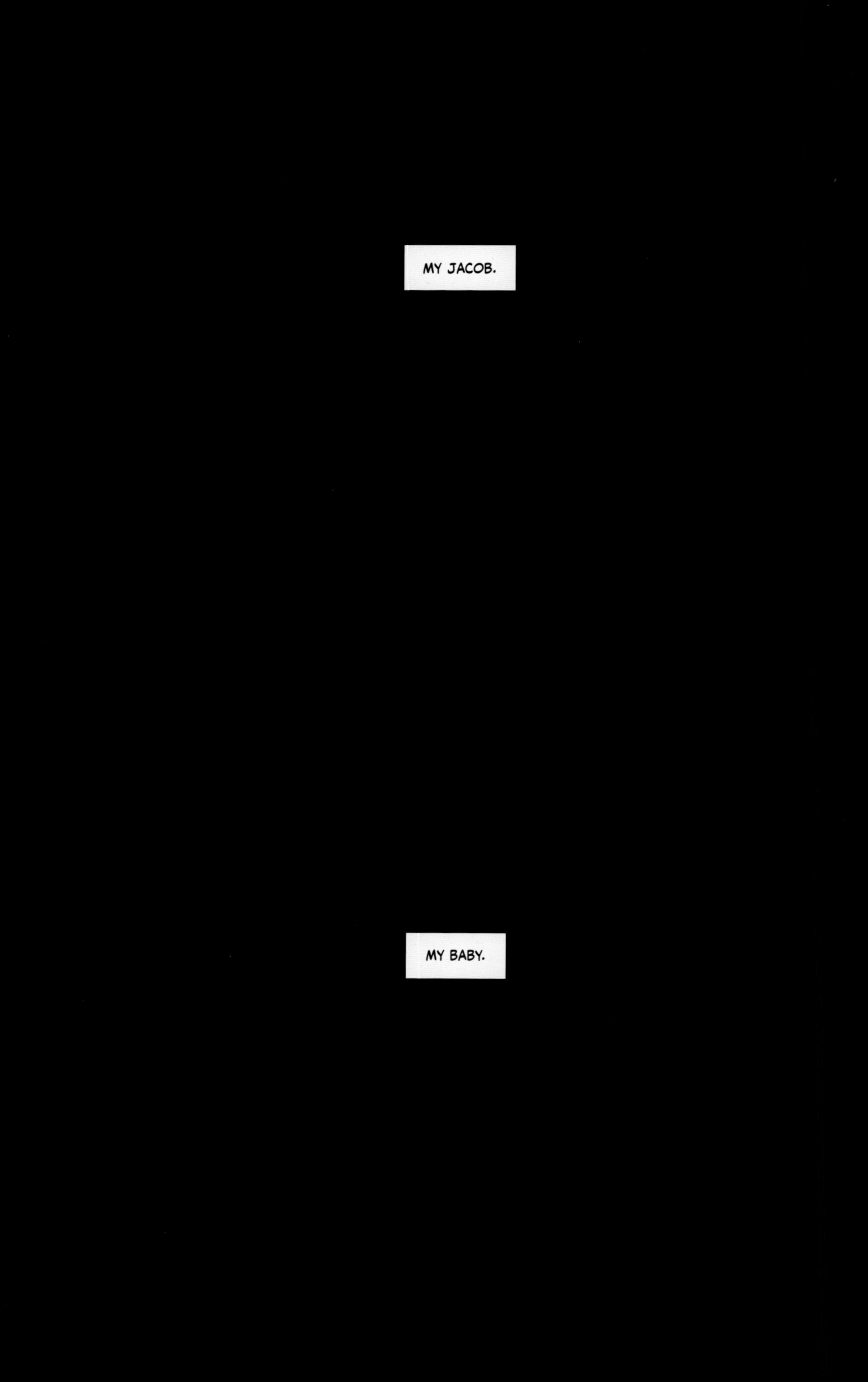
MY JACOB.
MY BABY.

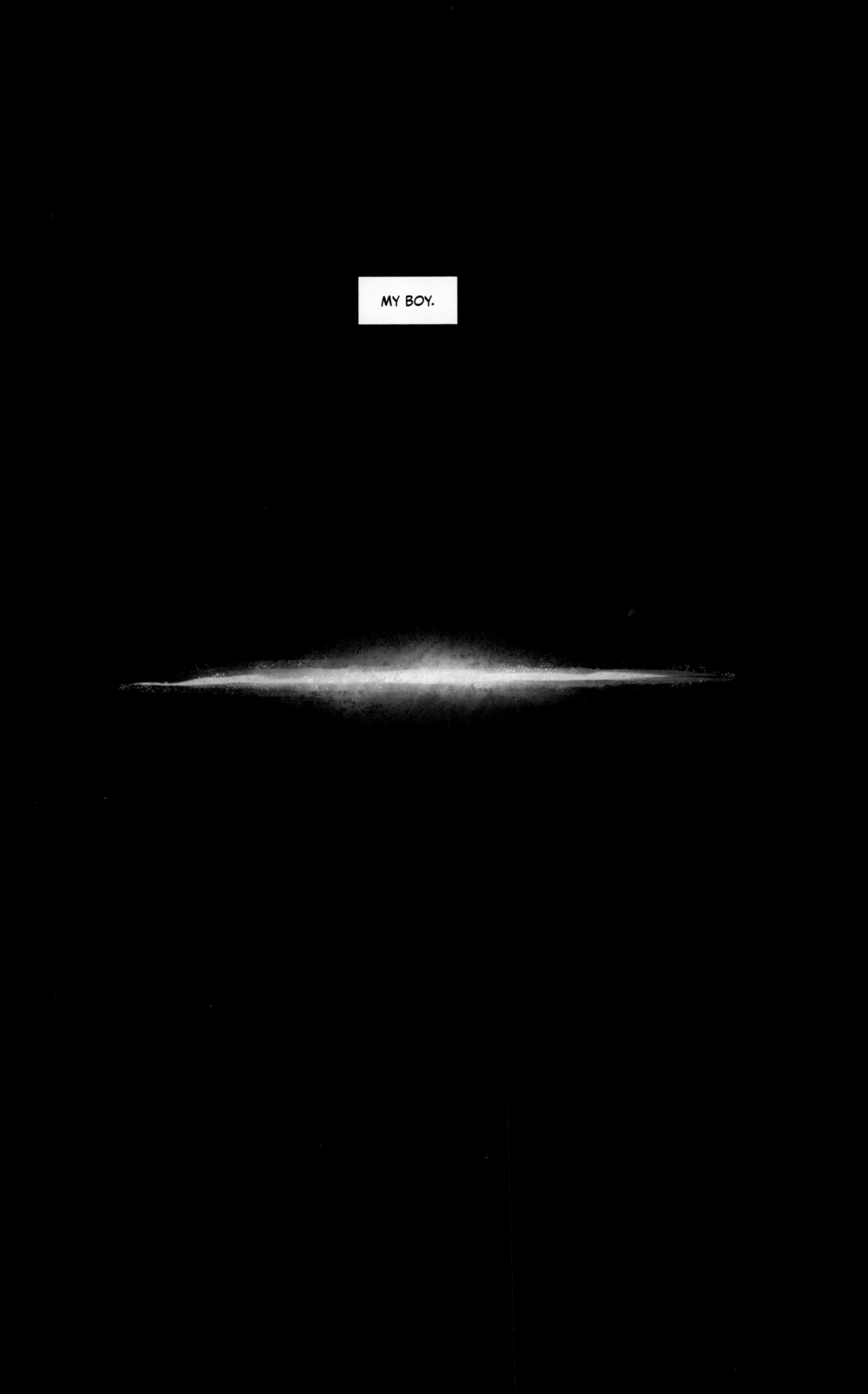
MY BOY.

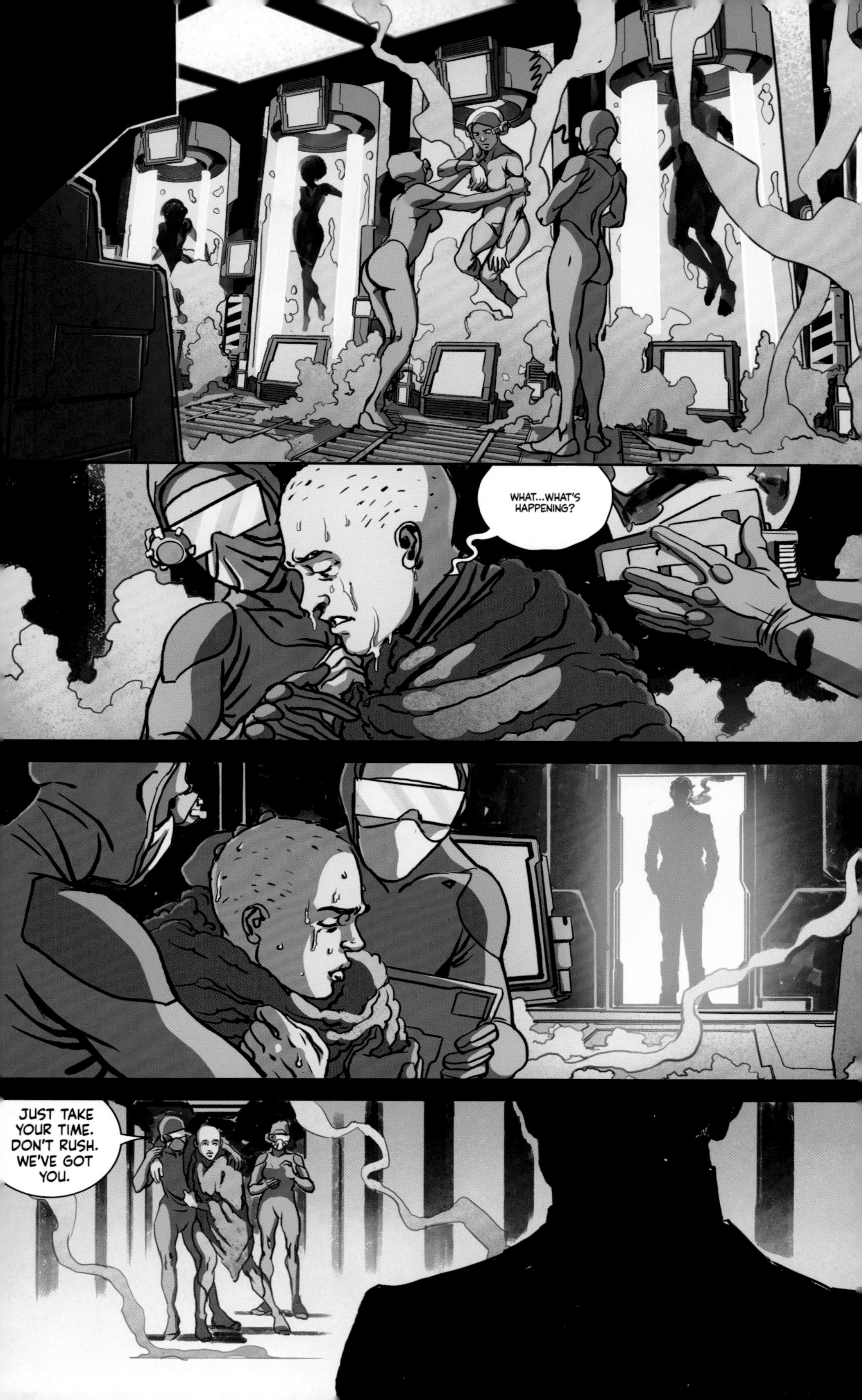
WHAT...WHAT'S HAPPENING?
JUST TAKE YOUR TIME. DON'T RUSH. WE'VE GOT YOU.

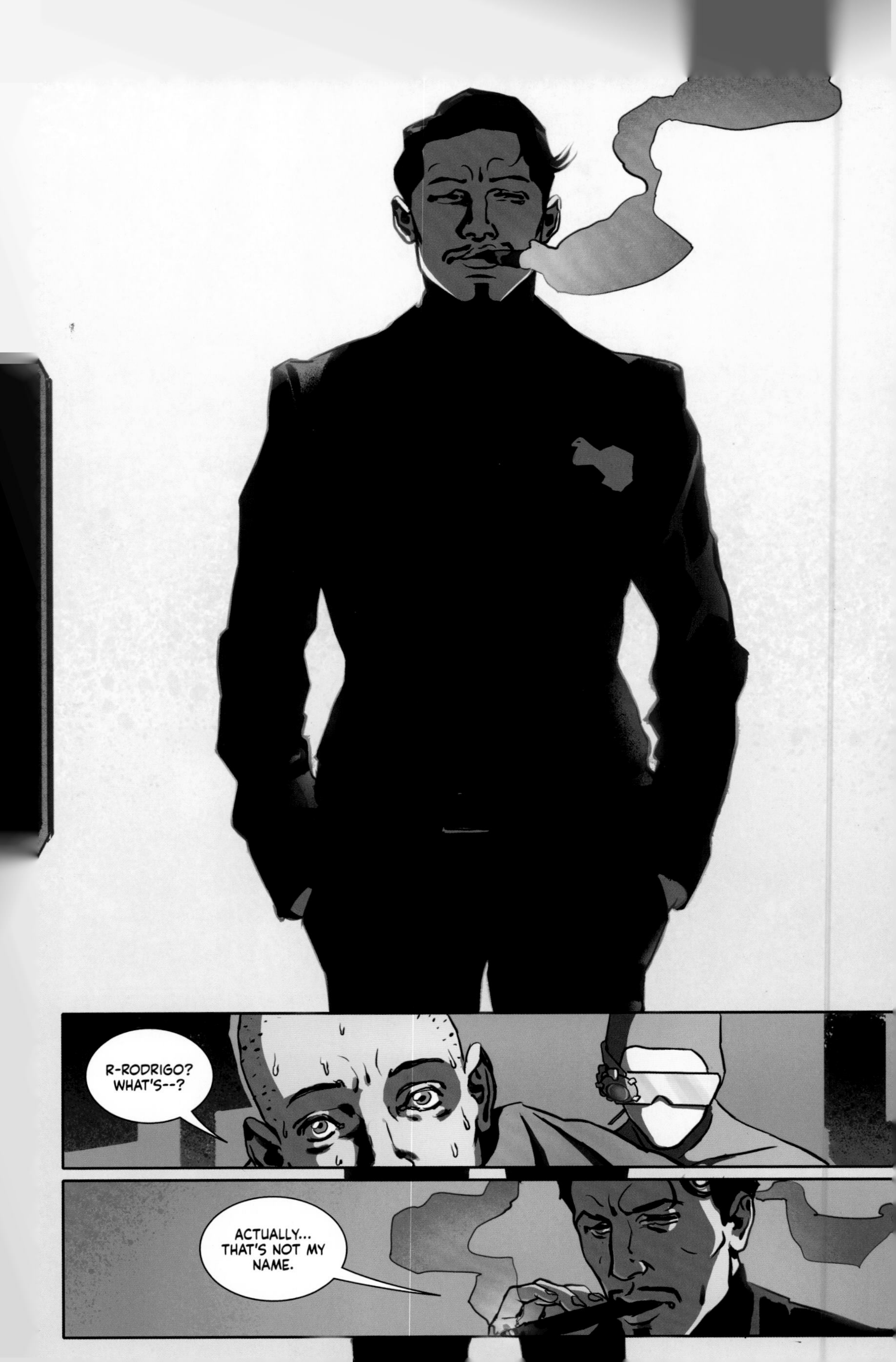
R-RODRIGO? WHAT'S--?
ACTUALLY... THAT'S NOT MY NAME.

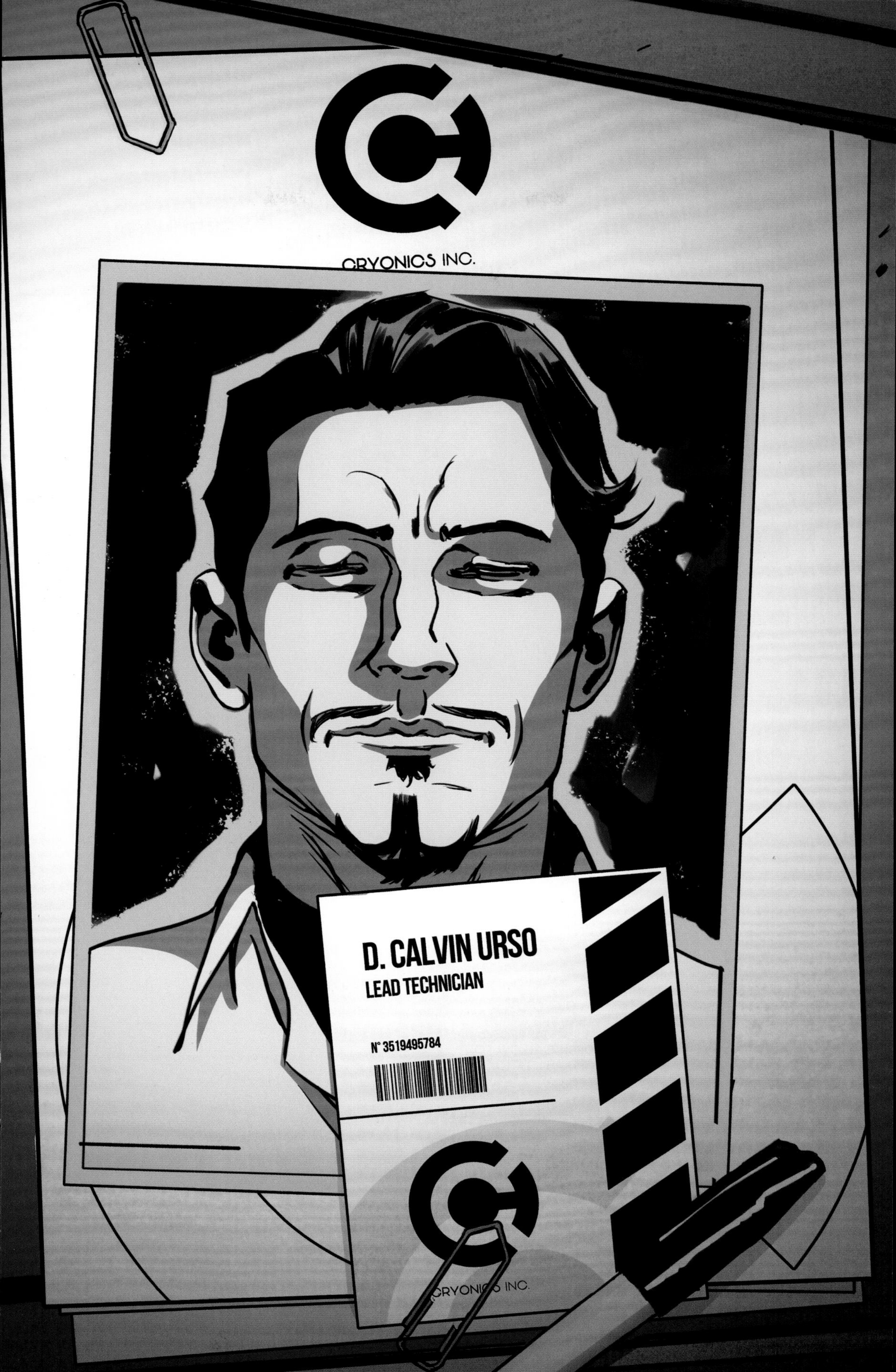
CRYONICS INC.
D. CALVIN URSO
LEAD TECHNICIAN
N° 3519495784
CRYONICS INC.

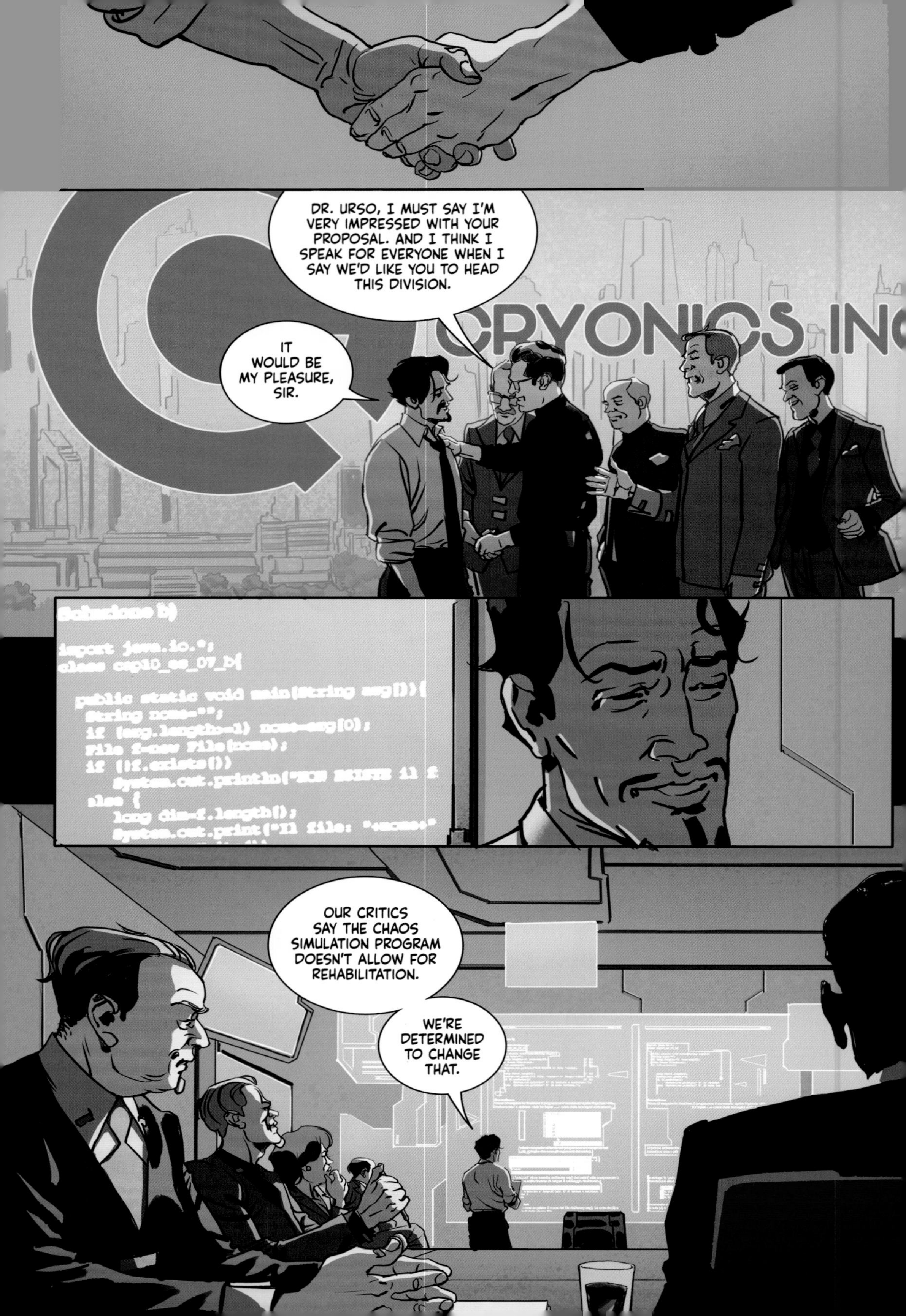
DR. URSO, I MUST SAY I'M VERY IMPRESSED WITH YOUR PROPOSAL. AND I THINK I SPEAK FOR EVERYONE WHEN I SAY WE'D LIKE YOU TO HEAD THIS DIVISION.
CRYONICS INC
IT WOULD BE MY PLEASURE, SIR.
OUR CRITICS SAY THE CHAOS SIMULATION PROGRAM DOESN'T ALLOW FOR REHABILITATION.
WE'RE DETERMINED TO CHANGE THAT.

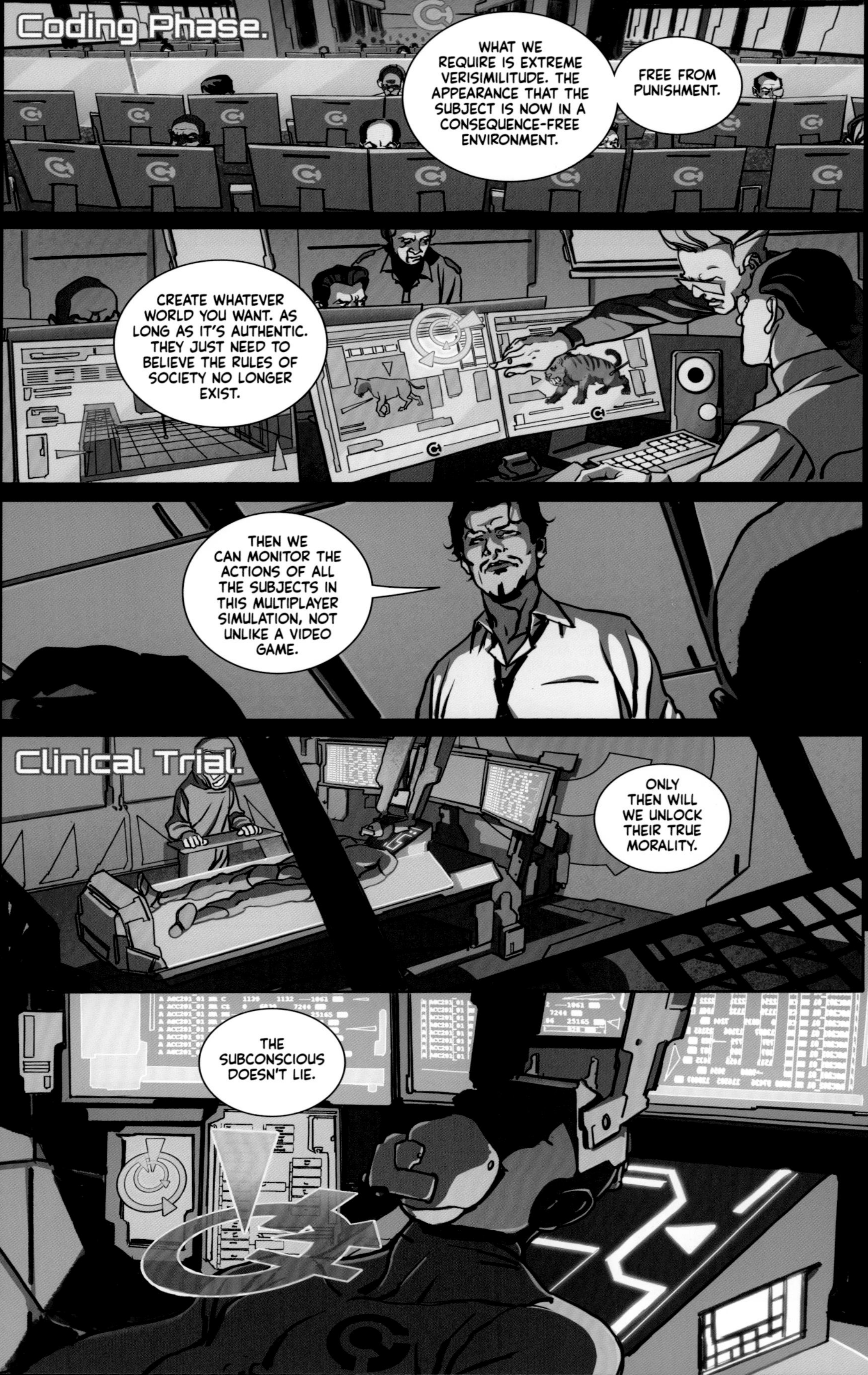
Coding Phase.
WHAT WE REQUIRE IS EXTREME VERISIMILITUDE. THE APPEARANCE THAT THE SUBJECT IS NOW IN A CONSEQUENCE-FREE ENVIRONMENT.
FREE FROM PUNISHMENT.
CREATE WHATEVER WORLD YOU WANT. AS LONG AS IT'S AUTHENTIC. THEY JUST NEED TO BELIEVE THE RULES OF SOCIETY NO LONGER EXIST.
THEN WE CAN MONITOR THE ACTIONS OF ALL THE SUBJECTS IN THIS MULTIPLAYER SIMULATION, NOT UNLIKE A VIDEO GAME.
Clinical Trial.
ONLY THEN WILL WE UNLOCK THEIR TRUE MORALITY.
THE SUBCONSCIOUS DOESN'T LIE.

Beta Test.

OUR SCORING ALGORITHMS THEN PRESENT A CASE FOR *ELIGIBILITY FOR PAROLE,* BASED ON COOPERATION, ALTRUISM, SELFLESSNESS...

...AND HONESTY.

WHEN PAROLE IS GRANTED, WE EFFECTIVELY "KILL" THEM FROM THE SIMULATION.

A MUCH SAFER INNOVATION THAN ALLOWING THEM TO GO FREE AND HOPING THEY WON'T RETURN TO A LIFE OF CRIME.

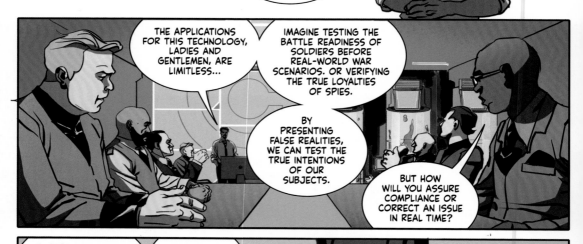

THE APPLICATIONS FOR THIS TECHNOLOGY, LADIES AND GENTLEMEN, ARE LIMITLESS...

IMAGINE TESTING THE BATTLE READINESS OF SOLDIERS BEFORE REAL-WORLD WAR SCENARIOS. OR VERIFYING THE TRUE LOYALTIES OF SPIES.

BY PRESENTING FALSE REALITIES, WE CAN TEST THE TRUE INTENTIONS OF OUR SUBJECTS.

BUT HOW WILL YOU ASSURE COMPLIANCE OR CORRECT AN ISSUE IN REAL TIME?

I, PERSONALLY, WILL BE UNDERTAKING THE SIMULATION WITH OUR INMATES. IN FACT, I'M QUITE LOOKING FORWARD TO PLAYING A ROLE.

IT MIGHT BE A GOOD BIT OF FUN TO PLAY "NOTORIOUS."

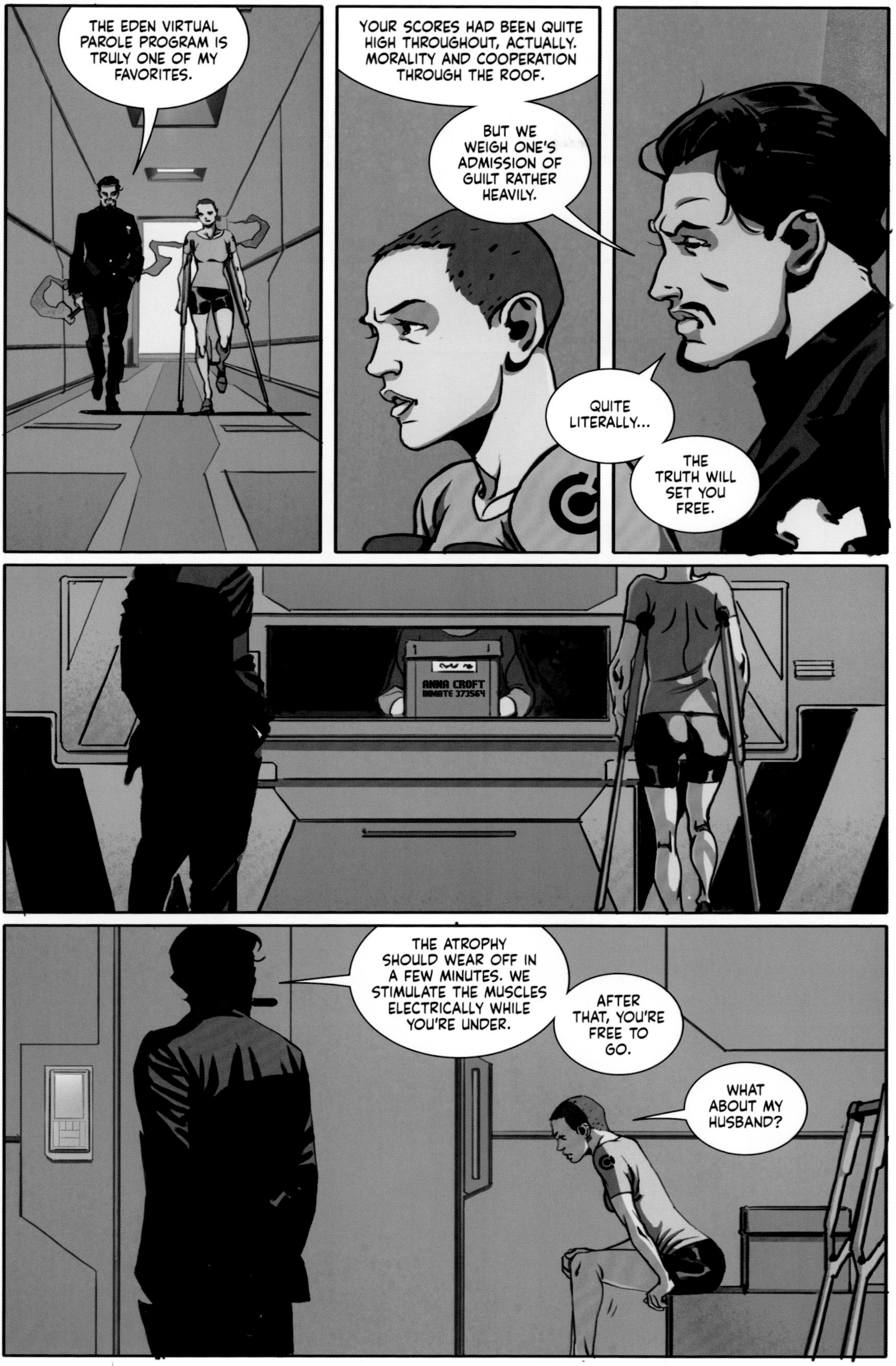
THE EDEN VIRTUAL PAROLE PROGRAM IS TRULY ONE OF MY FAVORITES.
YOUR SCORES HAD BEEN QUITE HIGH THROUGHOUT, ACTUALLY. MORALITY AND COOPERATION THROUGH THE ROOF.
BUT WE WEIGH ONE'S ADMISSION OF GUILT RATHER HEAVILY.
QUITE LITERALLY...
THE TRUTH WILL SET YOU FREE.
ANNA CROFT
INMATE 373564
THE ATROPHY SHOULD WEAR OFF IN A FEW MINUTES. WE STIMULATE THE MUSCLES ELECTRICALLY WHILE YOU'RE UNDER.
AFTER THAT, YOU'RE FREE TO GO.
WHAT ABOUT MY HUSBAND?

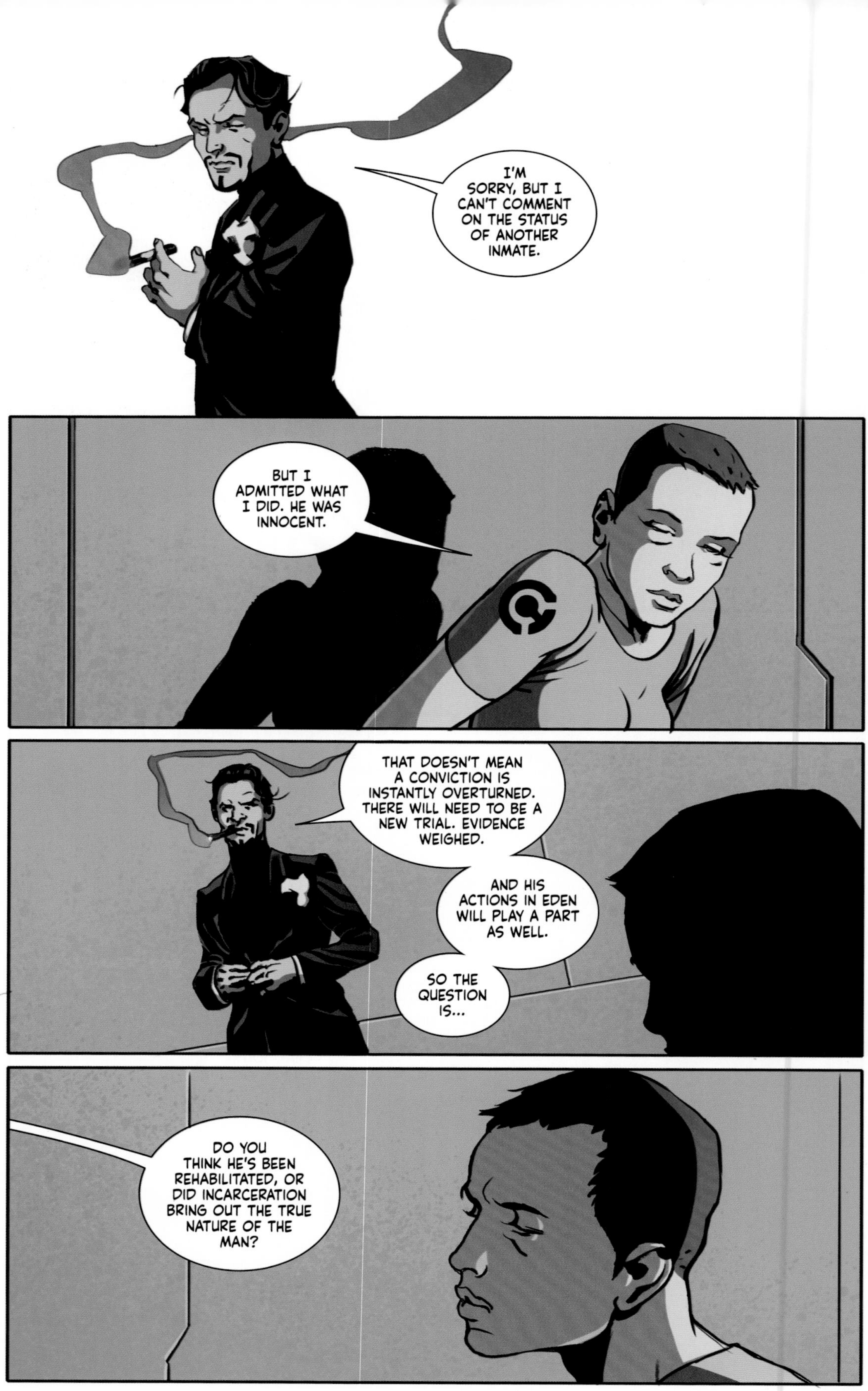
I'M SORRY, BUT I CAN'T COMMENT ON THE STATUS OF ANOTHER INMATE.
BUT I ADMITTED WHAT I DID. HE WAS INNOCENT.
THAT DOESN'T MEAN A CONVICTION IS INSTANTLY OVERTURNED. THERE WILL NEED TO BE A NEW TRIAL. EVIDENCE WEIGHED.
AND HIS ACTIONS IN EDEN WILL PLAY A PART AS WELL.
SO THE QUESTION IS...
DO YOU THINK HE'S BEEN REHABILITATED, OR DID INCARCERATION BRING OUT THE TRUE NATURE OF THE MAN?

I DIDN'T KNOW THE ANSWER TO THAT QUESTION.

BUT I WASN'T GOING TO GIVE UP. I'D MAKE SURE HE GOT THAT NEW TRIAL.

IT HAD BEEN TWENTY-FIVE YEARS.

WHAT WOULD THE WORLD BE LIKE NOW?

THEY SAY I'M REHABILITATED, BUT I DON'T FEEL IT. I DON'T FEEL ANYTHING. JUST A NUMBNESS.

IN SOME WAYS, I'D RATHER BE BACK INSIDE.

AT LEAST I HAD BEN.

NOW I HAVE NO ONE. NO HUSBAND. NO SON. AND NO LIFE TO RETURN TO.

I NEVER THOUGHT I'D END UP LIKE THIS.

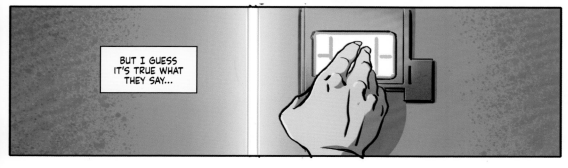

BUT I GUESS IT'S TRUE WHAT THEY SAY...

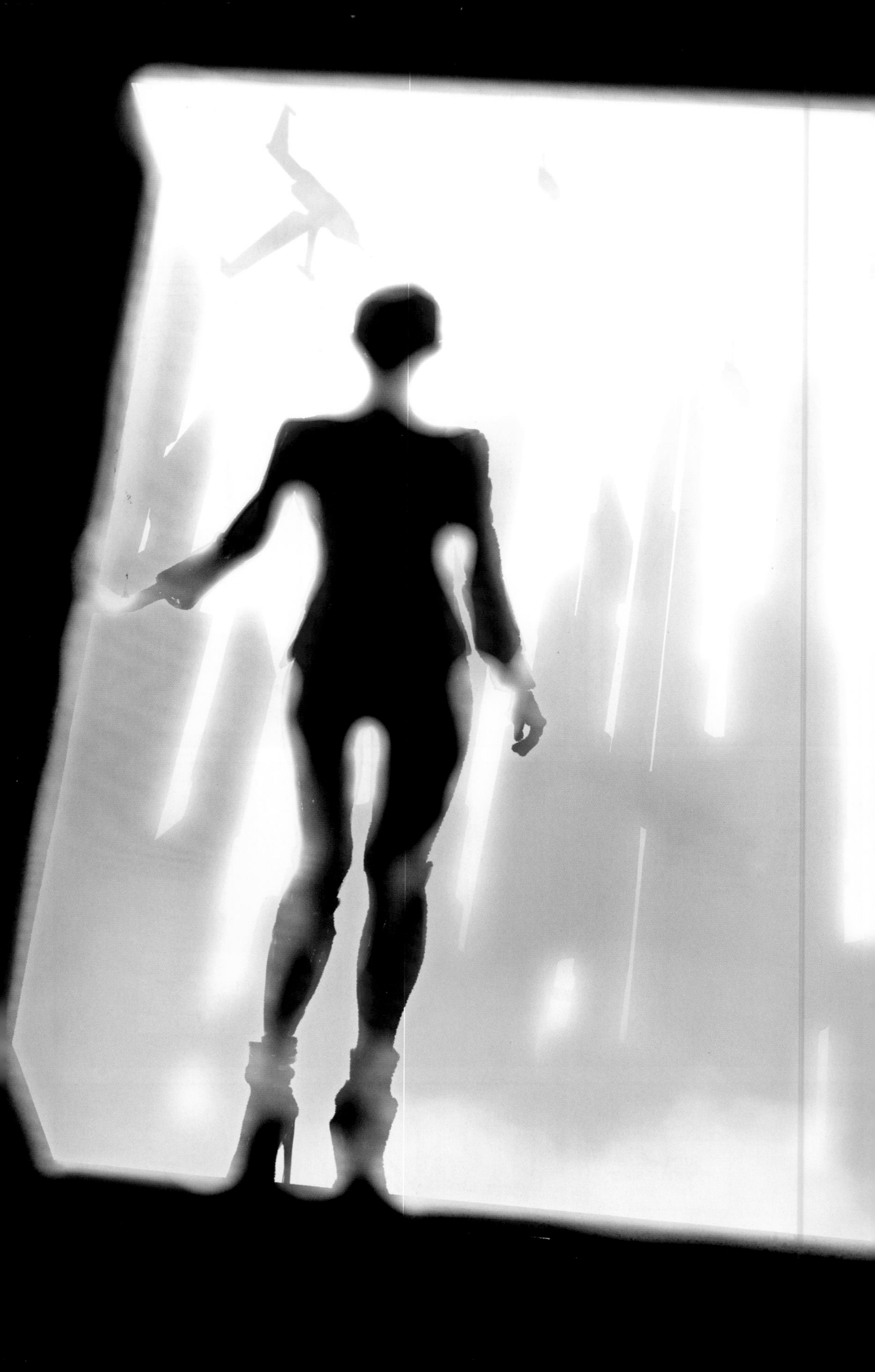

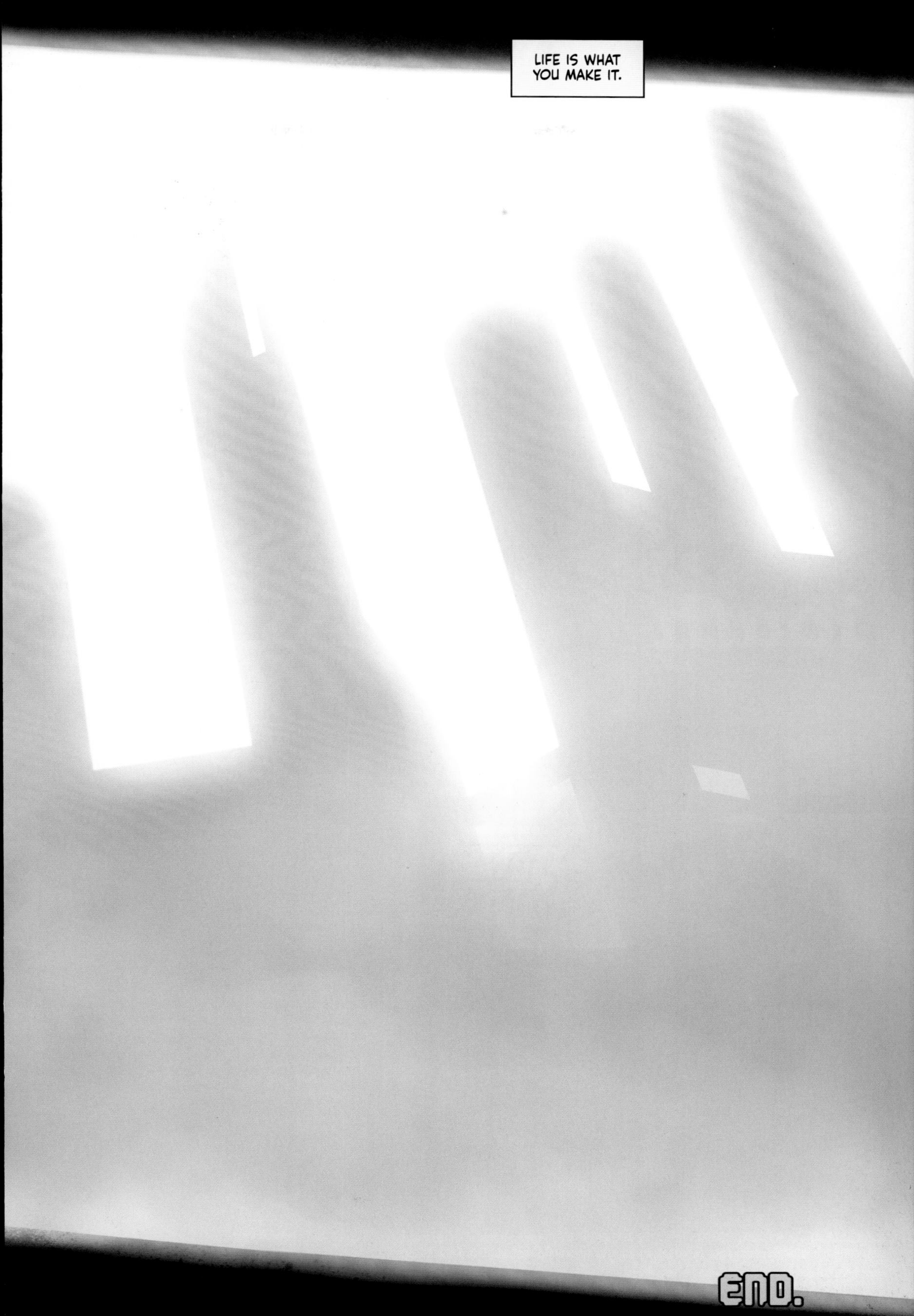
LIFE IS WHAT YOU MAKE IT.
END.

COMIXOLOGY COMES TO DARK HORSE BOOKS

ISBN 978-1-50672-440-9 / $19.99

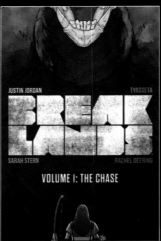

VOLUME 1: THE CHASE

ISBN 978-1-50672-441-6 / $19.99

curt pires
alex diotto
dee cunniffe
micah myers

Youth

ISBN 978-1-50672-461-4 / $19.99

ISBN 978-1-50672-446-1 / $19.99

ISBN 978-1-50672-447-8 / $29.99

VOLUME 1: FIGHT OR FLIGHT

ISBN 978-1-50672-458-4 / $19.99

AFTERLIFT
Written by Chip Zdarsky, art by Jason Loo

This Eisner Award–winning series from Chip Zdarsky (*Sex Crimina*
Daredevil) and Jason Loo (*The Pitiful Human-Lizard*) features c
chases, demon bounty hunters, and figuring out your place in th
world and the next.

BREAKLANDS
Written by Justin Jordan, art by Tyasseta and Sarah Stern

Generations after the end of the civilization, everyone has powe
you need them just to survive in the new age. Everyone exce
Kasa Fain. Unfortunately, her little brother, who has the potential
reshape the world, is kidnapped by people who intend to do just th
Mad Max meets *Akira* in a genre-mashing, expectation-smashi
new hit series from Justin Jordan, creator of *Luther Strode*, *Spre*
and *Reaver*!

YOUTH
Written by Curt Pires, art by Alex Diotto and Dee Cunniffe

A coming of age story of two queer teenagers who run away fro
their lives in a bigoted small town, and attempt to make their way
California. Along the way their car breaks down and they join a gro
of fellow misfits on the road. travelling the country together in a va
they party and attempt to find themselves. And then . . . somethi
happens. The story combines the violence of coming of age with t
violence of the superhero narrative—as well as the beauty.

THE BLACK GHOST SEASON ONE: HARD REVOLUTIO
Written by Alex Segura and Monica Gallagher, art by George Kamabda

Meet Lara Dominguez—a troubled Creighton cops reporter obsess
with the city's debonair vigilante the Black Ghost. With the help
a mysterious cyberinformant named LONE, Lara's inched closer
uncovering the Ghost's identity. But as she searches for the breakthrou
story she desperately needs, Lara will have to navigate the corruption
her city, the uncertainties of virtues, and her own personal demons. W
she have the strength to be part of the solution—or will she beco
the problem?

THE PRIDE OMNIBUS
Joseph Glass, Gavin Mitchell and Cem Iroz

FabMan is sick of being seen as a joke. Tired of the LGBTQ+ commun
being seen as inferior to straight heroes, he thinks it's about dar
time he did something about it. Bringing together some of the worl
greatest LGBTQ+ superheroes, the Pride is born to protect the wo
and fight prejudice, misrepresentation and injustice—not to mention
pesky supervillain or two.

STONE STAR
Jim Zub and Max Zunbar

The brand-new space-fantasy saga that takes flight on comiXolo
Originals from fan-favorite creators Jim Zub (*Avengers*, *Samurai Jac*
and Max Dunbar (*Champions*, *Dungeons & Dragons*)! The noma
space station called Stone Star brings gladiatorial entertainment
ports across the galaxy. Inside this gargantuan vessel of tournamer
and temptations, foragers and fighters struggle to survive. A you
thief named Dail discovers a dark secret in the depths of Stone S
and must decide his destiny—staying hidden in the shadows
standing tall in the searing spotlight of the arena. Either way, his l
and the cosmos itself, will never be the same!